Zhuge Liang
諸 葛 亮

Strategy, Achievements, and Writings

By

Ralph D. Sawyer
and
Mei-chün Sawyer

Cover calligraphy by Lee Mei-chün

Copyright © 2014 by Ralph D. Sawyer
All rights reserved.
ISBN: 1492860026
ISBN 13: 9781492860020
Library of Congress Control Number: 2013919128
CreateSpace Independent Publishing Platform,
North Charleston, South Carolina

Dedicated to the memory of Lee T'ing-rong

Contents

	Preface vi	
I	Historical Context and Developments 1	
	1	Introduction 3
	2	*San-kuo Chih* Biography 26
	3	Southern Campaign 54
	4	The Northern Campaigns 69
	5	Strategy and Achievements 108
II	Military Writings 145	
	6	Beliefs and Martial Writings 147
	7	Collected Military Passages 155
		兵 法 Military Methods 155
		兵 要 Military Essentials 157
		軍 令 Army Orders 163
	8	將 苑 *Chiang Yüan* 168
	9	便 宜 *Pien Yi* 217
III	Collateral Matter 257	
	Critical Sources 259	
	Suggested Martial and Contextual Reading 260	

Preface

When writing about Chu-ko Liang (Zhuge Liang), the question immediately arises: Which of his many manifestations should be the focus? The remote, rather aloof figure that appears in the earliest historical works; the prominent architect of Liu Pei's survival and Shu's policies as recounted in Ssu-ma Kuang's well-pondered synthetic history, the *Tz'u-chih T'ung-chien*; the brilliant strategist featured in streetside tales; the savant depicted in outlandish stories; the esoteric thinker who supposedly conceived at least two prognosticatory methods; the powerful but darkly shrouded tactician who emerges as the realm's most knowledgeable practitioner of real politics in the Ming dynasty novel known as the *San-kuo Yen-yi*; or any of the heroes found in contemporary action comics or even Internet compendia.

Chu-ko Liang continues to enjoy an enormous reputation, even reverence, and is often deemed China's greatest strategist, more than the equal of the T'ai Kung, Sun-tzu, Sun Pin, Chang Liang, or Liu Po-wen (Liu Chi), all of whom were instrumental in founding dynasties or preserving states. Moreover, befitting his tactical wisdom and acumen, he is credited not just with battlefield innovation, but also with the authorship of important martial works that fall well within the continuous tradition of Chinese military science literature that commenced with Sun-tzu's *Art of War* and includes Sun Pin's *Military Methods* and the T'ai Kung's *Six Secret Teachings*.

In concluding his biography of Chu-ko Liang in the *San-kuo Chih*, Ch'en Shou (233–297) indicated that he had compiled a separate work consisting of twenty-four chapters of what he deemed were the best of Chu-ko Liang's writings, and even listed the section titles. This volume was unfortunately lost within a few centuries, and current attempts to understand what Liang actually composed invariably have recourse to Chang Shu's (張澍) Ch'ing dynasty synthetic work, the *Chu-ko Chung Wu-hou Wen-chi* (諸葛忠武侯文集). Chang included the *Chiang Yüan* and *Pien Yi* commonly attributed to him and assiduously culled numerous sentences and paragraphs from the various books, commentaries, and compendia (such as the *T'ai-p'ing Yü-lan*) that had appeared over the centuries whenever Liang was cited as the speaker or the contents seemed to be closely associated with him.

Not unexpectedly, rather than uncontested, some of his choices have been considered dubious; others have been totally rejected, prompting acrimonious debate over their veracity.[1] Ever since the *Chu-ko Chung Wu-hou Wen-chi*'s initial circulation, Chu-ko Liang aficionados who decried the omission of many materials that they consider highly valid or otherwise representative have also produced a number of extensive works of varying reliability and academic competence. (A few of their selections are now included in the basically definitive *Chu-ko Liang Chi* (諸葛亮集), originally published by the Chung-hua Shu-chü in 1960 and slightly revised in 1974.) In addition, the numerous secondary works and contemporary vernacular translations that began to appear several decades ago have rapidly multiplied in recent years, resulting in both scholarly studies and wildly speculative expansions of his ideas and purported creations.

We basically undertook this work in response to numerous requests over the past two decades to provide a relatively comprehensive translation of his military writings. Being only partially cognizant of the difficulties besetting them, at the outset our intent was simply to follow the model previously employed in my version of the *T'ai-pai Yin-ching*'s strategic chapters (recently published under the title *Strategies for the Human Realm*): a minimal introduction that makes no attempt to ponder the era's political and military issues, but the inclusion of brief analytical and historical comments to explicate the contents of the individual chapters. However, it quickly became apparent that Chu-ko Liang's martial thoughts are not confined to his purported writings but must be winnowed out from his memorials and sought in his activities and accomplishments.

Ch'en Shou's twenty-four titles indicate that he ranked several important memorials and missives among Chu-ko Liang's essential writings, and most compilations include them today. In consonance with his appraisal, in addition to all the passages found in the first Ch'ing dynasty compilation (ranging from the *Chiang Yüan* through *Pien Yi* and *T'ai-p'ing Yü-lan* fragments), we have translated the important military memorials embedded in the *San-kuo Chih* and a number of other

---

[1] However, as the ancient Chinese philosopher Chuang-tzu early on pointed out, arguments for one or another position fail to achieve anything; further, detailed, and invariably tedious discussion has therefore been left to specialist articles.

letters and apparent contemplations. As is my usual practice, I have appended a few footnotes to explain various items in the text, and also added some brief comments to explicate certain passages and relate the contents to the classic military writings that preceded him and had by then become the foundation of military knowledge.

However, I have refrained from providing extensive translations of previous works, since they are readily available and would unnecessarily increase the bulk and expense. Moreover, since this book is intended for a broad audience rather than the handful of Sinologists who have an interest in military writings, unlike in my version of Sun Pin's *Military Methods*, neither textual emendations nor translation notes are included.[2] Because most of the materials are self-explanatory, I have also refrained from offering a lengthy analytical (and necessarily artificial) introduction. Nevertheless, in conjunction with the succinct historical overview, the somewhat irregular comments provided to the various passages will hopefully be adequate to allow readers to study the contents of Chu-ko Liang's probable writings and draw their own, however contradictory, conclusions.

Achieving any understanding of Chu-ko Liang's thought requires at least a cursory examination of the historical context and the significant developments that directly affected his life and undertakings. However, it was not our intent to write a military history of the period, even though one continues to be lacking in English. Therefore, despite their often intriguing nature, neither collateral events nor many fundamental military, political, and economic issues have been pursued. Although numerous specialized articles, historical works, and military histories in Chinese and Japanese have been consulted, just as all the secondary works published to date (including the 三國軍事史 in the modern 中國軍事通史 series), the brief historical introduction and my examination of Chu-ko Liang's strategic and command achievements are primarily based upon the *Chronicle of the Three Kingdoms* (三國志 *San-kuo Chih*), compiled by Ch'en Shou

---

2 Although there are slight variations in characters among different texts, few make a significant difference. However, despite the writing being relatively straightforward and largely based on earlier works, in some places condensation has made the exact meaning less clear and parts of the translation may well merit revision in the future. (For the convenience of readers, rather than replicating variations or references by title, individuals are generally referred to by a single name, such as Ts'ao Ts'ao for Ts'ao Kung, and Wu-ti. The numerous administrative and military titles that appear throughout the writings, being somewhat self-evident, are also largely left untranslated to avoid becoming entangled in the bureaucratic nightmare that characterized the three political entities and the era as a whole.)

about 274 CE and thus within a few decades of Chu-ko Liang's death, reportedly from records and memorials still extant in Chin's archives.

It should be noted that being a Chin official—Chin being the name of the successor state that evolved from the Han through Ts'ao Ts'ao's state of Wei—Ch'en Shou did not escape the need to express a certain perspective. Chin's subjugation of the realm had been based upon Ts'ao Ts'ao's emergence as well as his role as the forceful architect of the debilitated Han's evolution. Chu-ko Liang's campaigns are therefore described in terms of Shu's "bandits" and "brigands" making incursions into the Han because only the north qualified as a legitimate power, whatever Ch'en's personal appraisal of Chu-ko Liang and even Liu Pei.

The brevity of many *San-kuo-Chih* depictions requires that the information be supplemented by P'ei Sung's commentaries (completed about 429 CE) and other information found in the definitive Sung dynasty edition of the text. Further cognizance has been taken of Ssu-ma Kuang's chronologically synthesized account in his massive *Tz'u-chih T'ung-chien* (資治通鑒), because it not only integrates all the foregoing material but also provides additional insights and a dramatic retelling that merits reading in its own right. Remarkably, although it was soon accorded imperial sanction and support, rather than an official compilation undertaken by a staff of historians within the government itself, the *Tzu-chih T'ung-chien* was the private project of a dedicated Sung dynasty scholar, Ssu-ma Kuang, which required some twenty years to complete before being formally presented to the emperor in 1084 CE.

Generally rendered into English as *Comprehensive Mirror for Aid in Government*, the *Tzu-chih T'ung-chien* chronicles the period from 403 BCE to 959 CE in an essentially continuous narrative sweep that was intended to integrate what Kuang and his three main scholarly assistants felt to be the most reliable accounts for each event.[3] In contrast, the now well-known dynastic histories (including the *San-kuo Chih*) disperse the contents among basic annals, biographies, and specialized treatises, making it difficult to envision all aspects of particular events, including context and precursors, without consulting many sections and mentally integrating them.

Ssu-ma Kuang and his associates scrutinized hundreds of sources ranging from dynastic and official records through personal accounts and general writings, many

---

[3] For a historical analysis of the *Tzu-chih T'ung-chien*, see E. G. Pulleyblank's classic "Chinese Historical Criticism: Liu Chih-chi and Ssu-ma Kuang" in *Historians of China and Japan*.

of which are now lost. Although they subjected them to rigorous examination and applied standards that emphasized probability and consistency, the work probably has not escaped certain prejudices stemming from Kuang's conservatism and strong adherence to Confucianism beliefs, including a generally negative attitude toward martial power and a consequent tendency to emphasize the role of wisdom in wresting victory. Nevertheless, as might be expected, since the history of China is essentially a history of warfare, much of the *Tzu-chih T'ung-chien* is devoted to military activity, and it preserves a very comprehensive account of the Three Kingdoms period that transcends the *San-kuo Chih*'s annalistic fragmentation. (As has long been my practice, even though I lack the precision and perspicaciousness of my early teacher, Dr. Achilles Fang, rather than simply summarizing or paraphrasing, I have included lengthy translations from the text, in the belief that readers are best served by access to the original material.)

It should be noted that much of Chu-ko Liang's current approbation, his "superstar" status, derives not from historical works but from stories and tales that tended to be enhanced over the centuries with each retelling. Although two or three are mentioned in the introduction, our focus has been understanding the historical figure in order to ponder his probable writings, rather than to reprise and evaluate the potential veracity of his more legendary aspects. Accordingly, the rather amazing achievements attributed to him by later tradition, the very essence of his expanded reputation, can best be grasped by reading a translation of the *The Romance of the Three Kingdoms*, particularly that by Moss Roberts.

Finally, the ready availability on the Internet of detailed maps of China and satellite views of the topography where Chu-ko Liang's northern campaigns unfolded has obviated the need for more than a few sketchy indications of the northern campaign routes.[4] Although some of the details continue to be argued, there is general agreement about the thrust of each campaign and the location of the actual battles.

Ralph D. Sawyer
Summer 2013

---

4 The most extensive battle maps produced to date remain those found in the classic multivolume series *Chung-kuo Li-tao Chan-cheng-shih* (中國歷代戰爭史) and, although far fewer, the *San-kuo Chün-shih-shih* (三國軍事史) in the *Chung-kuo Chün-shih T'ung-shih* (中國軍事通史) series.

A Note on Pronunciation

As I have noted in my previous books, neither of the two commonly employed orthographies facilitates the pronunciation of Romanized Chinese characters for the uninitiated. Each system has its stumbling blocks, and I cannot imagine that *qi* in *pinyin* is inherently more comprehensible to unpracticed readers than the older, increasingly discarded (and now politically disdained) Wade-Giles *ch'i* for a sound similar to the initial part of "chicken" or *xi* for the simple "she," although they are certainly no less comprehensible than *j* for *r* or even *t* for *d* in Wade-Giles. However, as this work is intended for a broad audience, many of whom will have little experience with Romanized Chinese words—apart from a few occurrences in the news and my other works, in which Wade-Giles has exclusively been used—the hyphenated break between syllables facilitates pronunciation, and specialists should have equal facility in either system, so we have continued to employ Wade-Giles here with the exception of an idiosyncratic *yi* for *i* and contemporary provincial names.

As a crude guide to pronunciation, we offer the following notes on the significant exceptions to normally expected sounds:

t, as in *Tao*: without an apostrophe, pronounced like "d" (*pinyin d*); otherwise "t"

p, as in *ping*: without an apostrophe, pronounced like "b" (*pinyin b*), otherwise "p"

ch, as in *chuang*: without an apostrophe, pronounced like "j" (*pinyin j* and *zh*), otherwise "ch"

k, as in *kuang*: without an apostrophe, pronounced like English "g" (*pinyin g*), otherwise "k"

hs, as in *hsi*: pronounced like English "sh" (*pinyin x*)

j, as in *jen*: pronounced like "r" (*pinyin r*)

Thus, the name of the famous Chou (or Zhou in *pinyin*) dynasty is pronounced as if written "jou" and sounds just like the English name "Joe."

I
Historical Context and Developments

1
Introduction

Chu-ko Liang (181–234), a relatively minor historical figure appropriately credited with formulating strategic measures that prolonged the minor Han, looms astonishingly large in Chinese culture. Although active in the third century CE, consonant with China's subsequent fascination with the Three Kingdoms period,[5] his reputation continued to grow in later centuries as his measures and acumen became the subject of myths, street-side tales, plays, poems, operas, and finally a highly romanticized Ming dynasty novel generally known in English as *The Romance of the Three Kingdoms* (三國演義 *San-kuo Yen-yi*). In recent decades his exploits have been reprised in movies and books, his tactics collected and analyzed in dozens of works, and his purported writings reprinted in a variety of highly annotated compilations ranging from the scholarly and arcane through the imaginative and simplistic. His accomplishments are now the subject of comic book renditions, and he has become a powerful denizen in board and electronic games.

Two well-known but rather unsubstantiated incidents contributed greatly to his undying fame by fashioning an image for him as a true master of the unorthodox and a formulator of imaginative, invariably clever tactics. According to *The Romance* (but not the *Chronicle of the Three Kingdoms*, the most reliable history of the period), the first arose prior to the Battle of Red Cliffs when Chou Yü, Wu's commanding general, fearing Chu-ko Liang's potential, attempted to preclude any future adverse impact on the state of Wu. By openly opining that they would be short of arrows if these could not be acquired within ten days, he provoked Chu-ko Liang into offering to provide them. Moreover, he promised to produce the one hundred thousand needed within just three days, an obvious impossibility since they lacked the artisans necessary to fabricate them in such

---

5 Even the late Sung dynasty's *Hundred Unorthodox Strategies* (百戰奇法) employs a disproportionate number of incidents from the Three Kingdoms period as historical illustrations for the various tactical principles. (For a complete translation, see Sawyer, *One Hundred Unorthodox Strategies: Battle and Tactics of Chinese Warfare*.)

a short period, and Chou Yü could be expected to instruct his subordinates to obstruct Liang's efforts.

Chu-ko Liang allowed two days to pass without undertaking any visible action. However, he did manage to persuade Lu Su, a high-ranking, supposedly sympathetic official, into secretly furnishing twenty boats with high walls and bales of hay packed along the outside. Taking advantage of a heavy nighttime fog, Liang then had his few troops undertake a deliberately noisy reconnaissance along the perimeter of Ts'ao Ts'ao's tethered vessels. Their approach prompted a hastily mounted response that included thousands of archers chaotically firing into the impenetrable mist. Liang continued to maneuver his boats in order to provoke further volleys until the fog began to clear, after which he turned them back, gathered the undamaged arrows, and presented them just as the deadline loomed. Much to Chou Yü's astonishment and rising anger, the number easily surpassed the enormous amount of one hundred thousand.[6]

An epoch-making event, the Battle of Ch'ih-pi (Red Cliffs) contributed to vastly enhancing Chu-ko Liang's reputation. The battle unfolded when the northern usurper Ts'ao Ts'ao initiated a massive invasion of the southeast by sending a huge flotilla down the Yangtze River that threatened both the remnants of Liu Pei's forces and the incipient state of Wu, located in the area of the ancient states of Wu and Yüeh, with extinction. According to popular accounts, Chu-ko Liang conceived the strategy of employing an incendiary attack upon the two thousand wooden vessels anchored at Ch'ih-pi and accurately predicted when the wind's direction would change, even brought it about through magical means, allowing the fire boats commanded by a false traitor to approach their target with unstoppable speed. (Variations claim that Chou Yü, Wu's famous general and sometime strategist, simultaneously realized that only an incendiary attack would allow their terrifyingly outnumbered forces any chance for victory.)

The second and undoubtedly most cleverly conceived triumph of Chu-ko Liang's career has long been known as the "empty city ploy." Sun-tzu first

---

6 Although this tale does not appear in the *San-kuo Chih*, according to a passage from the *Wei Lüeh* preserved among the commentaries, it was actually Sun Ch'üan who perpetrated this trick against Ts'ao Ts'ao one night when he went out alone in a large vessel and came under an archery attack. Realizing that thousands of arrows had impaled one side, he turned the boat about to replicate the results on the other side.

articulated the interrelated concepts of vacuity and substance, but competent generals had been avoiding the substantial and striking the vacuous long before then.[7] Naturally the early military thinkers of the Warring States period (403–221) incorporated this tactical principle in their writings. Wu Ch'i accordingly advised: "In employing the army you must ascertain the enemy's voids and strengths and then race to take advantage of their endangered points." The *Six Secret Teachings* (六韜 *Liu-t'ao*) similarly asserts, "When you see vacuity in the enemy you should advance; when you see substance you should halt." Commanders simply had to detect gaps, vacuities, and weaknesses in the enemy and exploit them.

An additional complexity that arose over time was the use of feigned weakness to lure an unsuspecting or negligent enemy into an ambush, prompting wariness whenever the "vacuousness" became too obvious.[8] Chu-ko Liang's empty city ploy supposedly unfolded within this increasingly complicated context:

> During the Three Kingdoms period, General Chu-ko Liang of Shu remained in Yin-p'ing while Wei Yen and several other generals united their forces in the east and went downriver. Chu-ko Liang only retained about ten thousand men to defend the city. Ssu-ma Yi of Wei led two hundred thousand troops to crush Chu-ko Liang, moving along an alternate route to Yen's forces and halting about sixty *li* away to oppose Liang. An observer returned and reported to Ssu-ma Yi that there were few soldiers in Liang's city and that their overall strength was weak.
>
> Chu-ko Liang also knew that Ssu-ma Yi's armies would soon reach them and feared they would severely press them. He wanted to join his forces with Yen's army, but they were

---

[7] The vacuous and substantial are primarily discussed in two *Art of War* (兵法) chapters, "Strategic Military Power" and "The Vacuous and Substantial."

[8] The theory of empty facades became quite complex over time, as discussed in my forthcoming book on deception in theory and practice, *Lever of Power*. The "empty city ploy" was subsequently incorporated in the now well-known *Thirty-six Stratagems*.

too far apart and his own strategic power was insufficient to achieve it. His generals and officers all lost their composure, not knowing what their plans might be. However, Chu-ko Liang's spirit and determination were unchanged, and he issued an edict that everyone within the army should furl their battle flags and set their drums aside and no one should irresponsibly go forth. He also ordered the four city gates thrown wide open and instructed that they should sweep the grounds and sprinkle them with water.

Ssu-ma Yi had always regarded Chu-ko Liang as a grave commander, so when Liang manifested this weak appearance he suspected him of holding troops in ambush. Accordingly, Ssu-ma Yi led his numerous troops in a retreat to the northern mountains. By mealtime Liang and his assistants were clapping their hands and laughing. Liang said: "Ssu-ma Yi thinks I am deliberately displaying fear because I have troops in ambush, so he will go around the mountains and depart." An observer returned and reported that it was as Liang had said. Later, when Ssu-ma Yi learned of it, he hated him deeply.

Several variants of this story are known, including a slightly more melodramatic version found in the *The Romance of the Three Kingdoms* in which the city is far emptier, as just twenty-five hundred troops remained (but Ssu-ma Yi is only accorded one hundred fifty thousand men). For further theatrical effect Chu-ko Liang even obliviously played his zither atop the city wall after donning his famous cloak of crane feathers. The one translated here, actually quite close to that included as commentary in the Sung dynasty edition of the *San-kuo Chih*, is employed in the late Sung dynasty's *One Hundred Unorthodox Strategies* as the historical example for "The Vacuous in Warfare." The chapter's tactical discussion states: "If, when you engage an enemy in battle, your strategic power is vacuous, you should create the facade of a substantial disposition to make it

Introduction

impossible for the enemy to determine where you are vacuous, where substantial. When the enemy does not dare recklessly engage your forces, you can preserve your regiments and protect your army."

Chu-ko Liang's name is also associated with inventiveness, arcane knowledge, and esoteric practices ranging from magical military deployments through divination and omen interpretation. He has traditionally been credited with creating "wooden oxen" (木牛) and "flowing horses" (流馬), two reputedly self-moving devices that broadly resembled their namesakes but were probably some form of wheelbarrow, to facilitate transporting essential military provisions along the narrow paths of the constricted valleys that had to be traversed when undertaking incursions into the north. Several tales depict him interpreting celestial phenomena and baleful indications, and two prognosticatory works are associated with his name, the *Chu-ko Liang Shen Kua* (渚葛亮神掛 *Chu-ko Liang's Spiritual Graphs*) and *Chu-ko Liang Suan-fa* (渚葛亮算法 *Chu-ko Liang's Calculation Methodology*), both of which exist in contemporary book form, though of unknown derivation.[9]

Finally, more than Sun-tzu or the T'ai Kung, Chu-ko Liang has in recent centuries been honored as a master of strategic cleverness who, spirit-like, defeated Shu's battlefield enemies through manipulation and unorthodox techniques. His fame in this regard derives not just from his resounding success with the empty city ploy, but also the legendary southern conquest campaign during which he reputedly vanquished the same enemy seven times, having released him after each victory. Reportedly he undertook this imaginative exercise (which gave rise to a popular aphorism) to prove his superiority and convince Meng Huo to willingly submit in order to ensure that peace and stability would continue to prevail when they finally launched their first punitive expedition against Wei in the north.

In the current context of virtually worldwide belief in his surpassing achievements, talents, and powers, it will no doubt strike many readers as heretical to search for the man and his beliefs by scrutinizing his historical accomplishments prior to pondering his probable writings. Nevertheless, understanding the latter and the mission that Chu-ko Liang determinedly undertook requires examining what might be termed the most reliable historical writings, contemplating his

---

[9] Sometimes, without any justification whatever, authorship of the *Thirty-six Stratagems* (三十六計)—a synthetic work that did not appear until the end of the Ch'ing—is also credited to Chu-ko Liang.

activities as recorded in the chronicles and reflected in his memorials and missives, and evaluating the several military campaigns mounted under his direction. This effort is best commenced with a focused but brief overview of the era's tumultuous history, thereby setting the stage for a fuller understanding of the events preserved in his *San-kuo Chih* biography.

The Three Kingdoms

The collapse of the Later Han dynasty (23–220 CE) may have been hastened by the millenarian Yellow Turban uprising but was actually precipitated by a clash between the powerful eunuchs that had come to increasingly control the court and the emperor's relatives. Forces of every type and size, both locally spawned and governmentally raised, arose out of the chaos engendered by the rebellion and its suppression. Several powerful leaders emerged, and others who played collateral but still key roles, such as Chu-ko Liang, Kuan Yü, and Chang Fei, would become heroes. The era's complex intrigues ever after fascinated Chinese audiences, furnishing materials for a highly popular novel, tales, operas, movies, and three television serializations.

Ts'ao Ts'ao first achieved prominence in suppressing the Yellow Turbans, but eventually moved to establish himself as an independent despot after his forces were defeated in a clash with the eunuchs. Some seventeen years would be required before he finally managed to consolidate power south of the Yellow River in 207 CE. During this interval he became a military governor, but also encountered regional opposition and was once, early on, entangled with the stalwart warrior Lü Pu in a hundred-day standoff that ended only when both sides exhausted their supplies. In 195 CE he had successfully ambushed Lü Pu and gained control over two commanderies before going on to defeat remnants of the Yellow Turbans the next year. Surrounded by enemies and plagued by defections, Ts'ao Ts'ao still continued to expand his forces by absorbing allies, volunteers, clan members, local officials, and even subjugated enemies. Famous for his ability to "know men"—to recognize talent and fathom character, and employ them irrespective of their backgrounds or personal enmity—he also attracted

Introduction

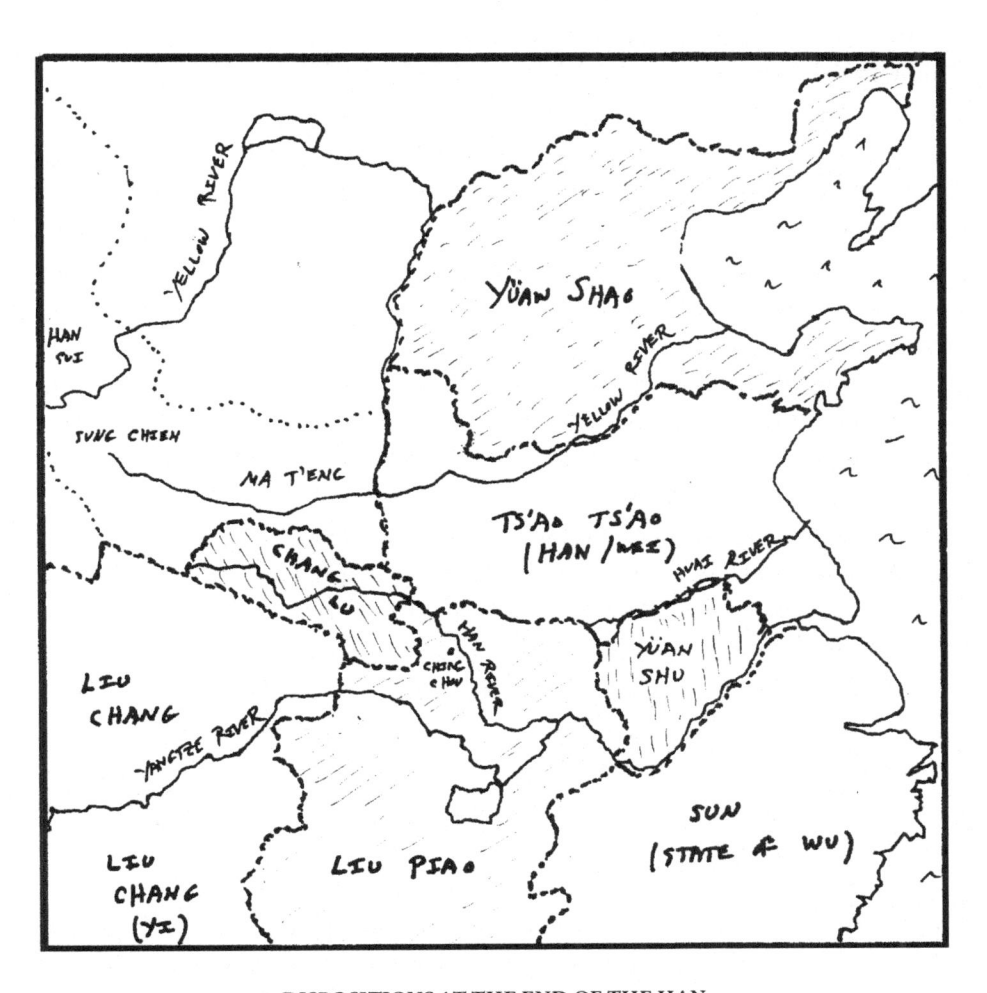

DISPOSITIONS AT THE END OF THE HAN

important defectors, strategists, and other talented individuals from throughout the empire.

Perceiving the economy's dire situation, Ts'ao Ts'ao strove to ensure social order, attract migrant peoples, and nurture agriculture. He also established the military field system (屯田 *t'un-t'ien*) in order to provide local structure and ameliorate logistical problems. To counter Yüan Shao's claims of nobility, he emphasized preserving the Han dynasty and shifted the puppet emperor to Hsü-ch'ang. However, several potent enemies continued to confront him south of the Yellow River, including, but not limited to, Lü Pu, Liu Pei, Yüan Shao and Yüan Shu (cousins but bitter rivals), Liu Piao (who occupied the core area of Ching-chou, but seemed disinclined to expand his holdings), and Chang Hsiu, who commanded roving forces.

Preliminary to attacking the weakest ones, Ts'ao Ts'ao seduced several of them with formal Han titles and subverted a few others. In 197 CE, while Yüan Shao was preoccupied in the north, he attacked Yüan Shu, who had just declared himself emperor, forcing him southward where he died. To counter Liu Piao and Chang Hsiu, he attacked the latter and then ambushed and defeated their coalition forces in the second month of 198 CE.[10] In the tenth month he again struck Lü Pu, who retreated but was subsequently destroyed with an aquatic attack. With his brother's assistance, over a two-year period Ts'ao Ts'ao vanquished several potent enemies, significantly expanding and consolidating his domain.

Meanwhile, Yüan Shao, a powerful military aristocrat, had amassed a force of perhaps one hundred fifty thousand men, of which one hundred thousand infantry, ten thousand cavalry, and eight thousand elite barbarian cavalry would be employed in the forthcoming southern campaign. Little unified and constantly suffering from a shortage of provisions, his armies were tired after three years of nearly constant warfare, whereas Ts'ao Ts'ao's troops remained animated despite their two years in the field. Nevertheless, Yüan Shao decided to attack Ts'ao, but failed to seek a preemptive victory. Furthermore, to reach Hsü-ch'ang, Yüan had to penetrate perimeter defenses established along the Yellow River and then defeat the primary holding force at Kuan-tu.

---

10 In their clash, Ts'ao Ts'ao was actually compelled to retreat, but he exploited the ravines to establish ambushes and then feigned further flight to lure Chang Hsiu into them. Therefore, the *Hundred Unorthodox Strategies* employed these developments as the historical illustration for the topic of "Retreats."

Introduction

Proceeding in measured fashion, Yüan secured his rear and ensured a continuous flow of supplies by employing ten thousand wagons for transport. He also neutralized external threats with judicious alliances and improved the army's command and control, but generally neglected the cavalry's maneuvering capabilities and chose to concentrate his overwhelmingly superior forces rather than segment them for multiple strikes. Conversely, still threatened by Liu Piao and Chang Hsiu, the embattled Ts'ao Ts'ao could only field thirty thousand men who were now precariously close to starvation. Fortunately, well in accord with Chinese martial writings on detecting and exploiting vulnerable traits in enemy commanders, his advisors had already discerned critical flaws in Yüan Shao's character whom they considered greedy, ignorant, cowardly, jealous, and suspicious.

Ts'ao Ts'ao dispatched twenty thousand troops to Li-yang, deployed numerous small contingents to key areas and strong points on the flanks and rear, including the historically important ford at Meng-chin, and shifted ten thousand soldiers to Kuan-tu. Chang Hsiu fortuitously shifted his allegiance to Ts'ao Ts'ao,[11] Liu Piao chose to remain neutral, and other groups either joined as allies or deliberately opted to remain inactive observers. However, Sun Ts'e's assassination precluded any immediate support from the incipient state of Wu located in the east.

Being an astute student of the classic military writings as well as said to have been the *Art of War*'s first editor and commentator, Ts'ao Ts'ao had mounted his primary defense at Kuan-tu, south of the Chi River, to compel Yüan's forces to ford the river.[12] Complicating his situation, Liu Pei renounced his nominal allegiance and moved to establish an independent, threatening position in the east at the end of 199 CE. Ts'ao Ts'ao then adroitly resolved his tactical quandary by mounting a rapid assault that vanquished Liu Pei before he could ensconce himself, compelling him to flee with his shattered forces and join Yüan Shao.

In the second month of 200 CE, Yüan Shao finally launched his southern offensive, with peripheral strikes that saw Ts'ao Ts'ao withdraw from Li-yang but

---

11 A development employed by the *Hundred Unorthodox Strategies* as the historical illustration for the topic of "Surrender."
12 See "Military Combat" in the *Art of War*.

one of Yüan's generals also defeated and slain in a collateral action at Pai-ma.[13] Exemplifying his frequent use of varying and imaginative tactics, Ts'ao Ts'ao managed to ambush the pursuing forces and gain another surprising victory. Yüan Shao then gingerly attempted to exploit his numerical advantage by deputing secondary forces to maneuver down through the west and having Liu Pei strike toward the capital while a second force proceeded in a smaller arc. Perhaps because their numbers were insufficient, both were summarily defeated by highly motivated troops under Ts'ao Jen and others.

Seeking a decisive confrontation, Yüan then moved the bulk of his forces south in the eighth month, by which time Ts'ao Ts'ao's own situation had further deteriorated. Although suffering constant shortages, increasing defections by both allies and his own troops, and even the risk of subversion, Ts'ao Ts'ao maintained a defensive posture because retreat would mean extinction. The six-month standoff was only resolved when one of Yüan's frustrated commanders unexpectedly defected and provided detailed knowledge of a supply depot roughly forty *li* to the north, where some ten thousand wagons and an equal number of troops were concentrated but neither perimeter defenses nor scouting operations had been undertaken.

Ts'ao Ts'ao immediately mounted a night assault with five thousand cavalry flying the enemy's banners and disguised in their uniforms. After proceeding by an indirect route and deflecting all incidental challenges by claiming they had been sent to reinforce the camp against sudden attack, they initiated their assault with incendiaries and then exploited the succeeding chaos to slaughter the defenders and complete the destruction, again just as advised in the *Art of War*, which states: "When fires are started within their camp, you should immediately respond with an attack from outside."[14]

Yüan Shao found himself in a dilemma: whether to immediately attack Kuan-tu en masse, since its already limited numbers had been significantly depleted, or dispatch a large force to rescue the supply depot and vanquish the

---

13 The battle at Pai-ma resulted from a thrust suggested by Hsün Yu to segment Yüan Shao's forces. His advice is cited in the historical illustration for "Disposition" in the *Hundred Unorthodox Strategies*. Another aspect is similarly employed for the topic of "Bait."
14 "Incendiary Warfare," *Art of War*. The attack provides the historical illustration for "Provisions" in the *Hundred Unorthodox Strategies*.

attackers. Ultimately he indecisively attempted to do both by ordering a massive, direct assault on Kuan-tu, despite having failed to reduce it over the previous six months, and simultaneously dispatching a cavalry contingent to the supply depot. Aware of the cavalry's imminent arrival, Ts'ao Ts'ao concentrated on destroying the depot rather than confiscating desperately needed provisions and then defeated the onrushing reinforcements before hastening back. Meanwhile, realizing that he was doomed for having failed to overrun the bastion at Kuan-tu, Yüan's assault commander surrendered with all his troops and equipment. Ts'ao Ts'ao then counterattacked Yüan Shao's remaining, highly dispirited troops and achieved total victory. Yüan barely escaped with just eight hundred men while his forces suffered a reported seventy thousand casualties.

Ts'ao Ts'ao's Reversals

Several governors and other high military officials held power south and east of the Yangtze River, but most of them were unmarked by any great ambition and incapable of quelling the disorder about them. Sun Chien's martial achievements had earlier prompted the Han to grant him increasingly prestigious, though unsupported, appointments, and with each victory his "righteous" army had grown. By 187 CE he had already been appointed governor of Ch'ang-sha and distinguished himself in the war against Tung Chuo before being assassinated. After inheriting his father's power base, Sun Ts'e, only seventeen, quickly targeted the east because he believed he could wrest power from the lethargic administrators posted there while being unfettered by major enemies such as Ts'ao Ts'ao. In view of Yüan Shu's conspicuous lack of ability and the impossibility of him attaining emperorship, Sun Ts'e's decisiveness, courage, and talent quickly attracted numerous adherents, and within four years he succeeded in gaining control of an extensive area in the southeast.

Sun Ts'e's approach to growing his power emphasized attracting people and winning their allegiance through beneficent measures coupled with strict military constraints that were intended to prevent pillaging and plundering. He similarly strove to recruit talented individuals and readily integrated defeated forces; employed unorthodox tactics and multiple techniques, including ruses and false letters to induce laxity or destabilize the enemy by coercing them into movement before attacking; and highly valued military intelligence because he not only had a strategic vision, but also the acumen to actualize it. After he was assassinated in 200 CE, his younger brother, Sun Ch'üan, retained the old generals and continued efforts to attract additional followers. Imbued with the same strategic vision, he first secured their fertile base in the east then redirected his attention westward and northward, making conflict with Ts'ao Ts'ao inevitable.

Liu Pei had also achieved his initial prominence as a minor commander when he battled the Yellow Turbans, but lacked real power himself. Nevertheless, early on he managed to attract the allegiance of two heroic warriors, the stalwart Kuan Yü (who would eventually be apotheosized as the god of war) and the irascible Chang Fei, and the three reputedly even pronounced themselves to be "brothers," comrades in arms who would live and die together (even though Liu Pei would always be accorded precedence). After Yüan Shao's defeat at Kuan-tu they fled to the province of Ching-chou, where Liu Piao attempted to employ Liu Pei's forces as a screen against Ts'ao Ts'ao. Pei's ostensibly righteous persona and visible potential soon began attracting many of Liu Piao's partisans, even before Pei learned of Chu-ko Liang. Shortly after Liang joined him, Liu Pei's forces jumped by some ten thousand.

From 201 to 206 CE, Ts'ao Ts'ao continued consolidating his domination of the north through astute military and administrative measures that included remitting taxes, fostering the people's welfare, rectifying their customs, stabilizing society, and establishing schools. The impetus for the famous Battle of Red Cliffs was his thrust to gain control of the crucial area of Ching-chou and thereby expand his empire, though precluding potential rivals from employing it against him doubtlessly was equally important. Meanwhile, Liu Pei had been clandestinely developing his own power and was seemingly well prepared to take advantage of Liu Piao's sudden demise in the eighth month of 208. However, Ts'ao Ts'ao decisively exploited the ensuing vacuum to wrest quick victories against Liu Piao's former armies and to drive Liu Pei southward, capturing and then annexing the northern part of Ching-chou, as well as absorbing its seventy thousand troops and acquiring some one thousand naval vessels. Since Liu Pei's situation

Introduction

had become desperate, and neither he nor Sun Ch'üan could withstand Ts'ao Ts'ao alone, they opted to unite despite their enmity and distrust once Chu-ko Liang persuaded Sun Ch'üan that he had little future if compelled to face Ts'ao Ts'ao in isolation.

To oppose Ts'ao Ts'ao's approximately one hundred fifty thousand infantry and seventy thousand naval forces Sun Ch'üan mobilized thirty thousand infantry. Although Kuan Yü commanded a mere ten thousand naval forces on Liu Pei's behalf, they decided to seek a decisive battle. Prior to the main clash, Ts'ao Ts'ao attempted to fragment Sun Ch'üan's power by dispatching secondary forces against him, but the crux of his campaign was simply a coordinated advance down the Yangtze River by his presumably well-trained, vast armada. After deploying to block a few key points, in preliminary skirmishes the southern coalition forces surprisingly defeated Ts'ao Ts'ao's onrushing infantry, perhaps a harbinger of the actual battle that would see his massive flotilla destroyed and his armies decimated.

Because Ts'ao Ts'ao chose to harbor his vastly superior forces in port after suffering minor setbacks and sacrificed the initiative, the Battle of Red Cliffs (Ch'ih Pi 赤壁) was essentially a static encounter. In addition, he foolishly sacrificed his mobility by lashing the vessels together, and apparently had wooden catwalks erected across them, thereby linking the entire undulating mass to their land encampments. Reportedly intended to ameliorate the discomfort plaguing his northern troops, who found the incessant rocking motion caused by the Yangtze's current and windblown waves insufferable, these measures were quickly detected when archers were witnessed practicing upon them. Immediately realizing that even a small fire would quickly spread, one of Sun Ch'üan's veteran commanders, Huang Kai, rather than Chou Yü or Chu-ko Liang, advised mounting an incendiary attack.

The carefully planned assault required extensive preparation and an unimpeded approach that was achieved through Huang Kai's feigned defection. Ten large vessels were filled with combustible materials that had been soaked in oil to produce a huge conflagration and ensure that massive casualties would be inflicted in the resulting confusion. Ts'ao Ts'ao negligently allowed Huang to sail his ships directly in, rather than arranging to accept his surrender at some distant, unthreatening location. After having rapidly closed on the heightening wind, once they forcefully collided and the spreading flames engulfed the fleet, escape became impossible. Archery volleys from Kuan Yü's naval forces quickly exploited the chaos, felling many who managed to avoid being trapped in the fire.[15]

The famous T'ang dynasty poet Li Po memorialized the debacle in his "Ode on Parting from Red Cliffs":

Two dragons battled to decide victor and vanquished,
Towered ships at Ch'ih Pi swept the land clear.
Fierce fires rose up to Heaven, illuminating the sea of clouds,
Here Chou Yü destroyed Duke Ts'ao.

With his navy in ruins and his forces decimated, the normally resilient Ts'ao Ts'ao surprisingly abandoned the field without making any attempt to gather his remnant forces, inspire a valiant defense, or otherwise thwart the enemy's advance. Thousands of weakened troops perished from illness on the northward trek, and many more were slaughtered by southern coalition forces as his now disorganized rabble fled for their lives. Torrential rains rendered the roads impassable, and when rescue forces finally arrived, Ts'ao Ts'ao galloped off virtually alone without rallying his troops.

Ts'ao Ts'ao suffered additional defeats the next year that compelled him to retrench and rebuild his forces. Liu Pei exploited the victory to recover some territory further south, but Ts'ao Ts'ao still retained control of the recently acquired northern portions of Ching-chou. The employment of hundreds of boats in what was then China's largest riverine campaign to date indicates the integral role that naval forces would play in military expeditions around and south of the Yangtze River. However, although massive infantry forces were also employed in this relatively well-coordinated campaign, the two were not yet fully integrated.

---

15 For further discussion and the evolution of incendiary warfare, particularly the developments that occurred in the Three Kingdoms period, see Sawyer, *Fire and Water: The Art of Incendiary and Aquatic Warfare in China*.

Introduction

Liu Pei's conquest of Yi

Populated by disparate peoples, including Yi minorities who detested the "northerners" increasingly dominating the province, Yi encompassed a highly fertile area that had been largely untouched by the chaos spawned by the Yellow Turbans. Despite his deliberately nurtured reputation for imperturbable righteousness, Liu Pei subjugated Liu Chang, the area's chief power holder, largely through subterfuge after Chang had requested his presence to blunt threats posed by Chang Lu and his possible defeat by Ts'ao Ts'ao in the north. After nearly three years (211–214) of dithering, conniving, and military campaigns, Pei finally compelled him to surrender the last remaining bastion of Ch'eng-tu, achieved only because Chang nobly shunned inflicting further casualties upon the less than supportive populace.[16]

Having gained control of Yi, Liu Pei strove to forge the stable bastion that he deemed necessary for recovering the realm by entrusting Chu-ko Liang with the major administrative responsibilities and initiating military actions in the north. However, his seizure of Yi infuriated Sun Ch'üan, who had been deceived by specious arguments about the nature of their alliance and whose advance into Ching (Ching-chou) had been forcefully blocked by Kuan Yü. Moreover, Wu had also been expanding southward ever since 211, and even though Ts'ao Ts'ao still occupied the conjoined cities of Hsiang-yang and Fan-ch'eng on the Han River, Sun Ch'üan continued to view Ching-chou as the springboard for any northern attack.

Liu Pei had been forced to nominally acknowledge Sun Ch'üan's authority, and he even enjoyed close familial relations after having married Sun's younger sister. Furthermore, Sun Ch'üan had only temporarily ceded administrative control over two of Wu's commandaries on the premise that Liu could unify the people in Ching-chou and constitute an active bulwark against Wei's vastly superior strength. When Sun Ch'üan demanded that they be returned, Liu justified retaining them on the pretext that they were necessary to withstand Ts'ao Ts'ao. He also immediately deputed Kuan Yü to occupy the potentially contested

---

16 The major stages of the process and a number of puzzling aspects are discussed in the concluding section.

regions, particularly Ch'ang-sha, resulting in the above-mentioned stalemate. Armed conflict was only aborted when Wei's advancing forces prompted a temporary reconciliation, the non-Wei-controlled portion of Ching-chou being split between them.

The battle for domination of Han-chung, initially under the control of Chang Lu, a powerful and extremely popular local leader whose authority had received grudging recognition from the Han, unfolded in two stages. In 215, concerned that Liu Pei might attempt to annex the region because of its strategic value and critical location between Yi-chou and Kuan-chung, Ts'ao Ts'ao advanced through several mountainous valleys with a sizable force, only to encounter unexpectedly strong opposition from indigenous groups and Chang Lu's brother. Eventually compelled to withdraw because of a lack of provisions, he yet managed to secure Chang Lu's voluntary surrender (whom he retained in place) and consolidate control of the so-called Three Pa commanderies in the northeastern region. He also moved the astonishing number of eighty thousand households to Luo-yang and Yeh-ch'eng.[17]

In 217, prompted by Fa Cheng's assessment of Han-chung's strategic value, Liu Pei led a large army into the area and attacked Yang-p'ing-kuan. When he managed to gain initial victories over Hsia Hou Yüan and Chang Ho, Ts'ao Ts'ao responded by coming forth with vastly increased forces, compelling Liu Pei to persistently avoid battle in an attempt to enervate Wei's troops who were already beginning to suffer from a shortage of provisions. However, only after an unexpected reversal brought about by Chao Yün's astute employment of an empty city ploy) did Ts'ao Ts'ao commence withdrawing, concluding the more than eighteen-month conflict and yielding the core, but not the peripheral areas, of Han-chung to Liu Pei.[18]

In the seventh month of 219, Wu and Wei clashed in the Huai-nan region, creating an opportunity for Kuan Yü to attack the important city of Fan-ch'eng. Heavy rains in the eighth month fortuitously inundated the northern encampments, forcing the surrender of seven Wei armies totaling some forty thousand

---

17 *Tzu-chih T'ung-chien, chüan* 67, "Han-chi, 59," Hsien-ti Chien-an 20th year (215).
18 *Tzu-chih T'ung-chien, chüan* 68, "Han-chi, 60," Hsien-ti Chien-an 22nd year.

Introduction

men.[19] Kuan Yü then surrounded Fan-ch'eng and attacked the companion city of Hsiang-yang on the southern bank of the Han River. (Much contested in future centuries, these twin cities would always be crucial to any military progress north or south, but were not yet directly linked.) Kuan Yü had momentum and looked invincible, but in moving north he had inadvertently left a vacuum in his rear.

Prudence dictated mounting a preventive defense against possible Wu perfidy, but Kuan Yü focused all his efforts on the assault, allowing Ts'ao Ts'ao to persuade Wu to launch an unexpected strike against him, despite Sun's purported alliance with Liu Pei.[20] Wei then deviously employed a secret letter of agreement received from Sun Ch'üan to stimulate the resolve of the beleaguered defenders and foster doubt in Kuan Yü's camp. Wary of the latter's strength, the Wu commander Lü Meng opted to diffuse his awareness rather than immediately undertake a strike. Feigning illness, he arranged for the appointment of a sub-commander (Lu Hsün), who sent laudatory letters of admiration that preyed upon Kuan Yü's vanity and surprisingly subverted the wariness appropriate to their somewhat precarious situation.[21]

Their apparently idyllic rapport was shattered when Sun Ch'üan found a pretext for initiating military action in Kuan Yü's having appropriated provisions from Wu's storehouses to feed the thirty thousand northern prisoners recently acquired. Lu Hsün cleverly cloaked his assault armada as a fleet of commercial vessels, concealed the troops, and dressed the sailors as ordinary boatmen. Traveling upriver both day and night, they overwhelmed all the lookouts before they could sound an alert and thus suddenly appeared on target, often startling the local commanders into surrendering without offering the least resistance. Venturing ever westward, Lu seized Yi-ling, subdued local opposition, and cut off Kuan Yü's retreat, leaving him vulnerable to a northern strike that never materialized

---

19 The historical illustration for the topic of "The Substantial in Warfare" in the *Hundred Unorthodox Strategies* is Yü Chin's failed attack on Kuan Yü.

20 Ssu-ma Yi persuaded Ts'ao Ts'ao that since Yü Chin's defeat had not been brought about by Kuan Yü's strategy but the ill fortune of torrential rains, Kuan could still be attacked, particularly from behind. (His discussion forms the historical illustration for the topic of "Alliances" in the *Hundred Unorthodox Strategies*.)

21 This readily accomplished manipulation, one well in accord with dictums to nurture arrogance and promote laxity in the enemy's commander, was subsequently chosen to illustrate the topic of "Arrogance" in the *Hundred Unorthodox Strategies*.

Zhuge Liang: Strategy, Achievements, and Writings

because Ts'ao Ts'ao wanted his enemies to reduce each other, just as advocated in the classic military writings and taught by historical examples.

In a classic manipulative effort, Wu's commander-in-chief, Lü Meng, then implemented a conspicuously humanitarian policy throughout the newly occupied territory that resulted in treating the populace so well that the glowing reports brought back by Kuan Yü's spies badly undermined Shu's fighting spirit.[22] Nearby Shu generals surprisingly refused to provide external support, and despite his valor, Kuan Yü actually experienced a high rate of desertion as he moved to a more advantageous position. In the twelfth month, Wu's forces finally captured and killed him, ignominiously ending the career of the much-glorified but somewhat headstrong warrior who would subsequently be apotheosized as the god of war.[23]

As a result of these victories, Wu now controlled all of southern Ching-chou, and the next year an important general defected to Wei, further reducing Shu's terrain. Sun Ch'üan's campaign had increased Wu's territory and augmented their overall strength through the absorption of captured troops, but it had also seriously damaged the military capability of their only possible ally and significantly subverted the geostrategic tenets of the realm's tripartite division, if only because it compounded the difficulties of communication between Yi and Ching. Furthermore, it compelled them to thereafter shoulder the full burden of Ching-chou's defense and can definitely be said to have precluded Shu from ever inflicting a substantial defeat on Wei, whether alone or in coordination with Wu.

Infuriated by the perfidious slaughter of his longtime comrade, Liu Pei promptly mounted an assault to exact revenge and recover Ching-chou, in the seventh month of 221 with nearly sixty thousand troops. Although Sun Ch'üan had anticipated this expeditionary campaign and prepared extensive defenses along the Yangtze River against Liu's probable retribution, the onslaught quickly achieved several victories, compelling Lü Meng to withdraw and undertake a persisting defense. The campaign also benefited from Wei's surprising failure

---

22 Another aspect chosen to illustrate a *Hundred Unorthodox Strategies* topic, in this case "Letters."
23 It should be noted that appraisals of Kuan Yü's culpability in this debacle vary, with his fervent fans claiming that he had basically been abandoned by Liu Pei or entrusted with an impossible task for a bold warrior.

to attack either of the belligerents, but was perhaps ill-fated by Chang Fei's assassination.

Lü Meng then adopted the classic withering strategy of allowing the invader to penetrate the interior, so as to stretch out their supply lines and disperse their forces while waiting for their strength to wane and their spirits to decline. After deliberately refusing battle for some six months despite virulent taunts and provocations, he then exploited Liu Pei's frustration and enervation by launching incendiary attacks in the dry summer heat against the forty camps scattered along the Yangtze River and then exploiting the chaos with fervent follow-on strikes. Liu Pei managed to escape with a very small contingent, but the majority of his troops perished, and their ships and supplies were largely destroyed. Finding himself isolated in the north, another Shu field commander, Huang Ch'üan, perversely opted to surrender to Wei rather than intercede with a flank attack. Only thereafter did Wei, despite Wu's now nominal submission, finally mount a three-pronged attack on the latter, with indifferent results.

Shu's Prolongation and Demise

Well protected by intervening mountains, the fertile Sichuan valley was situated in a natural bastion characterized by easily defended narrow passes. However, the highly constricted, often circuitous routes that thwarted invaders equally impeded furnishing the supplies required by Shu's northern expeditionary armies because draft animals and wide wagons could rarely be employed. In addition, the semitropical climate made warfare unbearable for northern invaders in the summer months and could debilitate even well-acclimated local forces. Under Chu-ko Liang's efficient leadership the state was unified and strengthened, and its limited military forces embarked upon a rebuilding program that stressed physical qualifications and training. About this time Liang also invented (or perhaps improved and exploited) both the single-wheel wheelbarrow and a multiple-bolt crossbow reportedly capable of firing ten arrows at once,[24] and formulated his famous (but now lost) Eight Deployments.

---

24 It should be noted that precursor weapons were already being employed late in the Warring States period.

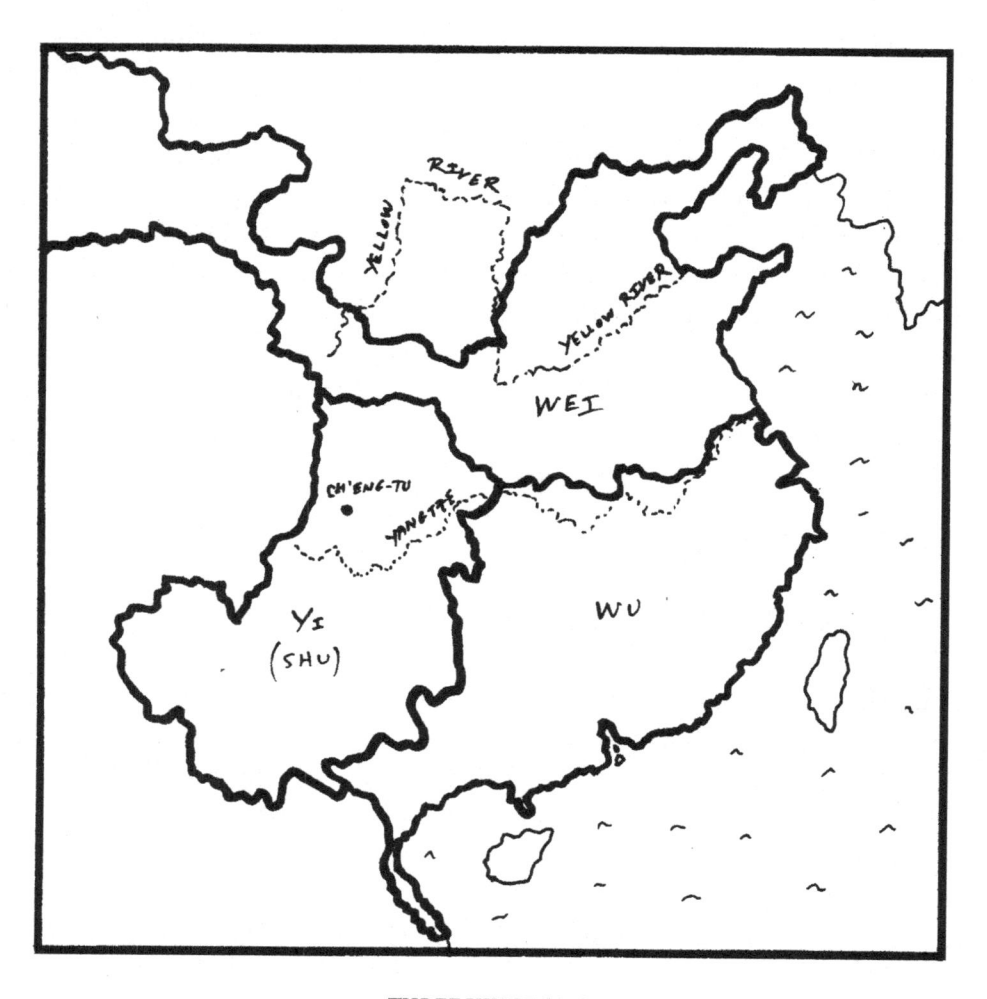

THREE KINGDOMS

Introduction

Still committed to their quest to restore the Han, and despite being compressed into China's southwestern quarter, Chu-ko Liang felt compelled to secure the northern approaches, expand up into the Wei River valley, employ it as a corridor to the major centers of Ch'ang-an and then Luo-yang, and thereby exterminate the northern usurpers. Unfortunately, Liu Pei's death not only postponed the great task of restoring the Han kingship but also prompted several southern commandaries to revolt. Only after subduing the rebellion-plagued area could Chu-ko Liang plan and then direct the five successive expeditions intended to subjugate Wei that would be mounted over the next seven years. However, as discussed below, none of them achieved their objectives or even noteworthy success. Furthermore, despite Chiang Wei's numerous martial efforts both the government and Shu's strategic situation quickly deteriorated after Chu-ko Liang's own death.

Throughout this period, the well-known strategist, commander, and eventual usurper Ssu-ma Yi had been consolidating both his and Wei's power. Although Chin (as it would now be known) consistently plotted against the weaker state of Shu, it deceptively strove to create the impression that Wu had been targeted for annihilation. About this time Shu shortsightedly vitiated its forward defenses to implement a new, ultimately futile strategy intended to entice Wei's invading forces onto the interior plains where they (theoretically) could be vanquished. At the end of 263, Wei launched a three-pronged attack whose western and central strike forces each numbered thirty thousand and whose eastern contingent, itself divided into three prongs, reportedly encompassed a vast one hundred twenty thousand troops. After rapidly transiting the undefended mountains, these armies overwhelmed the initial line of about fifty thousand defenders, leaving Shu's fate in the hands of the paltry forty thousand soldiers then held in reserve around the chief cities.

Despite the strategy's flaws and a tardy response by their secondary forces, a resolute effort surprisingly managed to block Wei's main advance, exposing its troops to flank and rear attacks and making their supply lines untenable. However, a minor but determined ten-thousand-man aggressor force negotiated a difficult circuitous route and suddenly materialized in Shu's rear, stunning many of the unprepared defenders into surrendering without a fight.[25] Another quick victory brought them to Ch'eng-tu's very walls, whereupon the ever-ineffectual emperor meekly surrendered.

The Conquest of Wu

The formidable Yangtze River would always prove a daunting obstacle against incursions, ensuring that southern states could survive if they defended the fords and prepared adequate vessels to repel small-scale riverine operations, especially during quiet seasons. Even major amphibious assaults could be thwarted because highly visible staging would be required, allowing the timely dispatch of opposition forces. Nevertheless, Wei's conquest campaign not only reduced the Yangtze to a surmountable inconvenience, but also redefined it as an exploitable topographical feature. As subsequent Chinese history would repeatedly show, self-contained fleets sweeping down from Sichuan could easily vanquish enemy forces, whether deployed on the river or ensconced along the banks. Little advance warning could ever be expected because their speed upon the current normally exceeded all but the fastest relay horses, and the upper Yangtze's winding course and mountainous terrain made the sighting of signal fires problematic.

Wei had significantly augmented their resources and already massive troop numbers through its conquest of Shu. Coincidentally, Wu's new emperor was not only greedy and debauched but also oblivious to the growing threat. Having concluded that Wu's strength lay in its naval forces but that its commanders lacked the will for sustained battle, Chin's strategists opted for another multipronged, conjoined land and river attack in order to draw Wu's defensive forces away from the water while simultaneously exploiting the river's flow. Their preparations extended over some fifteen years, the last seven being devoted to constructing several hundred large warships and training an aggressive naval force in Yi.

Some two hundred thousand troops embarked on the invasion in the second month of 280. Although unorthodox cavalry forces forded the river to establish a beachhead, and a floating bridge constructed across the Yangtze allowed troops to

---

25 The *Hundred Unorthodox Strategies* employs Teng Ai's innovative campaign as the historical illustration for the crucial topic of "The Unorthodox." (For further discussion of the unorthodox aspects, see Sawyer, *The Tao of Deception: Unorthodox Warfare in Historic and Modern China*, 158–161.)

cross over, the land forces actually made little contribution. However, the riverine components swept down the Yangtze largely unopposed after they eliminated the large chains that had been emplaced to block the river.[26] Unfortunately for Wu, the Yangtze's great length prevented its widely dispersed armies from mounting an adequate defense at any particular point, or even effectively communicating. Because their ill-prepared troops lacked the will for battle and several of their commanders simply rushed to preserve themselves, Chin's riverine assault forces achieved numerous victories in quick succession, often without having to engage in combat. Surging forward, they placed unremitting pressure on the defenders until the emperor finally surrendered without a fight.

---

26 For further information, see "Riverine Incendiary Strikes" in Sawyer, *Fire and Water*.

2
San-kuo Chih Biography

Succinct and insubstantial as it may be, Ch'en Shou's biography in the *Chronicle of the Three Kingdoms* remains the only comparatively reliable characterization of Chu-ko Liang's life and achievements. The core of his account may be translated as follows:

> Chu-ko Liang, who styled himself K'ung-ming, was a native of Yang-tu in Lang-ya and a descendant of Chu-ko Feng, [formerly] *Ssu-li Hsiao-wei* [under the Later Han].[27] His father, Kuei, had the style name of Chün-kung. At the end of the Han he had served as the *Chün-ch'eng* (Commandery Sub-prefect) of T'ai-shan [Commandery].
>
> Liang was orphaned early on. When his uncle, Chu-ko Hsüan, was temporarily assigned by Yüan Shu as *T'ai-shou* (Governor) of Yü-chang, he had Liang and his younger brother Chün come to his headquarters. However, it happened that the Han court appointed Chu Hao, who then replaced him. As Hsüan had previously been friends with Liu Piao, the *Mu* (Regional Governor) of Ching-chou, he went to throw in with him.[28] When Hsüan died Liang took

---

[27] Without extensive research and a comprehensive chart of the era's bureaucracies, translating many of these titles or even determining functional equivalents is unproductive, even meaningless, especially as their general sense is clear from the context. Therefore, only rough approximations have been provided for the more important ones. (For some of them, see Charles O. Hucker, *A Dictionary of Official Titles in Imperial China*.)

[28] The positions of governor (for a commandery) and regional governor (for a *chou* or province), *t'ai-shou* and *mu*, respectively, entailed both civil and military power and were often filled by officials who held a concomitant rank of general (*chiang-chün*). In times of weak central authority or fragmentation they could accumulate great power, with several of the *mu* (which originally meant "shepherd") becoming virtual warlords during the Later Han's disintegration.

up farming near Mount Lung-chung. He liked to recite the verses of the [old folk tune] "Liang-fu-yin."[29]

Liang was six foot six inches tall[30] and frequently compared himself to Kuan Chung and Yüeh Yi but none of his contemporaries agreed. Only Ts'ui Chou-p'ing of Po-ling district and Hsü Shu, personally styled Yüan-chih, made friends with Liang and believed him. At this time Liu Pei was encamped at Hsin-yeh where Hsü Shu went to visit him. Liu Pei regarded Hsü as a great talent. Hsü advised Liu Pei, "Chu-ko K'ung-ming is a sleeping dragon. Would you, General, be willing to see him?"

Liu Pei replied, "Bring him in with you."

Hsü then said, "It is possible to go see this man but he cannot be compelled to appear. It would be best, general, for you to condescend to visit him." Thereafter Liu Pei went to visit Liang three times before meeting him.

After dismissing his attendants, Liu Pei said: "The house of Han is about to be overturned, villainous ministers exercise authority,[31] and the ruler is covered in dust and has fled for refuge [to Hsü-ch'ang]. Without considering my virtue or measuring my strength I want to extend great righteousness throughout the realm, but my knowledge and measures have been inadequate and shallow. Despite employing them, perversity has continued up until the present.

---

29 Although there are later renditions of a poetic tune with this name, they are said to lack any connection with the original.
30 The modern equivalent for a Han era height of "eight feet," which would have been extremely rare in this period and made him a giant among men.
31 Referring primarily, but not exclusively, to Ts'ao Ts'ao.

Zhuge Liang: Strategy, Achievements, and Writings

Nevertheless, my will remains unbroken. What strategy might you suggest?"[32]

Chu-ko Liang replied: "Ever since Tung Chuo [revolted], the powerful and heroic have arisen and the number who bestride provinces or unite commandaries cannot be counted. Compared with Yüan Shao, Ts'ao Ts'ao's name was insignificant and his troops few, yet Ts'ao was subsequently able to conquer Shao. When the weak vanquish the strong, not only must it have accorded with the moments of Heaven but also had to be because of human plans. Ts'ao has now amassed a horde of a million and is coercing the Son of Heaven in order to command the feudal lords. In these circumstances it is certainly not possible to directly contend with him.

"Sun Ch'üan's [family] has occupied the area east of the Yangtze River for three generations.[33] The state is constricted, but the populace has given him their allegiance and he is able to employ the worthy and capable. Wu can be a source of support but cannot be planned against.

"The northern part of Ching is occupied by two rivers, the Han and Mien, and it profits extensively from the southern sea. To the east it connects with Wu and K'uai, to the west with Pa and Shu. This is a state that can employ the military but the ruler cannot preserve it. Heaven probably

---

32 His vaunted geostrategic analysis, known as the "Lung-chung Tui" or the "Ts'ao-lü Tui," follows. (It subsequently became so famous that the *Hundred Unorthodox Strategies* employs parts of it to illustrate the very first chapter on the crucial topic of "Estimation.")

33 Chiang-tung, the area east of the Yangtze River, encompasses the terrain where the Spring and Autumn states of Wu and Yüeh formerly existed, explaining why Wu and Yüeh subsequently appear as references. (Not really three generations in the normal sense, as Sun Chien, the founder, was succeeded by his son, Sun Ts'e, but Ts'e by his brother.)

intends to provide this resource to you. Do you have any inclinations about this?

"Within Yi's constricted and isolated territory lie a thousand *li* of fertile fields, it is the terrain of a Heavenly kingdom. Emperor Kao-tsu relied on it to achieve emperorship.[34] Liu Chang is obtuse and weak while Chang Lu occupies the area to the north. The people are flourishing and the state prosperous, but Liu Chang does not know how to be solicitous of the people. His wise and capable officers long for an enlightened ruler.

"You, general, are a descendant of the imperial house and your good faith and righteousness are prominent within the four seas. You seize upon stalwart heroes from all about and think of the worthy as if thirsty. If you were to bestride Ching and Yi, seeking preservation in their cliffs and narrows, establish harmonious relations with the various Jung in the west and be solicitous toward the Yi and Yüeh in the south, conclude an alliance with Sun Ch'üan in the east, and internally cultivate good government, when the realm's situation changes you could order a high-ranking general to lead Ching's armies in advancing into Wan [Nan-yang in Henan] and Luo [Luo-yang in Henan] while you personally lead Yi's troops out along Ch'in's rivers.[35] Who among the populace would dare not welcome these armies with baskets of food and jars of soy sauce? If events truly proceed in this

---

34 Having been vanquished by Hsiang Yü, Liu Pang, who eventually succeeded in defeating Hsiang to establish the Former Han dynasty, fled for refuge to Shu (Sichuan), also known as Yi, where he reordered his forces and replenished his supplies before resurging into the central plains area.

35 The rivers within Kuan-chung where the former state of Ch'in arose and the Chou flourished before conquering the Shang.

fashion, the task of hegemony can be achieved[36] and the house of Han can again be made to flourish."

Assenting by saying "good," Liu Pei then established a friendly relationship with Chu-ko Liang that grew closer every day. Kuan Yü, Chang Fei, and others were displeased, but Liu Pei defused [their unhappiness] by saying that "my having gained Chu-ko Liang is like a fish having water. I hope you honorable men will not speak of it again." Kuan Yü and Chang then desisted.

Liu Piao's eldest son Ch'i also deeply respected Liang's talent. It happened that Piao heeded his later wife's words and loved their young son Ts'ung, and thus became displeased with Ch'i. Every time Ch'i wanted to plan measures for his self-preservation, Liang abruptly refused and remained silent, so Ch'i was never able to formulate any plans with him. Ch'i then had Liang take a tour of the rear garden and ascend a high tower with him. While they were eating and drinking he ordered men to remove the steps and then addressed Liang. "Today we are not so high as Heaven nor so low as Earth. Any words that come out of your mouth will enter my ears alone. Can you discuss [my plight] or not?"

Liang replied, "Has my lord not noticed the case of Shen Sheng, who remained within [the palace] and was endangered while Ch'ung Erh was preserved outside it?"[37]

---

36 Chu-ko Liang seems to be thinking of hegemons who sustained the waning majesty and authority of the Chou king, however fictitiously, in the Spring and Autumn period.
37 One of two disfavored sons due to the influence of a new concubine, Ch'ung Erh fled to avoid death, initiating a lengthy period of wandering that gave rise to many dramatic stories and ended only when he regained the throne and initiated a glorious period for Chin.

Having been enlightened, Ch'i secretly formulated plans to go out. It happened that Huang Tsu [*T'ai-shou* of Chiang-hsia] died and Ch'i was able to escape by being appointed as Chiang-hsia's governor. Shortly thereafter Piao died, and when Liu Ts'ung heard that Ts'ao Ts'ao was coming to attack him, he dispatched an emissary to request that he be allowed to surrender.

When Liu Pei learned about it at Fan-ch'eng, he led his troops into the south with Chu-ko Liang and Hsü Shu behind him. Ts'ao Ts'ao pursued and shattered their forces, capturing Hsü's mother. Hsü therefore took leave of Liu Pei by pointing to his heart and saying, "I had originally wanted to plan the affairs of kingship and hegemony with you, great general, using this square inch. Now that I have lost my old mother this inch is very turbulent and of no use in [planning] affairs. I therefore request permission to take my leave." Subsequently he went [to join] Ts'ao Ts'ao.

When Liu Pei reached Hsia-k'ou, Liang then said, "Affairs have reached a critical point! I would like to undertake your mandate to seek rescue from General Sun Ch'üan."

At this time Ch'üan had assembled his troops at Ch'ai-sang and was observing who would be victorious and who defeated. Liang spoke with Ch'üan as follows: "Within the seas there is great chaos. You, general, have mobilized an army and hold the area east of the Yangtze River, while Liu Pei has also assembled troops south of the Han River in order to contend with Ts'ao Ts'ao for all under Heaven. Ts'ao Ts'ao has now exterminated the great obstacles [confronting him in the north], largely pacified the area, and destroyed [his enemies] in Ching-chou, resulting in his awesomeness shaking the four seas. The heroic and valiant having nowhere to employ their military skills, Lu Pei fled.

"General, you should measure your strength and make a decision. If you can contend with [the forces of] the central state across the land, why not sever relations with [Ts'ao Ts'ao] early on? If you cannot oppose him, why not have your army stand down, tie up your armor, face north, and serve him? Right now you are submissive in name while harboring hesitant and doubtful plans. The situation has become critical. If you do not make a decision, misfortune will arrive in a few days!"

Ch'üan replied, "If the situation is as you describe, why doesn't Liu Pei serve him?"[38]

Liang replied, "T'ien Heng, although only a stalwart warrior in Ch'i, still maintained his righteousness rather than be insulted. How much more so will Liu, a descendant of the royal house, a hero for our age whom the troops and officers think of and respect the way the water [in rivers] returns to the sea. If this [great] undertaking is not successful then it will have been due to Heaven. How could he then turn about and again submit to him?"

Ch'üan angrily retorted, "I cannot place all of Wu's terrain and our one hundred thousand troops under the control of others. I have already decided my plans! Other than Liu Pei, no one can oppose Ts'ao Ts'ao. But after his recent defeat, how can he put up any resistance against such a difficult opponent?"

---

38 Throughout they refer to Liu Pei as governor Liu of Yü-chang because he had formerly been assigned there by Ts'ao Ts'ao.

Liang replied, "Although Liu Pei's forces were defeated at Ch'ang-fan, his warriors still include Kuan Yü's naval contingent of ten thousand elite men while Liu Ch'i and the fighters at Chiang-hsia similarly do not number less than ten thousand. Having come from afar Ts'ao Ts'ao's troops are fatigued and depleted. I have heard that in pursuing Liu Pei they covered three hundred *li* in a day and night. This is what is termed being at the end of a strong crossbow's range, where the bolt lacks the power to even penetrate silk from Lu. Accordingly, the *Art of War* counsels against it by saying that 'it will cause the general of the army to stumble.'[39] Moreover, northerners are not accustomed to riverine warfare, and although Ching-chou's populace has given their allegiance to Ts'ao Ts'ao, they were compelled by military power rather than submitting in their hearts.

"Now, general, if you can sincerely appoint a fierce general who can take command of several tens of thousands of soldiers and unite with Liu Pei in exerting their strength, it is certain that they will destroy Ts'ao Ts'ao's army. When his army has been destroyed he will certainly return north, in which case Ching and Wu's strategic power will become strong and compose the legs of a bronze cauldron with three feet.[40] Victory and defeat lie before you today."

Elated, Ch'üan then deputed Chou Yü, Ch'eng P'u, Lu Su, and others with thirty thousand naval forces to accompany Liang in going to Liu Pei and then uniting their strength to resist Ts'ao Ts'ao. After Ts'ao Ts'ao was defeated at Ch'ih-pi he withdrew his army to Yeh. Liu Pei then took control of

---

39 "Military Combat."
40 The extremely famous enunciation!

the commanderies south of the Yangtze River, appointed Liang as *Chün-shih Chung-lang Chiang*, and tasked him with supervising the three commanderies of Ling-ling, Kuei-yang, and Ch'ang-sha, as well as adjusting their military impositions and taxes in order to supply the army's substance.

In the sixteenth year of Chien-an [211 CE] the Yi-chou *Mu*, Liu Chang, dispatched Fa Cheng to meet Liu Pei and request that he attack Chang Lu. Entrusting Liang and Kuan Yü with Ching-chou's occupation, Liu Pei returned from Chia-ming to attack Chang. Subsequently, Liang, Chang Fei, and Chao Yün led troops up the Yangtze, segmenting some off to settle the various commandaries and districts before they besieged Ch'eng-tu together with Liu Pei. After Ch'eng-tu was pacified, Liang was appointed *Chün-shih Chiang-chün* (general of the army) and became responsible for administering the affairs of the office of the *Tsuo Chiang-chün* (general of the Left Army). Whenever Liu Pei went out [on campaign] Liang undertook responsibility for defending Ch'eng-tu and providing adequate food and soldiers.

In the twenty-sixth year of Chien-an [221 CE], all of Liu Pei's subordinates encouraged him to assume the esteemed title [of emperor] but he would not accede. Liang then said: "Formerly when Wu Han, Keng Yen, and several others first encouraged [the progenitor of the Later Han] Liu Hsiu to assume the position of emperor, he declined four times. After this Keng Yen advanced and said, 'All the heroes of the realm are clamoring, hoping for what they expect. If you do not follow their suggestion, these warriors and high officials will all turn away and seek another ruler and no one will follow you.' The founding emperor was deeply moved by these sincere words and thereafter acceded to them.

"Now that Ts'ao Ts'ao has usurped power in the Han the realm has no ruler. You, great king, are a descendant of the Liu family, so if you respond to the age and arise, accepting the position of emperor, it would be appropriate. The warriors and high officials who have long followed you, great king, who have labored and suffered, also expectantly hope to receive [some acknowledgement] of their minor achievements, just as Keng Yen said."

Thereupon Liu Pei assumed the position of emperor and designated Liang as *Ch'eng-hsiang* [Chancellor], saying: "My family met with misfortune, compelling me to assume the task of great unification. Fearful and attentive, I have not dared to relax for a moment, always thinking how to provide tranquility to the hundred surnames and fearing that I would not be able to fully comfort them. Fortunately Chancellor Liang fully understood my intentions and was never remiss in assisting where I was deficient. He has assisted me in again bespreading [the Han's] glory so that it radiantly illuminates the realm. Sir, exert yourself!" The chancellor then had the responsibility of *Lu-hsian Shu* added to his position as chancellor, and when Chang Fei died he also exercised the authority of *Ling-ssu-li Hsiao-wei*.

In the spring of the third year of Chang-wu [223 CE] Liu Pei's illness became severe while he was at Yung-an, so he summoned Liang to Ch'eng-tu and entrusted him with his post-demise affairs, saying: "Your talent is ten times that of Ts'ao P'i, you are certainly capable of providing security to the state and finally achieving the great affair [of uniting the realm]. If the heir-apparent (Liu Shan) can be bolstered, assist him, but if he proves to lack talent, you can take [the emperorship] yourself."[41]

Weeping, Liang replied: "How would I dare not exhaust my inner strength and loyally fulfill my responsibilities until I die!"

Liu Pei then summoned the heir apparent and instructed him as follows: "As you and the chancellor undertake responsibility for the state's affairs, you should serve him as you would your father."

In the first year of Chien-kuang [223 CE] Emperor Liu Shan enfeoffed Liang as Lord of Wu-hsiang [martial village] and established an administrative office for him to manage affairs. Shortly thereafter he was also designated as the *Mu* for Yi-chou. All the government's affairs, no matter how large or small, were decided by Liang. At this time the commanderies in the south rebelled, but in view of the rites of mourning attendant upon the emperor's recent death, Liang decided it would not be prudent to conduct a punitive expedition against them. Moreover, he dispatched an emissary to invite Wu into [renewing] their alliance, with the result that they established peaceful relations[42] and became allies.

---

41 According to information from the *Liang-chi* preserved in the *San-kuo Chih*'s commentaries (and abstracted as the "Cheng Yi" found in many contemporary editions), Chu-ko Liang received letters encouraging him to assume control of the government but he declined on the grounds of virtue.
42 The actual term is *ho-ch'in*, formerly used in Han to refer to alliances based upon marriage relations, highly appropriate insofar as Liu Pei had married Sun Ch'üan's sister.

In the spring of the third year of Chien-kuang [225 CE], Liang led the army on a campaign into the south and by autumn the [rebellious commanderies] had all been thoroughly pacified. All the military expenses incurred were recovered and the state grew rich and prosperous. Thereafter Liang focused on organizing the army and discussing military affairs in order to await a grand mobilization.

In the fifth year, before he led their armies north to occupy Han-chung, he presented a memorial [known as the "Ch'u-shih Piao"]:

"The former emperor had accomplished less than half of his great undertaking before departing. The realm is presently divided into three and Yi-chou is fatigued and depleted. This is truly an autumn of extreme crisis, of survival and extinction. Nevertheless, the ministers responsible for defense are not lax within while our loyal and resolute warriors are willing to sacrifice themselves without, no doubt because of the special treatment they received from the former emperor, which they want to repay to you. Your majesty should be open to and sagaciously listen to their advice in order to gloriously manifest the former emperor's bequeathed virtue and cause the courageous *ch'i* of your determined warriors to flourish everywhere.[43] Do not deprecate yourself and accept unrighteous advice, thereby stopping up the path of loyal remonstrance.

"The palace and administrative offices act as one body, so promotions and punishments, rewards and dismissals

---

43 The Chinese concept of *ch'i*, roughly the essential breath or *pneuma* of the universe, entailed martial spirit and morale in a military context. (For a discussion, see Sawyer, "Martial Qi in China: Courage and Spirit in Thought and Military Practice" in the *Journal of Strategic and Military Studies*, Winter 2008/2009, available at www.jmss.org.)

should not differ. If there are those who commit villainous acts and contravene the ordinances or who are loyal and excel, it would be appropriate to have your officials discuss their punishments and rewards in order to manifest your equitable and enlightened management and avoid any partiality that might result in inner and outer having different regulations.

"Among your *tai-lang*[44] Kuo Shou-chih, Fei Yi, Tung Yün, and other such men are all excellent and substantial, their thoughts and intentions are loyal and pure. For this reason the former emperor selected them to bequeath to your majesty. I humbly believe that you should question them about all the court's affairs, no matter how large or small, before implementing them because they can supplement deficiencies and extensively contribute.

"General Hsiang Ch'ung's character is composed and his actions equitable, he understands and can explicate military affairs. When he was tried in earlier times the late emperor pronounced him capable and after a general discussion Lung was appointed as a *Tu* [military supervisor]. I humbly believe that he should be questioned on all military affairs because he can certainly bring about harmony in the deployments and ensure that superiors and inferiors attain their appropriate places.

The Former Han flourished by bringing worthy ministers close and keeping menial persons distant. [In contrast], by embracing menial persons and keeping worthy ministers distant the Later Han was overturned. When the late emperor was still alive, every time we discussed this affair he

---

44 High civil officials.

sighed and felt pain and hatred for Emperors Huan and Ling. The *Shih-chung, Shang-shu, Chang-shih,* and *Ts'an-chün* are all upright, good ministers who are willing to die for the state. I would like your majesty to keep them close and trust them, for then the days until the glory of the Han house can be restored can be counted.

"I was originally a common person who personally tilled fields at Nan-yang. I sought only to preserve my nature and life in a chaotic world, not to become known among the feudal lords. Despite my lowliness and rusticity the late emperor did not regard me as inferior and unrefined, but instead perturbed himself three times to see me at my grass hut and inquire about the affairs of our world. Because of this I was extremely moved and agreed to share his efforts as he raced about the realm. Later, when he encountered a severe reversal, amid the defeated army I was entrusted with responsibility, and received a mandate during that time of duress twenty-one years ago.

"The late emperor knew that I was fastidious and cautious and therefore entrusted me with great affairs just before his death. Since receiving his mandate I have been worried and troubled morning and night, fearing that I will fail in my responsibilities and thereby detract from the late emperor's illustriousness. Therefore, in the fifth month I crossed the Lu River and penetrated deeply into the desolate land of the south. Now that the southern quarter has been pacified and our weapons and armor are adequate, I ought to exhort the Three Armies and lead them northward to settle the central area, exhaust my inadequate abilities to drive out the villainous and eliminate the brutal, restore the house of Han, and return it to the old capital. In this way I will repay the former emperor and loyally fulfill my responsibility to your majesty.

"It is the responsibility of Kuo Shou-chih, Fei Yi, and Tung Yün to consult about disadvantages and advantages and advance the loyal who will exhaustively remonstrate. I ask that your majesty entrust me with the task of extirpating the brigands and revitalizing [the Han]. If I am not effective, then punish me [with death] in order that I may announce it to the former emperor's spirit. If no words are advanced that promote Virtue, then upbraid Kuo Shou-chih, Fei Yi, and Tung Yün for their laxness in order to make evident their errors.

"Your majesty should also make plans yourself, inquiring and deliberating about the Tao of goodness, investigating and appropriating elegant words, and deeply pursuing the late emperor's instructions. Then I will receive immeasurable beneficence and be extremely grateful. Now that I am about to depart for far-off places, in presenting this memorial I weep and do not know what to say."

Then he set forth, finally encamping at Mien-yang. In the spring of the sixth year he proclaimed that he would seize Mei-yeh by advancing along the Yeh-ku[45] road and deputed Chao Yün and Teng Chih to occupy Chi-ku with a decoy army. Wei's commanding general, Ts'ao Chen, mobilized his troops to resist them. Liang then personally led several armies in an assault on Ch'i-shan. The martial formations were well-ordered, the rewards and punishments strictly respected, and the commands and orders clear. The three

---

45 The character for *yeh* (斜) is normally pronounced *hsieh*.

commanderies of Nan-an, T'ien-shui, and An-ting rebelled against Wei and responded to Liang and Kuan-chung reverberated.

Emperor Ming of Wei went west in the defensive effort and ordered Chang Ho to resist Liang. Liang had general Ma Su supervise the several armies deployed to the fore and engage Chang Ho in battle at Chieh-t'ing. Su contravened Liang's constraints, took inappropriate actions, and was severely destroyed by Ho. Liang plucked some thousand households from the district of Hsi-hsien and shifted them back into Han-chung. He subsequently executed Ma Su to atone to the troops [that were lost].

Liang presented a memorial to the emperor that read: "Because of my feeble talent I incompetently undertook great obligations. I personally grasped the flag [of command] and great battle-axe [of punishment] in order to steel the Three Armies, but was incapable of instructing them in the ordinances or making the laws clear and they became fearful when they approached danger. As for [Ma Su] having disobeyed orders at Chieh-t'ing and the defeat of our forces at Chi-ku, the blame all lies with your minister. I lacked the ability to fulfill my responsibility.

"I clearly do not know men and have been obtuse in my management of affairs. According to the practice of upbraiding commanders recorded in the *Ch'un Ch'iu* (*Spring and Autumn Annals*), since I undertook responsibility I ask to be degraded three ranks to reprove me for my errors."

Thereupon the emperor made Liang *Yu Chiang-chün* [General of the Right], but had him retain concurrent responsibility for implementing all the chancellor's affairs, just as before.

In the winter Liang once again went forth from San-kuan (San pass) and besieged Ch'en-ts'ang. Ts'ao Chen resisted him, and when Liang's provisions were exhausted he returned [to Shu]. When the Wei general Wang Shuang pursued Liang with a cavalry contingent, Liang engaged him in battle, destroyed his forces, and slew him.

In the seventh year, Liang dispatched Ch'en Shih[46] to attack Wu-tu and Yin-p'ing. Yung-chou's *Tz'u-shih* (Regional Inspector), the Wei general Kuo Huai, led his troops in an attempt to attack Shih. Liang then came forth himself as far as Chien-wei, and when Huai turned about and retreated Liang pacified the two commanderies.

The emperor summoned Liang and issued an edict that stated: "In the clash at Chieh-t'ing the error was Ma Su's, but you, sir, accepted the blame and severely degraded yourself. Rather than strongly contravening your thoughts I accepted and implemented what you indicated.

Last year you managed the army brilliantly, slaying Wang Shuang, and this year you continued with a punitive expedition that caused Kuo Huai to flee and also brought about the surrender of several groups of the Ti and Chiang and gloriously repatriated two commanderies. Your awesomeness has shaken the evil and brutal, your achievements are manifest. At this moment the realm is turbulent and troubled, the great source of evil has not yet been extirpated.

---

46 Some texts have Chieh rather than Sh'ih.

You have received great responsibility and the weight of handling the state's weighty affairs but have long deprecated yourself. This is not the way to gloriously raise the vast accomplishments. Today I restore you to the position of chancellor, do not decline."

In the ninth year Liang once again went out to Ch'i-shan, employing "wooden oxen" to transport their provisions. When they were exhausted he withdrew the army but was engaged in battle by Chang Ho, who was slain by archers.

In the spring of the twelfth year Liang led all their forces out through Yeh-ku, relying on the "fluid horses" [*liu ma*] for transport. He occupied Wu-chang-yüan in Wu-kung and engaged in battle with [future] King Ssu-ma Yi south of the Wei River. On every expedition Liang had worried that failing to sustain their provisions would keep him from fully realizing his intentions. For this reason he divided up the soldiers and had them encamp and farm in order to create a foundation for long occupation. Although these farmers were interspersed along both banks of the river and dwelled among the inhabitants, the hundred surnames remained untroubled because the soldiers did not act wantonly.

After a standoff of more than a hundred days, in the eighth month of the fifth year Liang became severely ill and died in the army, being at that time fifty-four years old. When the army retired King Hsüan (Ssu-ma Yi) conducted a tour of inspection about their camps and fortifications and remarked that "he was one of the realm's unique talents."[47]

---

[47] A *ch'i ts'ai* (奇材), somewhat ironic in the sense that *ch'i* refers to the unorthodox, but Chu-ko Liang never employed unorthodox techniques.

Zhuge Liang: Strategy, Achievements, and Writings

Liang's bequeathed instructions ordered that he should be interred at Ting-chün-shan in Han-chung, that the mountain be employed as his funeral mound, that his grave should be just adequate to contain his coffin, and that he should be dressed in whatever he was wearing, with no need for commemorative vessels [to be interred with him].

The emperor issued a laudatory pronouncement that said, "You embodied the civil and martial, were wise and sincere. Orphaned, when I was entrusted to you, you corrected and assisted me. You continued the severed, made the minute flourish, and always harbored an intent to impose order on the chaotic. Furthermore, you ordered the six armies, and there was no year when you did not conduct expeditionary campaigns. Your spirit and martial [achievements] frightened the realm, your awesomeness suppressed the remotest areas in all eight directions, and you achieved outstanding success here in minor Han comparable to the great contributions of Yi Yin and the Duke of Chou. How could I not mourn for you, as just when affairs are nearing the point of completion you died from illness?

"I am profoundly saddened, my heart feels as if it is breaking. To venerate your virtue, display your achievements, and record your actions, I am mandating the award of a posthumous title to thereby glorify you for future generations and establish an immortal record. Today I am ordering *Tso-chung-lang* general Tu Ch'iung to convey and present the seal of chancellor and lord of Wu-hsiang [at your grave] and posthumously title you Lord of Chung-wu. If your ghost has sentience, may it feel glorified by this imperial honor. Alas, the grief, the grief [that I feel]."

At the beginning Liang had presented a memorial to the emperor that said: "At Ch'eng-tu I have eight hundred mulberry trees and some fifteen *ch'ing* of poor land. If my children rely on these for their clothes and food it will be more than adequate. Whenever I shouldered responsibilities outside the state I never took anything other than that provided by the army, and whatever I wore or ate I received through my offices, without otherwise seeking to nurture my life or increase my wealth in any way at all. On the day I die I will not allow any extra silks to be found within or great wealth outside my home that would betray your majesty's trust." When he died, it was as he had said.

In the spring of the sixth year of Ching-yao [263 CE], by imperial order a memorial temple for Chu-ko Liang was erected at Hsien-yang.[48] That autumn Wei's Suppressive Western Commanding General Chung Hui invaded Shu. When they reached Han-ch'uan he sacrificed at Liang's temple and ordered that neither the army nor officers could pasture animals or cut firewood around the temple. Liang's younger brother Chün reached the post of Hsiao-wei at Ch'ang-shui. Liang's son Tan inherited his title.

Ch'en Shou appended a number of additional paragraphs to his reprisal of Chu-ko Liang's life and accomplishments. These include a list of extant writings, some twenty-four titles in all that are discussed below, a reiteration of his life, a basic appraisal, and one or two other comments worth noting. In a paragraph that appears just before the final one translated above, Ch'en Shou states:

> By nature Liang excelled in clever thoughts. The improvement of the repeating crossbow and the [creation] of the

---

48 Nearly thirty years therefore elapsed between Liang's death and the authorization of a memorial temple.

"wooden oxen" and "fluid horses" all came out of his ideas. He investigated and extended the methods of war and created the diagram of the eight formations, all of which express the essence of his discussions. Many of Liang's instructional works and memorials can be still seen and I have compiled them in a separate work.

This rather tepid appraisal is actually augmented by an additional paragraph in which he marvels that Chu-ko Liang managed to engineer the survival of Liu Pei's faction and even nurture its growth. Finally, in a concluding appraisal of the sort that he attaches to all the *San-kuo Chih*'s chapters, Ch'en Shou summarized Chu-ko Liang's approach to government and his administrative accomplishments:

In his role as prime minister for the state Chu-ko Liang nurtured the hundred surnames, displayed the rites and regulations, constrained the bureaucratic offices, and governed through the application of authority. He opened the path of sincerity and implemented the Tao of public service. Those who exhausted their loyalty and contributed to the times were invariably rewarded even though they might be regarded with enmity, those who broke the laws or were lazy and dilatory were invariably punished even though they might be close relatives.

Those who acknowledged their offenses and confessed the truth would be released even if their offenses were severe but those who prevaricated and made pretenses would be executed, however slight the offense. No matter how small, good acts were rewarded; no matter how minute, those who committed offenses were degraded. In his management of affairs he was focused and controlled the foundation of things. He ensured that names accorded with reality while the vacuous and artificial never passed his lips. In the end everyone within the state both feared and loved him. Even when the severest punishments were imposed there was no rancor because he judged impartially and his actions and constraints were clear. He can be termed an outstanding talent who understood administration, someone comparable to Kuan Chung and Su Ho.

Ch'en Shou's comments apart, his biography of Chu-ko Liang contains several important sections that merit emphasis, particularly his initial consultation with Liu Pei, which thereafter became known as the "Lung-chung-tui" ("Reply at Lung-chung"), wherein he articulated his vision of a tripartite, strategic division of the realm, likening it to the three legs of a cauldron. (Although the abstract idea is obvious, given their respective strengths one of the legs would have had to be at least three times wider than either of the other two.) It also preserves the two memorials that Liang submitted to the youthful Liu Shan to justify undertaking the first and second expeditionary campaigns into the north, the "Ch'u-shih Piao" and "Hou Ch'u-shih Piao," respectively.

The biography also notes the difficulty that Chu-ko Liang encountered in gaining acceptance among Liu Pei's initial comrades, hardly an unexpected reaction since they had long valiantly fought at Liu Pei's side and presumably were accustomed to acting as his sole advisers. Despite China's lengthy tradition of esteeming esoteric wisdom and honoring unknown gurus, finding themselves suddenly displaced by an inexperienced "armchair general," these consummate men of action must have felt a mixture of anger and jealousy.

Certainly the Warring States story of Ch'ao Kua, the totally inexperienced but textually expert son of the great Chao commander Chao She, would have been quite familiar to Chang Fei and Kuan Yü.[49] (Through the astute use of double agents Ch'in managed to have Chao Kua placed in command of Chao's forward forces and then easily vanquished him, inflicting upward of four hundred fifty thousand casualties at the battle of Ch'ang-p'ing in 260 BCE.) Moreover, warriors have always had a natural antipathy toward strategists and fighters toward

---

[49] For a reprisal of this incident, which turned upon the effective use of disinformation agents, see Sawyer, *Tao of Spycraft*, 106–108.

planners. The Warring States work known as the *Ssu-ma Fa* early on insightfully characterized the disjuncture between the civil and the martial:[50]

> In antiquity the form and spirit governing civilian affairs would not be found in the military realm; those appropriate to the military realm would not be found in the civilian sphere. If the form and spirit [appropriate to the] military realm enter the civilian sphere the Virtue of the people will decline. When the form and spirit [appropriate to the] civilian sphere enter the military realm, the Virtue of the people will weaken.
>
> In the civilian sphere words are cultivated and speech languid. In court one is respectful and courteous and cultivates himself to serve others. Unsummoned, he does not step forth; unquestioned, he does not speak. It is difficult to advance but easy to withdraw.
>
> In the military realm one speaks directly and stands firm. When deployed in formation one focuses on duty and acts decisively. Those wearing battle armor do not bow; those in war chariots need not observe the forms of propriety [*li*]; those manning fortifications do not scurry. In times of danger one does not pay attention to seniority. Thus the civilian forms of behavior [*li*] and military standards [*fa*] are like inside and outside; the civil and martial are like left and right.

Across history a few civilians who had suddenly been entrusted with military power clearly recognized the nature of the problem and took steps to ensure that their authority would be unquestioned. They include Ssu-ma Jung-chü to whom the composition of the *Ssu-ma Fa* just quoted above is attributed:

---

50 "Obligations of the Son of Heaven."

Ssu-ma Jang-chü was a descendant of T'ien Wan. During the time of Duke Ching of Ch'i, Chin attacked [the major cities of] Ah and P'in, and Yen invaded [the river district] Ho-shang. Ch'i's army suffered complete defeat and Duke Ching was sorely troubled. Yen Ying then recommended Jang-chü, saying: "Even though Jang-chü is descended from T'ien's concubine, still, as a man, in civil affairs he is able to attach the masses and in martial affairs able to overawe the enemy. I would like my Lord to test him."

Duke Ching summoned Jang-chü and spoke with him about military affairs. He was greatly pleased and appointed him as General of the Army to lead the soldiers in resisting the armies of Yen and Chin.

Jang-chü said, "I was formerly lowly and menial. If my lord pulls me out from amidst my village and places me above the high officials, the officers and troops will not be submissive and the hundred surnames will not believe in me. Since the man is insignificant and his authority light, I would like to have one of my Lord's favored ministers, someone whom the state respects, appointed as Supervisor of the Army. Then it will be possible." Duke Ching assented and had Chuang Ku go forth.

Jang-chü, who had already taken his leave, made an agreement with Chuang Ku, saying: "Tomorrow, at midday, meet at the army's gate." Jang-chü raced ahead to the army, set up the gnomon and let the water [drip in the water clock], awaiting Ku. Ku, who had always been arrogant and aristocratic, assumed that since the commanding general had already reached the army while he was [only] the Supervisor, it was not extremely urgent. His relatives from all around, who were sending him off, detained him to drink.

Midday came and Ku had not arrived. Jang-chü then lay down the standard, stopped the dripping water, and went into [the encampment]. He advanced the army, took control of the soldiers, and clearly publicized the constraints and bonds. When the constraints had been imposed it was already evening and then Chuang Ku arrived. Jang-chü said: "How is it that you arrive after the appointed time?"

Ku acknowledged his fault, saying, "High officials and relatives saw the simple one off, thus he was detained."

Jang-chü replied: "On the day a general receives the mandate [of command] he forgets his home; when he enters the army and takes control of the soldiers he forgets his loved ones; when he takes hold of the drumsticks and urgently beats the drum he forgets himself. At this moment enemy states have already deeply invaded [our land]; within the state there is unrest and movement. Our officers and soldiers lie brutally cut down and exposed at the borders. Our ruler does not sleep soundly nor enjoy the sweet taste of his food. The fate of the hundred surnames hangs upon you, so what do you mean by being seen off?"

He summoned the provost marshal and inquired: "What is the army's law regarding those who arrive after the appointed time?" He replied: "They should be decapitated!"

Terrified, Chuang Ku ordered a man to race back and report to Duke Ching, asking to be saved. He had already left but not yet returned when [Jang-chü] beheaded Ku in order to publicize [the enforcement of discipline] within the Three Armies. All the officers within the Three Armies shook with fear.

Somewhat later the emissary that Duke Ching had dispatched, bearing a tally to pardon Ku, raced to the army. Jang-chü said: "When the general is with the army there are orders of the ruler that are not accepted." He asked the provost marshal, "What is the law regarding racing into the army?" The provost marshal said: "He should be beheaded."

The emissary was terrified. Jang-chü said, "We cannot slay the ruler's emissary." He then beheaded [the emissary's] attendant, severed the carriage's left stanchion, and decapitated the horse on the left in order to instruct the Three Armies. He dispatched the Duke's emissary to return and report, and then moved [the army] out.

Without doubt Chu-ko Liang was well familiar with this passage, for he not only mentions Jang-chü's name in his writings but also incorporates many passages and extensive language from the *Ssu-ma Fa*, including the need to impose punishments without allowing any exceptions for rank or position.[51] Jang-chü obviously understood the dynamics of authority and must have known that Ku would be remiss in his duties, thereby providing him with an opportunity to manifest the awesomeness of punishments. In this regard he mirrored Sun-tzu's dramatic (but probably apocryphal) action in beheading two of King Ho-lü's concubines in the ancient state of Wu when they failed to adhere to the commands he had issued, while illustrating formations and the importance of discipline at his first interview.[52]

---

[51] The description of Jang-chü's surpassing qualities, his behavior in the army, and his solicitude for his men, is essentially transformed and incorporated in the admonitions directed to commanders in the commissioning ceremony and other chapters found in the *Chiang Yüan*.
[52] Even if fabricated by his disciples, the story would have been widely known in the Three Kingdoms period. (It is also preserved in Sun-tzu's *Shih Chi* biography.)

Chu-ko Liang simply insisted that Liu Pei humble himself by conspicuously visiting him to elicit his advice. Certainly, perhaps because of Mencius's behavior and writings, the idea that the powerful had to personally venture forth in order to acquire the services of sagacious but reclusive figures enjoyed great currency in his era.[53] Naturally the wise but disenfranchised (rather unrealistically) felt that their surpassing knowledge and virtue more than deserved such exertions, even as they feigned disinterest in the realm's affairs. Even Chu-ko Liang would subsequently claim that "he had been seeking only to preserve his nature and life in a chaotic world, not to become known among the feudal lords" before encountering Liu Pei, but reportedly had been so moved by Liu's persistence that he decided to (condescend and) assist him.

However, the tension inherent in relationships initiated under these deliberately humbling circumstances can also prove problematic. A little contemplation and several well-known historical examples suggest that the enormity of entrusting one's fate to someone completely unknown and untested[54] may result in lingering annoyance suddenly exploding after unexpected reversals or at stressful moments. Moreover, the dynamics reflect the perennial battle between the truly powerful and erstwhile pretenders that frequently became visible in conflicts between the literati and the imperial family, as well as (derivatively but still crucially) civil bureaucrats and military commanders.

Whether Chu-ko Liang was vain and arrogant, as some of his critics have asserted, or merely self-confident remains an open question. His biography in the *San-kuo Chih* and other materials incorporated in the *Tzu-chih T'ung-chien* (rather than *The Romance of the Three Kingdoms*) depict a dedicated individual who worked selflessly to achieve Liu Pei's great yet highly personal quest to reestablish the Han ruling house. Whatever his own motivation, Liang obviously harbored an overwhelming ambition to achieve this objective, thereby ensuring

---

53 See the lengthy discussion in *Mencius*, VB6 and VB7, "Wan-chang, hsia."
54 Despite the incomprehensible propensity for voters to continue making this error!

his own place among such great historical strategic advisers such as the T'ai Kung and undying fame within the great wisdom tradition.[55]

However, the T'ai Kung had apparently positioned himself so that King Wen could discover him while fishing, and the story of Liu Pei visiting Liang three times, a virtual impossibility, has long been questioned.[56] Moreover, Chu-ko Liang hoped to encounter a powerful individual who combined intelligence and virtue, and he lacked any martial adherents himself, precluding any pretensions to direct power. For a realist such as Chu-ko Liang, a single visit from a realistic candidate, however dim the latter's political prospects, should have provided honor enough.

Finally, even though the historical records note little friction between Liu Shan and Chu-ko Liang, the youthful emperor must have resented his mentor's prestige and authority, because he did not authorize a memorial temple until persuaded nearly thirty years later that the spontaneous erection of edifices to honor him was eluding governmental control. Just as Sun Ch'üan's heir and the descendants of many future strong emperors, he had increasingly fallen under the control of inner palace attendants who catered to his personal whims and desires, and turned him away from the great task of reviving the Han and administering the state.

---

55 All the classic military writers, but especially the T'ai Kung and Li Ch'üan, emphasized the importance of worthies and even sages in advising the ruler and therefore the need to seek them out. (Naturally this means that the ruler should essentially delegate all the responsibility for planning and strategy and then simply rubber-stamp and implement their recommendations.)

56 The T'ai Kung's traditional biography is found in the *Shih Chi*.

3
Southern Campaign

Despite his reputation as the era's consummate strategist, Chu-ko Liang is not noted as having played a key role in formulating any campaign tactics prior to Liu Pei's demise. Furthermore, even though he was reportedly entrusted with overall directorship of one of the northern thrusts during the conquest of Yi, there is no record of him having personally commanded any contingents prior to this undertaking. This may simply be the result of historical omission, but it is more likely that in the early days of their association Liu Pei continued to make all the strategic decisions in conjunction with his experienced, if intemperate, comrades, resulting in Chu-ko Liang being confined to a broad advisory role. In addition, from his biography it appears that he devoted his efforts to administrative matters ranging from organizing and training the army, two concerns broadly reflected in his probable writings, through restructuring the government and implementing the legal and economic measures necessary to sustain their essentially orphaned forces. Following Shu's conquest he continued to fulfill this role until Liu Pei's death, after which he also assumed the actual mantle of command and undertook sole responsibility for their strategic decisions.

Chu-ko Liang's first real test as a field commander arose when several southern commanderies exploited the uncertainty occasioned by the emperor's death to forcibly reject Shu/Han domination. Populated by an intermixture of Han descendants and disparate minority peoples, primarily Yi, the area known as Nan-chung encompassed modern Guilin, Yünnan, and southwest Sichuan, or roughly half of Shu's claimed territory. Because of its mineral and agricultural resources it was thought to be crucial to funding and supplying expeditions intended to reconquer the north.

Nan-chung was not just remote and tortuously inaccessible; the inhabitants also had a well-deserved reputation for being fiercely independent. Throughout imperial history they would continue to resist externally imposed control, and whenever the central government weakened, became fragmented, or was preoccupied with threats, independent enclaves, even kingdoms, tended to arise. Ch'in had previously undertaken vigorous measures that included road building to master the area and the Former Han had struggled to control it. Liu Chang's weak administration had engendered widespread disdain and essentially fostered the growth of localized powers. According to the *Tzu-chih T'ung-chien*'s account of the rebellion:

> Initially, in Yi-chou Commandery the tribal leader Yung K'ai killed the *T'ai-shou* Cheng Ang and through [the Wu border official] Shih Hsieh sought to attach himself to Wu. In addition he seized the [new] *T'ai-shou*, the Ch'eng-tu native Chang Yi and turned him over to Wu. Wu made K'ai the *T'ai-shou* of Yung-ch'ang. Lü K'ai, the *Kung-ts'ao* for Yung-ch'ang, and Wang K'ang, the *Fu-ch'eng*, led the officials and officers in closing the border and defending it. Being unable to advance, Yung K'ai had his fellow commandery leader Meng Huo beguile the various Yi groups into following him [in rebelling]. In response to Yung K'ai, Chu Pao, the *T'ai-shou* of Tsang-k'o, and Kao Ting, Yi king of Yüeh-sui, both rebelled.

Ostensibly because they were immersed in the grief-ridden process of state mourning, Chu-ko Liang deferred mounting an immediate response: "Because Shu was just in the midst of their mourning for Liu Pei, instead of undertaking a punitive expedition Chu-ko Liang adopted a conciliatory approach in every case and concentrated upon agriculture and augmenting their grain reserves. He closed the passes and rested the people. After the people were at peace and their food supplies sufficient, he employed them."[57] However, in actuality he probably realized

---

57 *Tzu-chih T'ung-chien*, "Wei-chi 2," Wen-ti Huang-ch'u 4th year. Liu Shan's annals in the *San-kuo Chih*, probably the *Tz'u-chih T'ung-chien*'s source, contain a similar account: "In the summer of the first year of Chien-hsing (223) the Tsang-k'o *T'ai-shou* Chu Pao took advantage of his commandery to rebel. Even before this the leader of one of the great clans in Yi-chou Commandery, Yung K'ai, had rebelled, removed the *T'ai-shou* Chang Yi to Wu, and occupied Yi-chou Commandery but [the local officials] were not willing to go along. The Yüeh-sui Yi king Kao Ting also mobilized forces and rebelled. In the second year Shu concentrated upon agriculture and augmenting the grain reserves, closed the passes, and rested the people. In the spring, the third month of the third year, Chancellor Liang went south on a punitive campaign against the four commandaries. The four were all pacified."

that his authority was not yet unquestioned and that the army was insufficiently prepared for a punitive expedition under the harsh conditions prevailing in the south.

The *San-kuo Chih* account of the southern campaign found in his biography is brevity itself: "In the spring of the third year of Chien-kuang [225 CE] Liang led the army on a campaign into the south and by autumn the [rebellious commanderies] had been thoroughly pacified." Surprisingly, rather than depleting the state's coffers and debilitating the army, "all the military expenses incurred were recovered and the state grew rich and prosperous."

The *Tzu-chih T'ung-chien* provides a slightly expanded account of the campaign's progress over the several months required:

> After Chu-ko Liang reached Nan-chung he proved victorious everywhere that they engaged the enemy. Liang entered via Yüeh-shui Commandery [Hsi-ch'ang-hsien in Sichuan] and executed Yung K'ai and Kao Ting. He dispatched the supervisor of Lai-chiang, an Yi-chou native named Li Hui, to advance through Yi-chou and the *Men-hsia-tu* Ma Chung, a native of Pa-hsi, to penetrate Tsang-k'o. After attacking and destroying [the forces in] several districts they reunited with Liang.

Contrary to this highly martial summation, from the outset the campaign reportedly had a rather different orientation because it was supposed to emphasize the psychological impact rather than just forcefully subjugate or exterminate the rebellious. According to Chu-ko Liang's abstracted "Instructions on the Southern Campaign of Rectification": "In the Tao for employing the military attacking their minds is foremost, attacking their cities inferior. Psychological combat is superior, military combat inferior."[58] Although this formulation obviously coheres with Chu-ko Liang's orientation to winning through wisdom, it should properly be credited to close confidant Ma Su:[59]

---

58 His pronouncement essentially echoes fundamental concepts found in the *Art of War*.
59 Ma Su's brief biography may be found in *chüan* 39 of the *San-kuo Chih*.

When Chu-ko Liang was leading the troops in a punitive expedition against Yung K'ai the *Ts'an-chün* Ma Su escorted him several tens of *li*. Liang said, "Although we have been making plans for several years, perhaps you can advise me further?"

Su replied, "Relying upon the precipitous of their terrain, [the inhabitants in] Nan-chung have long been unsubmissive. Even if you destroy them today, they will rebel again tomorrow. At the moment you have been turning the state over to prepare for a northern expedition to engage our strong enemies. When the [southern peoples] learn that the government's strategic power has become vacuous, they will quickly rebel. But fully exterminating them in order to eliminate later misfortune would be inhumane and cannot be hastily accomplished. Now in the Tao for employing the military attacking their minds is superior, attacking their cities inferior. Psychological warfare is superior, military combat inferior. So I would hope that you can just cause their minds to submit." Liang accepted his words.

If this approach had succeeded it would certainly have reduced the damage inflicted and thereby maximized the wealth that might be confiscated (just as advocated in the *Art of War*).[60] Moreover, it might well have somewhat ameliorated local outrage at being compelled to yield their wealth, much of which would no doubt have been concealed prior to the enemy's onslaught. However, whether the inhabitants ever accepted their subjugation, not to mention "willingly submitted," is far more dubious.

Interesting details about the campaign are preserved in the biographies of the subordinate commanders found in the *San-kuo Chih*. Lü K'ai's biography begins similarly by noting that Yung K'ai had perceived an opportunity in Liu Pei's death: "When Yung K'ai and the others heard that the former ruler had died

---

60 See "Planning Offensives," the *Art of War*.

at Yung-an, they acted perfidiously and arrogantly and stirred up the people."[61] It then somewhat oddly notes that Li Yen (rather than Lü) had tried to dissuade Yung K'ai from rebelling by sending him a six-page letter discussing the advantages and disadvantages of his actions.

K'ai replied with a single page whose contents reflect his intention to exploit the realm's fragmented authority: "You have probably heard that Heaven does not have two suns and earth does not have two kings.[62] Today the realm is set up like [a three-legged cauldron] and there are three new years. For this reason people at a distance are fearful and confused and do not know whom to give their allegiance." Ch'en Shou's comment, "such was his haughtiness," certainly illuminates the pervasiveness of the literati's belief in unified rule.

Li Hui's biography depicts an innovative and resourceful commander who was in fact a native of Chien-ning:[63]

> When the former king died Kao Ting commenced acting brutally in Yüeh-sui, Yung K'ai stomped across Chien-ning, and Chu Pao rebelled in Tsang-k'o. When Chancellor Liang went south on his punitive expedition he first proceeded through Yüeh-sui while Hui followed the road toward Chien-ning. Gathering together, the [rebels] in the various districts surrounded Hui's army at K'un-ming.[64] At the time Hui's troops were few so the enemy was double his strength.
>
> Not having heard any news of Liang he deceptively said to the southerners, "The provisions for the government's forces have been exhausted so I am about to plan their withdrawal. I have been in the middle region [of Shu] for a long time and

---

61 *San-kuo Chih, chüan* 43. Lü similarly tried to persuade K'ai to abandon his course with a lengthy missive that is preserved in his biography, but to no avail.
62 Although certainly a common saying, it reputedly originates with Confucius and is found quoted in *Mencius*, "Wan-chang, Shang," VA4
63 *San-kuo Chih, chüan* 43.
64 Not present-day K'un-ming.

away from my village. Now that I have managed to return I do not want to go back north again. Instead, I would like to return and plan strategy with you and have therefore sincerely advised you of our situation."

The southerners trusted him and those mounting the siege became lax. Hui then broke forth in a strike, severely destroying them, and pursued the fleeing remnants into both the north and south until he reached P'an-chiang in the south. Thereafter he connected up with Chu-ko Liang in the east at Tsang-k'o. In pacifying the south Hui's army had the greatest accomplishments.[65]

The *Tzu-chih T'ung-chien* also includes the famous but highly improbable tale of how Chu-ko Liang captured and released Meng Huo, one of the rebel leaders, seven times:[66]

Meng Huo gathered K'ai's remnant troops together in order to resist Liang. Meng Huo had previously been well regarded by both the Han and Yi so Liang wished to bring him in alive. When he succeeded, he had Meng observe the arrangements within their camps and deployments and then inquired: "What do you think of our army?"

Meng Huo replied, "Previously, I did not recognize the vacuous and substantial points, but now that I have been fortunate enough to observe your camp and deployments, if they are just thus, I am certain that victory can be easily gained."

---

[65] One *San-kuo Chih* commentary asserts that several thousand families were also resettled along the border between Chien-ning and Yün-nan.

[66] According to unreliable accounts in *The Romance of the Three Kingdoms*, Chu-ko Liang used the lure of being vulnerable to an incendiary attack to defeat him the first time. (As discussed in our *Fire and Water*, in the nonhistorical records Liang is frequently associated with innovating and employing incendiary techniques.)

Zhuge Liang: Strategy, Achievements, and Writings

Laughing, Liang released him and had him renew the conflict. Even after he had been captured seven times and released seven times Liang still was ready to send him off. However, Huo stopped him, saying: "My lord has the awesomeness of Heaven. We southerners will not again rebel." Liang subsequently went to Tien-ch'ih.

Perhaps partly because he realized that Meng Huo had merely accepted the reality of defeat rather than willingly submitted, Liang reportedly decided to avoid provoking the people by not imposing Han (foreign) officials who would invariably cause resentment and friction. According to his rather astute analysis:

After the districts of Yi-chou, Yung-ch'ang, Tsang-k'o, and Yüeh-sui had been pacified Liang put them to great use. When someone offered a remonstrance he replied, "If we leave foreigners here [in an administrative capacity] we will have to leave soldiers. But the soldiers stationed here will lack provisions. This is the first inconvenience. Adding to this, the Yi have just been wounded and destroyed, fathers and elder brothers have lost their lives, so leaving foreigners here without any soldiers would result in disaster. This is the second inconvenience. Furthermore, the Yi and other minority peoples have long been guilty of displacing and slaying our officials. They will suspect severe reprisals will be forthcoming so if we retain foreigners they will never believe them. This is the third inconvenience. So today if I do not want to leave troops behind or transport provisions it is because I want to see the basic relationships reestablished and the Yi and Han dwell in security."

Liang then gathered all the [native] heroes and highly capable men such as Meng Huo and entrusted them with official positions as well as responsibility for furnishing copper, silver, cinnabar, lacquer, oxen for plowing, and horses for warfare for the state and army's use. Throughout Liang's life the Yi did not again revolt.[67]

Being sensitive to the provocative (and often exploitive) nature of foreign administrators and the vexatious nature of occupation troops, Liang opted to exploit the resources while maintaining a semblance of order through minimalist measures. Based upon the accounts just reprised, the southern campaign would therefore seem to have accomplished its original objectives and more. The rebels were suppressed; rather than impoverishing the state, the finance and supply of essential war materials was improved; a threat to the rear was eliminated; and the army benefited from campaigning under actual combat conditions, thereby preparing it for the forthcoming, far more arduous expeditions into the north against Ts'ao/Wei.

Several other points might be noted in conjunction with this campaign. First, it was undertaken in deliberate fashion rather than immediately after news of the rebellion had reached them. Second, Chu-ko Liang segmented Shu's troops and employed a three-pronged attack to reduce the enemy in detail, thereby preventing them from combining into a more significant force, much in accord with admonitions in the *Art of War* to keep the enemy's contingents from being able to unite.[68] Proceeding as three distinct forces along separate routes also reduced the congestion on the relatively narrow tracks that led into the south and minimized the foraging and plundering that might be required in any one area, diminishing local antagonism. Third, as attested by the awareness shown in his chapters in the *Chiang Yüan*, he modified his operational tactics to suit customs and attitudes of the Yi and Man.[69]

The accuracy and validity of the *Tzu-chih T'ung-chien* account of the southern campaign and its results have traditionally been unquestioned. However, the vestiges already seen in the biographies and Liu Shan's annals indicate that, rather

---

67 *Tzu-chih T'ung-chien*, "Wei-chi, 2," Hsüan-ti Huang-ch'u 6th year.
68 "Nine Terrains."
69 The last four chapters of *Chiang Yüan* characterize the contiguous external peoples. Although these groups are invariably referred to as Yi in the biographical account of the campaign, the Man should have been the primary inhabitants.

than a psychologically focused effort, it was a brutal military expedition that failed to proceed in accord with its purported method or achieve its proclaimed psychological objective because none of the rebels willingly submitted and their armed opposition had to be summarily crushed. Conciliatory measures were conspicuously absent, apart from the highly dubious tale of Meng Huo's manipulation, and only the subterfuges conceived by individual commanders ever exploited any psychological aspects. The ferocity of their opposition must have resulted in a high casualty rate that certainly would have engendered intense and lasting enmity among the Yi survivors.

Perhaps because he recognized the difficulty of actually pacifying the south, Chu-ko Liang quickly reorganized the four commanderies into six, thereby imposing a greater degree of control and dividing up the troublesome areas so that no single official would have responsibility for tribal conglomerations. The original four commanderies that hosted the rebellious were Yi-chou, Yung-ch'ang, Tsang-k'o, and Yüeh-sui, but "he then changed Yi-chou Commandery to be Chien-ning Commandery, split off parts of Chien-ning and Yung-ch'ang to form Yün-nan Commandery and similarly Chien-ning and Tsang-k'o to form Hsing-ku. In the twelfth month he returned to Ch'eng-tu." However, being primarily an administrative restructuring rather than an effort that entailed the creation of barriers, control points, and other military measures to isolate potential trigger points and keep groups from uniting for inimical purposes, it merely ensured that each official was responsible for less territory and presumably had more detailed knowledge of the evolving situation.

The repeated capture and release of Meng Huo, reputedly a knowledgeable and fierce warrior, greatly augmented Chu-ko Liang's reputation for surpassing tactical acumen. Ssu-ma Kuang's inclusion of the incredible sequence in his well-pondered *Tzu-chih T'ung-chien* certainly enhanced the account's credibility and it is known by almost all Chinese today. However, commentators began questioning its veracity early on and the tale's origination, not to mention its source, remains problematic. Moreover, no commander—especially one as acutely aware of the difficulties of campaigning in the south and as tactically conservative as Chu-ko Liang—would ever have risked the potential losses in time, men, and materials that would have been required for another six clashes to play out.

Only one explanation seems possible if the incident is not to be rejected as just another fabrication by Chu-ko Liang's ardent fans. Instead of actual physical battles that would have jeopardized the soldiers' lives, the two may have engaged in an early form of war gaming, either purely intellectual or played out with some physical props. In the former case, having already studied Shu's disposition and identified vulnerabilities, Meng might have verbally outlined tactics that would exploit apparent weaknesses. In reply, Liang would then have indicated how he would employ his formations to again thwart and capture him.

Because the sand table had come into use many centuries earlier, their tactical initiatives and responses could have been illustrated by recourse to markers on a miniaturized battlefield. Relative superiority could then have been determined by evaluating the many factors outlined in the *Art of War* and Chu-ko Liang's chapter "Assessing Ability" found in the *Chiang Yüan*, including the comparative advantage of different components, characteristics of weapons, relative strength of the contingents, and their positioning to exploit strategic advantages of terrain, all appropriately modified for their respective fighting styles and maneuver capabilities.[70]

It might also be asked what the southern revolt really entailed, and to what extent the fiercely independent disparate groups inhabiting Nan-chung had ever been integrated into the province's administrative framework, whether before or after Liu Pei's seizure of the government. Even if their revolution had simply amounted to a general refusal to recognize the authorities deputed by the central government (and their sometime brutal elimination), the degree to which they had ever given their allegiance and actually contributed to the state's resources should also be questioned. Given their reluctance to cooperate with each other, it is unlikely that they would ever have constituted a significant threat or been capable of mounting more than a brief incursion focused on pillaging and plundering. Thus, Chu-ko Liang's only real concern would have been the danger of

---

70 The first chapter in the *Art of War*, aptly titled "Initial Estimations," which outlines five critical factors for assessment, initiated the thrust to undertake warfare on a calculated basis so closely associated with traditional Chinese military science. (The *Art of War* actually contains some forty or so paired criteria for evaluation purposes.)

somewhat more extensive predatory actions should Ch'eng-tu's defenses become depleted when their armies ventured northward.[71]

If many of the various southern groups had chosen to visibly ally themselves with Wu or, although highly unlikely, Ts'ao/Wei, as Yung K'ai did, Shu would have faced further isolation or even virtual encirclement. Certainly Ts'ao/Wei would have welcomed the onset of guerilla activity virtually in the enemy's heartland, but they seem never to have conceived of the possibility nor deputed emissaries to encourage it. However, unless the groups inhabited the border between Shu and Wu, these defections would never have been more than nominal because of the vast distance that intervened between them and Wu's forces. Thus, even though the threat had only been ameliorated, Chu-ko Liang and the other oligarchs deemed the region to have been sufficiently pacified for Liang to redirect his energies to the primary task "of organizing the army and discussing military affairs in order to await a grand mobilization."

The report that Chu-ko Liang acquired an enormous amount of wealth, metal, and other materials that enriched the state and not only paid for the campaign but also helped sustain the upcoming northern campaigns indicates that the northern invaders fundamentally plundered the land. Their rapaciousness, however much justified in their eyes because of the suppressive efforts that had been required, and in view of the greater objective of conquering Wei, certainly must have caused enormous hatred.

An assertion contained in Liu Hui's biography confirms its extensiveness: "The military taxes imposed on the Sou and P'u, oxen for plowing, war horses, copper and silver, and water buffalo hide were employed to supplement the army's resources. At that time they had no insufficiency in their requirements."

Liu Hui's retention of the materials acquired through this splinter action, hardly unexpected given local needs and the problems inherent to transporting goods over the south's minimal road network (whether up to Ch'eng-tu or down for sustainment purposes) raises doubts as to the actual contribution to the greater military effort against the north.

---

71 Chu-ko Liang's apparent (but never explained) reluctance to forward additional troops to Liu Pei during the Han-chung campaign may have stemmed from his concerns with the south.

Southern Campaign

The traditional account gives prominence to Chu-ko Liang's decision not to impose foreign officials over the indigenous populace. However, Nan-chung could not be administered (nor said to be part of Shu) without emplacing central government authorities. A mixture of southern natives of Han origin and minority peoples with the rank of *t'ai-shou* and similar titles were accordingly appointed to oversee these commanderies. The lower echelons may have been staffed by local people and a few tribal leaders compelled to immigrate to the north, primarily to the Ch'eng-tu region, to preclude further antagonistic activity, but they seem to have been granted purely nominal positions, if any at all. Contrary to assertions that Han troops would not be retained in the south because of logistical and political reasons, as shown by their employment (such as by Li Hui) in suppressing subsequent uprisings, the administrative entities clearly had significant contingents attached.

Despite Liang's apparently sweeping success and the *Tzu-chih T'ung-chien*'s assertion that "throughout Liang's life the Yi did not again revolt," the area did not remain tranquil long. At least three biographies—those of Liu Hui, Lü K'ai, and Meng Chung—as well as Liu Shan's annals indicate that the region continued to be inhabited by belligerents who had no compunction about murdering local *t'ai-shou* and other high Han representatives. Although particularly odious officials may have individually prompted these assassinations, their recurrence must be considered symptomatic of seething disaffection. Even Lü K'ai, who had been appointed as Yün-nan's *T'ai-shou* after Chu-ko Liang's victorious southern campaign, subsequently died in the chaos of an Yi rebellion.

Before Chu-ko Liang undertook the northward campaign in 229 CE, Li Hui had already been called upon to suppress a significant uprising: "After the armies had returned to the north the southern Yi again rebelled and killed the local *shou-chiang* (defending general). Hui personally took command of a punitive strike force that went and vanquished the rebels. He then transferred their leaders to Ch'eng-tu."[72]

Again in 233 CE, the year before the final northern campaign, "Liu Wei, a southern Yi, rebelled, and general Ma Chung smashed and pacified him."[73]

---

72 *San-kuo Chih*, chüan 43 (Liu Hui's biography).
73 *San-kuo Chih*, chüan 33 (Liu Shan's annals).

According to the *Tzu-chih T'ung-chien*, the rebellion had been triggered by the abrasive behavior of a Han official:

> The *Tu-tu* of Lai-chiang in Shu, Chang Yi, was extremely harsh in applying the laws and the powerful southern Yi leader [in Yün-nan Ch'ü-ching-hsien], Liu Wei, rebelled. Chancellor Chu-ko Liang had the *Ts'an-chün* Ma Chung, a Pa-hsi native, replace Yi and sent orders for Yi to return. The messenger advised him to quickly go back for disposition of his offense.
>
> Yi replied: "Not so. The Yi have become restless so I have been recalled for failing to fulfill my responsibility. However, my replacement has not yet arrived while we are about to engage in warfare. We should transport the provisions and accumulate the grain needed as resources for exterminating the brigands. How can I abandon my public duties just because I have been dismissed and recalled!"
>
> Retaining responsibility, he worked diligently until his replacement arrived and then departed [for the capital]. Taking advantage of the resources he had accumulated Ma Chung destroyed Wei's forces and executed Liu Wei.[74]

How perniciously or pervasively Chang Yi exceeded reasonable bounds remains unknown. Paradoxically, although Chu-ko Liang's avowed policy and his writings show he was sensitive to governmental abuse, strictly applying the laws should have accorded well with his emphasis upon thoroughly implementing them.

According to his biography in the *San-kuo Chih*, the Pa-hsi native and noted military commander Ma Chung served as an effective, even ideal Shu official in the south. He was well regarded by the local populace, both Han and native peoples, and many of the latter showed considerable consternation at his death

---

74 *Tzu-chih T'ung-chien*, chüan 72, "Wei-chi 4," Ming-ti Ch'ing-lung 1st year.

and participated in his mourning ceremonies. Having supervised the suppression of the Wen-shan Ch'ing rebellion with Chang Ni, he seems to have excelled at fighting minority groups and was responsible for restoring order in Tsang-k'o and resettling displaced inhabitants after the main revolt. He would replace Chang Yi when Liu Wei rebelled, and was eventually responsible for defeating and slaying him. His habit of dwelling among the people rather than administering from afar made him a familiar and effective leader.

Somewhat earlier, in 227 CE, when Chu-ko Liang was in Han-chung, the mountain people in the area of Kuang-han and Mien-chu (north of Te-yang-hsien) started plundering and the Pa-hsi native Chang Ni (張嶷) was chosen to repress them:[75] "In the fifth year of Chien-hsing Chancellor Liang moved north to dwell in Han-chung. The mountain bandits in Kuang-han and Mien-chu, Chang Mu and others, pillaged the army's resources and plundered the officials and people. Chang Yi [was deputed] to quash them with the local provincial forces. Yi calculated that if they scattered it would be difficult to capture them through military means so he pretended to be friendly toward them and set out wine for them. When they had become somewhat inebriated Yi then led his attendants in slaying Mu and some fifty other leaders before thoroughly seeking out and extirpating the others. Within ten days tranquility had been restored." Liu Pei's emphasis upon righteousness clearly did not deter Chang Yi from cleverly employing the ploy of a false friendship to gain a critical advantage and coldly slaughter them all.[76]

The revolts naturally continued even after Chu-ko Liang's demise. "In the spring of the third year [240 CE] of Yen-hsi [the emperor] dispatched the *T'ai-shou* of Yüeh-sui, Chang Yi, to pacify Yüeh-sui Commandery." Meanwhile, other Yi groups in the north would also attempt to throw off what they viewed as oppressive Han control. For example, "In the 10th year [247], the Yi in Wen-shan P'ing-k'ang rebelled and Chiang Wei pacified them; in the 11th year the Yi populace in P'ei-ling in Han-chung rebelled and Teng Chih pacified them."[77]

---

[75] *San-kuo Chih*, *chüan* 43.
[76] For a discussion of the use of feigned treaties and false surrenders in warfare, see Sawyer, *Lever of Power*, forthcoming.
[77] *San-kuo Chih*, *chüan* 33 (Liu Shan's annals).

Not only did Chu-ko Liang's supposedly restrained southern campaign therefore fail to deter southern leaders from mounting further rebellions in the immediate future, it had little deterrent effect in other regions either, including Han-chung, despite its visible military accomplishments.

4
The Northern Campaigns

Following their generally acclaimed success against the south's limited but inspired forces, Chu-ko Liang began to plan for the first of five northern campaigns that would eventually extend over seven years. Although ostensibly intended to vanquish Ts'ao/Wei and reestablish the Han as the realm's legitimate authority, insofar as they always targeted locations within Kuan-chung that would eliminate the enemy's blocking forces and thereafter be employed as staging areas, they were invariably marked by conservative objectives from the outset. Furthermore, the problems posed by the terrain and Ts'ao/Wei's vast resources were considerably different than those they had encountered in the hot, desolate, but heavily vegetated south.

Their expulsion from Ching-chou severely hampered their conquest efforts because they had lost a vital source of provisions as well as a geographically advantageous position for staging attacks against prime northern cities. Without Wu's acquiescence their armies could not transit Ching-chou before striking upward, an arduous task under the best of circumstances, and were therefore tactically limited to targeting enemy enclaves in the Wei River valley. However, the latter could only be accessed by employing Han-chung as a staging area and laboriously traversing the intervening mountain ranges whose peaks could soar to six thousand feet or more, in every case a minimum distance of several hundred *li*. Only a portion of the Western Han River could be used for transport purposes; the local population density was low, precluding local support, whether coerced or not; and the often extremely narrow, rocky passages on three of the four possible approaches (indicated on the accompanying maps) precluded employing wagons for transport purposes, dramatically increasing the burden on the troops and causing them to become exhausted even before they reached the battlefield.

Even around 500 BCE, at the end of the Spring and Autumn period, it had become apparent that prolonged warfare and the distant transport of provisions debilitated states. The *Art of War*, which stresses the need for maneuver, rapidity, and wisdom throughout its laconic passages, provides a telling analysis that would often tend to be ignored in the turmoil of reality. After describing the expenses incurred in actual combat and for the sustainment effort, a key section in "Waging War" concludes:[78]

> One who excels in employing the military does not conscript the people twice or transport provisions a third time. The state is impoverished when it transports provisions far off. When provisions are transported far off, the hundred surnames will be impoverished. When their wealth is exhausted they will be extremely hard-pressed to supply their village's military impositions.

The chapter also includes a quantitative estimate of the expenses incurred. Not including the manpower diverted to warfare (which itself reduces the state's prosperity), the people could be expected to suffer the loss of some seventy percent of their material wealth, and the ruler sixty percent. In addition to weapons and provisions, according to the *Art of War*, "ruined chariots, exhausted horses, armor, helmets, arrows and crossbows, axe and spear-tipped large movable shields, strong oxen, and large wagons" would all require major outlays.

Conversely, even though Ts'ao/Wei also suffered from the need to supply forward positions located at a considerable distance from their primary bases, Kuan-chung's limited access vastly simplified their overall defensive requirements. In addition, they managed to acquire provisions from the disparate Yi and Ch'iang groups inhabiting the upper Wei River valley and greater Han-chung area through coercion and seizure, displaying little compunction whether or not it would leave them bereft of food.[79] Nevertheless, despite knowing the very few points at which Shu's forces could possibly emerge from the mountains, they did not mount vigorous standing defenses at these locations or in the mountain passes themselves, but instead tended to respond to incursions by hurriedly dispatching troops from the east, including the Ch'ang-an area, as needed. These

---

[78] "Superior Strategy" in the *Three Strategies* includes a variant of this passage.
[79] Note Kuo Huai's biography in the *San-kuo Chih*.

tactics probably resulted from their preoccupation with Wu's sometime aggressive activities and a general disdain for Shu's potency after they became ensconced in Sichuan and Liu Pei died.

The First Campaign

Following the south's successful pacification, the first northward thrust was initiated in the spring of 228 CE, roughly a year after Chu-ko Liang had moved substantial forces into the Han-chung area and submitted the memorial embedded in Chu-ko Liang's biography that subsequently became known as the "Ch'u Shih Piao." According to the "Ch'u Shih Piao," as well as reiterated in the "Hou Ch'u Shih Piao" (translated below), he clearly believed that "Yi is fatigued and depleted. This is truly an autumn of extreme crisis, of survival and extinction." According to the summary preserved in this same biography:

> He set forth, finally encamping at Mien-yang. In the spring of the sixth year he proclaimed that he would seize Mei [Mei-yeh] by advancing along the Yeh-ku road and deputed Chao Yün and Teng Chih to occupy Chi-ku with a decoy army. Wei's commanding general Ts'ao Chen mobilized his troops to resist them. Liang then personally led several armies in an assault on Ch'i-shan. The martial formations were well-ordered, rewards and punishments strictly respected, and commands and orders clear.
>
> The three commanderies of Nan-an, T'ien-shui, and An-ting rebelled against Wei and responded to Liang. Kuan-chung reverberated. Emperor Ming of the Wei then went west in a defensive effort and ordered Chang Ho to resist Liang. Liang entrusted General Ma Su with supervising the several armies deployed to the fore and had him engage Chang Ho in battle at Chieh-t'ing. Su contravened Liang's constraints, took inappropriate actions, and was badly destroyed by Ho.

Liang plucked some thousand households from the district of Hsi-hsien and shifted them back into Han-chung. He subsequently executed Ma Su to atone to the troops [that had been lost].

Ssu-ma Kuang's integrated account in the Sung dynasty *Tzu-chih T'ung-chien* includes significant material from earlier commentaries and works, including the *Han Chin Ch'un-ch'iu*. Perhaps most importantly, it integrates additional information about the course of battlefield developments, particularly Ma Su's actions. Reportedly, Ma "contravened the constraints [that Chu-ko Liang had imposed], his actions were troublesome and chaotic, he abandoned sites near water [sources] and ascended the mountain without occupying the fortifications below. Chang Ho severed their path to water, attacked, and greatly destroyed them. The officers and troops scattered. Lacking any forward position to occupy, Liang plucked some thousand households from Hsi-hsien and returned them to Han-chung."[80]

Ma Su's actions were inexplicable for two reasons: they not only contravened Chu-ko Liang's orders, but also ran contrary to widely known tactical admonitions that emphasized the need to secure water supplies and avoid becoming isolated. As summarized in the earlier *Liu-t'ao* (*Six Secret Teachings*), "Whenever the Three Armies occupy the heights of a mountain they are trapped on high by the enemy."[81]

Since no force can possibly survive without access to water, Ma Su's stupidity ever after became a lesson in command failure.[82] Wang P'ing, one of his subordinates, had even remonstrated with him, though unsuccessfully, thereby compounding his offense. In contrast, P'ing performed admirably:

---

80 *Tzu-chih T'ung-chien*, chüan 71, "Wei-chi, 3," Ming-ti T'ai-ho 2nd year. Chang Ho's biography in the *San-kuo Chih* (chüan 17) clearly states that he cut off Ma Su's routes to water.
81 "Crow and Cloud Formations in the Mountains." However, the passage also continues, "Whenever they hold the land below the mountain, they are imprisoned by the forces above them." Apparently the only effective solution would be to hold both the mountainous heights and the contiguous terrain below.
82 For a discussion of the recognition of water's importance and several examples of dramatic success achieved through denying water sources, see Sawyer, *Fire and Water: The Art of Incendiary and Aquatic Warfare in China*, especially the chapter "Negating Water Sources."

The Northern Campaigns

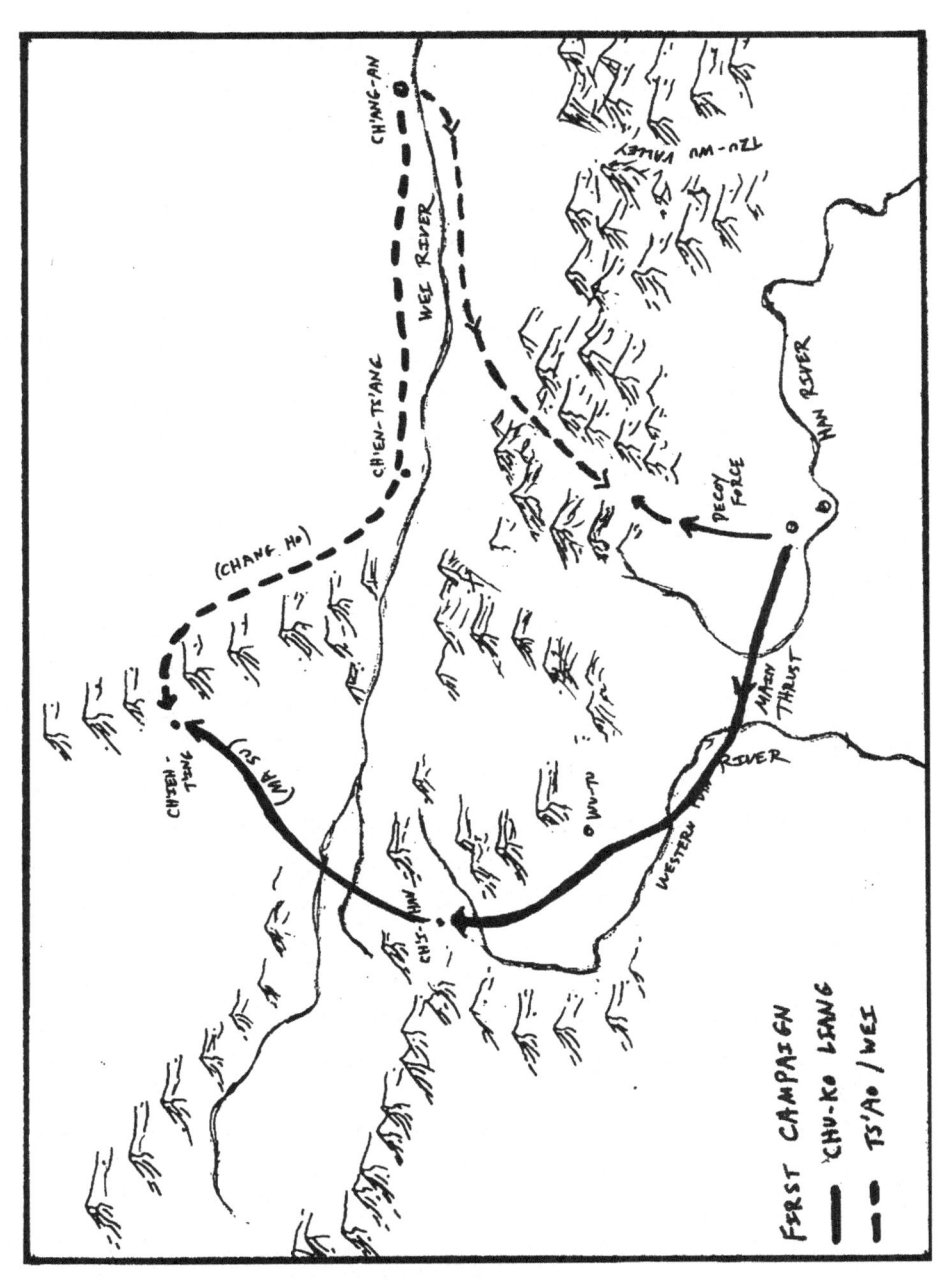

FIRST NORTHERN CAMPAIGN

Before Ma Su's defeat a subordinate general, the Pa-hsi native Wang P'ing, repeatedly admonished him to adhere to standard practices but Su did not heed him. When he was defeated and the troops scattered like stars, only the one thousand men that P'ing was leading beat their drums and defended themselves. Chang Ho suspected that there might be an ambush and did not go forward to press them. Thereupon P'ing leisurely gathered the scattered remnants of the several camps and led his generals and officers in returning. After Liang executed Ma Su and *Chiang-chün* (General) Li Sheng and seized control of the troops under Huang Hsi and other commanders, P'ing was especially honored and given increased titles and responsibilities.

Perhaps because of the numerous discussions that they had enjoyed on tactical matters, Chu-ko Liang's acceptance of his advice before they undertook the southern campaign, and their generally close relationship, the overconfident Ma never questioned the validity of his own wisdom. No doubt he would have justified his rejection of Liang's explicit instructions by referring to the *Art of War*'s assertion that a commander in the field can ignore his orders. (Well-known and widely believed long before the Three Kingdoms period, the concept of the commander's necessary independence also appears in "Sending the Army Forth," found in the *Chiang Yüan* and in Liang's analysis of Ssu-ma Yi's behavior during the last campaign.)

According to the *Art of War*'s "Nine Changes": "There are commands from the ruler that are not accepted." More generally, "If the Tao of warfare indicates certain victory, even though the ruler has instructed that combat should be avoided, if you must engage in battle it is permissible. If the Tao of warfare indicates that you will not be victorious, even though the ruler instructs you to engage in battle, not fighting is permissible."[83] However, Sun-tzu's famous statement refers to a field commander not being required to heed the *ruler's* edicts

---

[83] "Configurations of Terrain." "Planning Offensives" describes the several ways in which rulers hamper or balk battlefield operations.

(whether because of his ignorance or the difficulties of communication), not to a subordinate general disobeying the commander-in-chief's orders, an act that would subvert the very concept of hierarchical authority and thwart the successful implementation of operational tactics in the turmoil of warfare.[84]

Confronted by the blatant disregard of his orders, the disastrous results that had ensued, loss of valiant fighters, and waste of Shu's limited resources, Chu-ko Liang had no alternative but to execute Ma Su and thereby assuage the spirits of those who had needlessly died. Nevertheless, noting that defeat is an inescapable aspect of warfare, over the centuries a few commentators condemned Liang's decision as archaic and inappropriate, and some of Chu-ko Liang's own contemporaries were not averse to arguing that, as talent was in short supply, Ma Su should be spared and otherwise employed.

From another perspective, Chu-ko Liang's own culpability in employing Ma Su as the forward commander for the main contingent could not have been more obvious. According to Ma Su's biography in the *San-kuo Chih*, even though Su was the younger brother of the accomplished general Ma Liang, the other important officers believed that an experienced commander such as Wei Yen or Wu T'ai should have been appointed rather than a mere tactician. Furthermore, although Liu Pei had employed Ma Su in an administrative capacity, prior to his death he had specifically warned Chu-ko Liang that "Ma Su's words exceed his substance and he should not be given serious responsibility." He had also admonished him "to investigate it," no doubt through the employment of the measures then commonly advocated for scrutinizing men such as seen in Liang's "Knowing Human Nature" in the *Chiang Yüan* and widely found in the classic military writings.

Probably because he found Ma Su's wisdom enticing, Chu-ko Liang had differed in his assessment and therefore, in direct contradiction, confidently appointed him to a key position as *Ts'an-chün* or military advisor. (The historical texts note that "Ma Su's talents surpassed other men and he loved to discuss military strategy.") Certainly as commander-in-chief, Liang had to rely on his own judgment if he were to achieve surpassing results, yet he had also encouraged (the

---

84 Obviously, this immensely complex issue cannot be resolved so simply because commanders need to exercise initiative under changing circumstances, yet reflect the commanding general's intent and work toward achieving the mission's objectives.

clearly incompetent) emperor to thoroughly consult with his subordinates and heed their suggestions before making judgments or implementing plans.

In the aftermath of their defeat "Someone exhorted Liang to mobilize more troops but he replied: 'In both cases our large armies at Ch'i-shan and Chi-ku were more numerous than the brigands. Our error in not destroying them but instead being destroyed did not result from the fewness of our troops but instead lies with one man. I now intend to reduce the number of soldiers and generals, make punishments clear and have them think of their mistakes, and correct and vary our measures for the future.[85] If I do not succeed, what good will more troops be? From now on all those who are loyal and think on behalf of the state must attack my deficiencies because then our affairs can be settled, the brigands can be slain, and success can be awaited in as brief a time as standing up on tiptoe.'"

According to the *Tzu-chih T'ung-chien*, rather than simply making idle pronouncements to exculpate himself, Chu-ko Liang resolutely implemented his proclaimed intentions: "Thereupon he investigated the most minute contributions and scrutinized the sacrifices of their stalwart warriors, upbraiding himself for all his errors and making them known within their borders. He trained and disciplined the soldiers and held military discussions in order to make future plans. The martial officers were selected and instructed and the people forgot his defeats."

In this context, it should be noted that despite their previous training the troops dispatched to Chi-ku had also performed poorly. Fortunately, the commanders managed to retain control and extricate their contingents:

> Chou Yün and Teng Chih were also defeated at Chi-ku but Yün gathered the troops and maintained a solid defense and thus did not suffer any great harm. (However), he was also degraded to the rank of *chiang-chün* (general).

---

[85] An acerbic reaction perhaps made out of pique, his retort seems to suggest he planned to create a smaller, more elite force.

The Northern Campaigns

> Chu-ko Liang asked Teng Chih, "When the army retreated from Chieh-t'ing the soldiers and commanders did not have any concern for each other. How come when the army retreated from Chi-ku, even from the start the soldiers and commanders did not lose their order?"
>
> Teng replied, "Chou Yün personally cut off the rear and none of the army's materials and supplies were left behind so the soldiers and generals had no reason to lose their order."
>
> Yün had some leftover provisions so Liang wanted him to divide them among the commanders and soldiers but Yün said, "How can rewards be granted when military undertakings fail to be successful? Please put all these things into the Ch'in-an storehouse and wait until the tenth month to use them in making winter allotments." Liang therefore regarded him highly.

Accordingly, the only even minimally positive outcome was the defection of the great commander Chiang Wei to Shu. Liang's self-imposed castigation and degradation of three grades could therefore be, and in fact has been, deemed inadequate because he not only had erred in assessing or "knowing men," but had also fielded an army incapable of engaging the enemy without crumbling, despite his having long been responsible for the state's military training and administration.

A far greater, persistent question is how their initial campaign could have failed so miserably. It had actually benefited from the element of surprise because Wei had continued to expect a period of inaction consequent to Liu Pei's death, despite the prominence of their recent southern activities:[86]

> Initially, because Liu Pei had already died and nothing had been heard from [Shu] for several years, Wei had not really

---

86 Thus, even the emperor found it puzzling that Liang would abandon the natural strategic advantages that ensured their survival to venture forth, a further indication of the shortsightedness of his plan, as will be discussed below.

made any preparations. Thus, when they suddenly learned that Liang had come forth, both the court and countryside became afraid. At this moment T'ien-shui, Nan-an, and An-ting rebelled and turned to Liang. Within Kuan-chung his fame resounded and the ministers in the court pondered what sort of plan to put forth. However, the [Wei] emperor said, "Liang has been relying on the mountains for solidity but by now coming forth of his own accord he conveniently coheres with the technique advocated in the military books of 'compelling men.' Liang's destruction is certain." He then had a force of fifty thousand infantry and cavalry assembled and dispatched *Yu-chiang-chün* (General of the Right) Chang Ho to go west to resist Liang. On *ting-wei* the emperor went to Ch'ang-an.

Second, the initial campaign sought to exploit Wei's ongoing difficulties and fatigue in having chosen to confront Wu in the east, a decision that reduced the numbers immediately available to blunt an invasion. Wei was also suffering from internal problems and dissension following Ts'ao P'i's demise and the installation of a new emperor. Moreover, they had been forced to hastily dispatch forces an equal or greater distance at a double pace rather than been able to proceed in Shu's orderly, well-prepared mode. In addition, Chu-ko Liang's planning had resulted in local tactical superiorities (known as *ch'üan* in the *Art of War*'s crucial conceptualization) that should have allowed them to prevail in battlefield encounters and in achieving their limited objectives against outnumbered defenders.

The need to defend multiple, albeit well-known, locations posed some problems for Wei because they were compelled to similarly segment their forces into operational contingents. Although they had vastly more men under arms, the numbers that were eventually deployed had somehow remained inferior. (Commentators who criticize Chu-ko Liang's decision to weaken the main thrust by segmenting his troops erroneously overlook this localized numerical superiority.) Nevertheless, whether because of better commanders or the aggressor's errors, the defenders managed to blunt the onslaught and avoid being seduced by a decoy army that performed poorly.

The Second Campaign

The second campaign, undertaken that winter, was a thrust late in 228 CE through San-kuan Pass under Chu-ko Liang's personal command toward the middle of Kuan-chung that targeted the vast warehouses at Ch'en-ts'ang, a name that itself means "Ch'en storehouses." In view of the severe reversals suffered earlier that year, Chu-ko Liang's seemingly rash decision to undertake another effort was not only surprising but also aroused opposition within the court. The latter prompted him to justify the need for immediate, rather than much-deferred, action in a memorial ostensibly directed to the young emperor but certainly intended to dissuade his critics at large:[87]

> The late emperor deeply felt that the Han and the brigands [in Wei] could not coexist and that the task of kingship could not be secure in a limited peripheral area. He therefore entrusted me with responsibility for extirpating the brigands. Because of the late emperor's perspicaciousness, when he measured my abilities he knew that my talent for attacking the brigands was weak and that the enemy was strong. However, unless the brigands were to be attacked, the task of kingship would also perish and we would merely be sitting about awaiting death. But who should attack them? Accordingly he entrusted me with the responsibility and never had any doubts.
>
> From the day I received the mandate I have not been able to sleep quietly on my mat and my food has had no sweet flavor. Although constantly thinking of this northern campaign, it

---

[87] Evaluations of the authenticity of what has come to be known as the "Hou Ch'u-shih Piao" range from complete credence to suggestions that the language is too rustic for Chu-ko Liang as well as that, even though parts may be authentic, there are numerous later accretions.

was appropriate to first invade the south. Thus, in the fifth month we crossed the Lu River and penetrated deeply into that desolate land, eating once every two days. It was not that I did not have any concern for myself but that I realized that the task of kingship could not be preserved on the periphery at the Shu capital. I therefore risked danger and hardship in order to uphold the late emperor's bequeathed intentions but disputants [in the court] did not consider it a [viable] strategy.

Presently the brigands have become fatigued from hastening about in the west[88] and making focal efforts in the east. Military tactics exploit fatigue so this is the time to race forward. Let me array the justifications:

Emperor Kao-tsu's brilliance rivaled the sun and moon, his strategists were deep and profound, yet only after they overcame difficulties and endured wounds were they secure. Today your majesty does not come up to Kao-tsu while your strategists are not the equal of Chang Liang and Ch'en P'ing, yet you want to employ a long-range plan to gain victory, to sit about and settle the realm. To me this is the first inexplicable point.

Liu Yu and Wang Lang each occupied provinces and commanderies, discussed security and spoke about plans, and in their actions cited sagacious men, but a host of doubts filled their bellies and a mass of difficulties stopped up their chests so that one year they did not engage in warfare, the next year they did not conduct punitive campaigns. They allowed Sun Ts'e to become great and annex the area east

---

88 As a result of the first campaign.

The Northern Campaigns

of the Yangtze River. To me this is the second inexplicable point.

Ts'ao Ts'ao's wisdom and planning greatly surpassed other men and in his employment of the army he may be compared with Sun Pin and Wu Ch'i. Nevertheless, he still encountered difficulty at Nan-yang, was constricted at Wu-ch'ao, endangered at Ch'i-lien, pressed at Li-yang, nearly defeated at Pei-shan, and almost perished at T'ung-kuan, and only thereafter perversely managed to gain temporary success. Moreover, as my talents are weak, the third inexplicable point is wanting to settle the realm without becoming endangered.

Ts'ao Ts'ao attacked Ch'ang Pa five times without subjugating him, crossed Ch'ao Lake [to attack Sun Chien] four times but was not successful, employed Wang Fu yet Wang plotted against him, and entrusted Hsia Hou (Yüan) with responsibility but he was defeated and perished. The late emperor always praised Ts'ao Ts'ao's ability yet he still suffered these losses, so how can inferior talents like your minister invariably be victorious? This is the fourth inexplicable point.

It has been just a year since I went to Han-chung but we have [in the interim] lost Chao Yün, Yang Ch'ün, Ma Yü, Yen Chih, Ting Li, Pai Shou, Liu Ho, and Teng T'ung together with more than seventy contingent commanders and camp officers. Our generals capable of suddenly penetrating the enemy, other men who can command the vanguard, and more than a thousand men from the Pin Sou and Ch'ing Chiang tribes, including highly martial cavalry that can disperse the enemy, are all elite warriors that have been gathered over dozens of years from the four quarters, not the contribution of a single province. In another few years we will lose two-thirds of them so how will we be able to make plans against the enemy? This is the fifth inexplicable point to your minister.

Today the people are weary and the army fatigued yet we cannot desist from military affairs. If we cannot desist, the labor and expenses for remaining [in a defensive posture] and campaigning will be of the same order. Accordingly, not planning for it now but wanting to hold off the enemy for a lengthy period with just one province's resources is the sixth inexplicable point to your minister.

It is always difficult to attain balance in affairs. Formerly when the late emperor was defeated in the area of [ancient] Ch'u, Ts'ao Ts'ao rubbed his hands together [in glee] as he believed that the realm had now been settled. But then the late emperor formed an alliance with Wu and Yüeh [Sun Ch'üan] in the east and seized Pa and Shu in the west, mobilized the army for a northern expedition, and Hsia Hou Yüan lost his head. Ts'ao Ts'ao made a strategic error and the Han's affairs were about to be successful but then Wu violated the alliance, Kuan Yü was defeated and died, we suffered a debacle at Tzu-k'uei, and Ts'ao P'i proclaimed himself emperor. It is very difficult to foresee affairs such as these. I can only bow and undertake this task, continuing to exhaust my strength until I die. Whether we will succeed or fail, whether our efforts will proceed advantageously or be blunted, cannot be anticipated beforehand.

In this memorial Liang almost offhandedly mentions what was probably the real reason he chose to undertake another campaign so quickly: "Presently the brigands have become fatigued from hastening about in the west and making focal efforts in the east. Military tactics exploit fatigue so this is the time to race forward." The first, that the enemy had become fatigued from rushing to defend against his multipronged initial campaign, of course applied equally to their own forces. More importantly, Wu had lured a major force under Ts'ao Hsiu into southern territory, compelling Wei to shift soldiers apparently no longer required for Kuan-chung's defense out of the valley into the southeast, thereby creating a temporary power vacuum that could not be remedied in less than a few weeks should Shu's forces suddenly reappear, particularly after Hsiu suffered a severe defeat.[89]

Before the engagement commenced Chu-ko Liang wrote a brief letter of explanation to his older brother Chin, ironically a high-ranking adviser in Wu, discussing his strategic intent and the difficulties involved: "Even though the mountains are precipitous, the valley constricted, and a stream passes through the small valley of Sui-yang making it difficult to maneuver the army, in the past we have had reconnaissance scouts pass back and forth and there is an important road that penetrates it. Now I have had our advance army improve the road toward Ch'en-ts'ang so it should be sufficiently [wide] for us to entangle the enemy's strategic power, keeping them from dividing their forces and moving eastward."

As usual, his *San-kuo Chih* biography contains a succinct reprisal of the actual campaign: "In the winter Liang once again went forth from San-kuan (San pass) and besieged Ch'en-ts'ang. Ts'ao Chen resisted him and when Liang's provisions were exhausted Liang returned [to Shu]. When the Wei general Wang Shuang pursued Liang with a cavalry contingent, Liang engaged him in battle, destroyed his forces, and slew him."

The second campaign thus had a moderate but well-defined objective, capturing the storehouses that sustained Wei's defensive forces near the middle of Kuan-chung. If they could have been taken intact, the effort would not only have denied crucial supplies to the enemy but also accorded with the *Art of War*'s behest to seize provisions from opponents: "The wise general will concentrate on securing provisions from the enemy. One bushel of the enemy's foodstuffs is worth twenty of ours, one picul of fodder is worth twenty of ours."[90]

---

89 Ts'ao Shu's defeat, which resulted in part from him being another theoretical expert rather than an experienced battlefield commander, is discussed in the concluding section.
90 "Waging War," the *Art of War*.

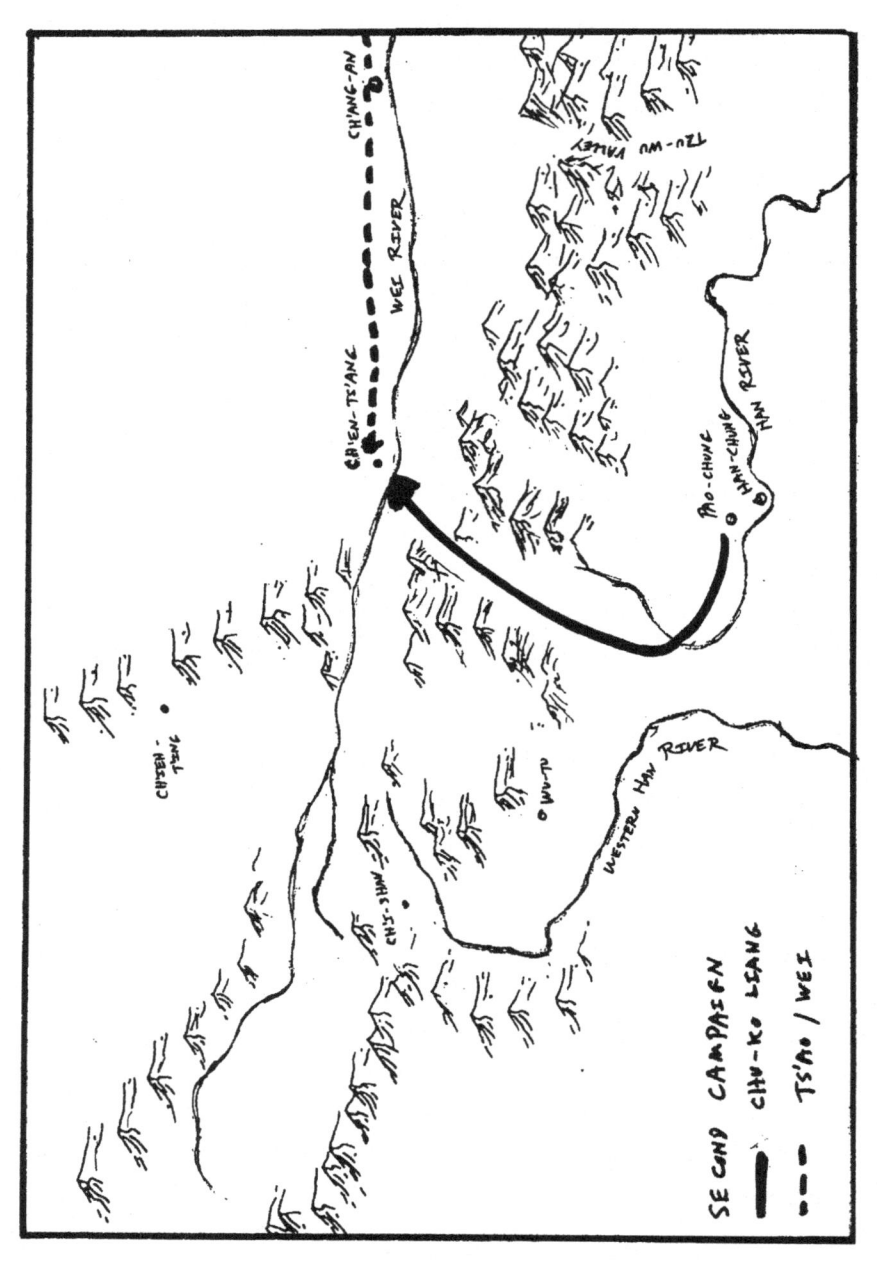

SECOND NORTHERN CAMPAIGN

As expressed in the tactical discussion incorporated in the *Hundred Unorthodox Strategies* for the topic of "Hunger":

> In general, whenever you mobilize the army to go forth on a punitive campaign to extirpate an enemy and have deeply penetrated their territory, fodder and provisions will be scarce and lacking, so you must segment your troops to forage and plunder. If you occupy the enemy's storehouses and granaries and seize his accumulated resources in order to continuously provision your army, you will be victorious. A tactical principle from the *Art of War* states: "If one relies upon gaining provisions from the enemy, the army's food will be sufficient."

Success would have also facilitated establishing a semipermanent base for the eastward thrust inevitably required to vanquish Wei, one that would have to be undertaken before the locally stored supplies were themselves exhausted. However, the *Tzu-chih T'ung-chien* indicates Ts'ao Chen had by then not only retaken the three rebellious commandaries of Nan-an, T'ien-shui, and An-ting, but had also anticipated the attack:

> Ts'ao Chen conducted a punitive expedition against An-ting and the others, three commanderies in all, and pacified them. Chen believed that because Chu-ko Liang had suffered a painful lesson at Ch'i-shan he would next come forth at Ch'en-ts'ang. He therefore dispatched General of the Army Hao Chao and others to defend Ch'en-ts'ang and put their fortifications in order.

Chu-ko Liang thus failed to achieve the operational ideal of keeping the enemy ignorant as advised in the *Art of War*: "The location where we will engage the enemy must not become known to them. If it is not known then the positions that they must prepare to defend will be numerous. If the positions that the enemy prepares to defend are numerous, the forces we will engage will be few."[91]

Cities and the techniques of urban assault had evolved considerably from the end of the Spring and Autumn period, when the *Art of War* condemned attacking fortified positions as the lowest form of strategy and strongly advised commanders to eschew them. Nevertheless, defenders ensconced within city walls still retained a considerable advantage and enormous efforts might be required to vanquish them. The battle for Ch'en-ts'ang provides a particularly painful example of how determined fighters exploiting every available method could succeed in consistently thwarting even astute, fervently implemented assault measures:[92]

> Liang noted that he had several tens of thousands of troops while general Chao's soldiers [in the bastion] only amounted to somewhat more than a thousand. Moreover, he estimated that rescue troops could not easily arrive from the east so he advanced the army to assault Chao. They raised cloud ladders and employed assault wagons in order to approach the walls but Chao countered them by using incendiary arrows to shoot the ladders and all the men on them were burned to death.[93] Chao also smashed the assault wagons with [large] stones attached to [swinging] ropes and they were crushed.
>
> Liang then had a hundred-foot enclosed aerial tower constructed in order to shoot arrows into the city and used dirt balls to fill up the moat in order to directly attack the walls but Chao erected a second wall within the fortifications. Liang also had tunnels dug so that his troops could leap

---

91 "Vacuity and Substance."
92 *Tzu-chih T'ung-chien*, *chüan* 71, "Wei-chi, 3," Ming-ti T'ai-ho 2nd year.
93 For a discussion of Chinese siege techniques, see Robin D. S. Yates, "Early Poliorcetics: The Mohists to the Sung" in Joseph Needham, *Science and Civilisation in China*, Volume V, part 6. For the role of incendiaries in attacks and defense, see Sawyer, *Fire and Water: The Art of Incendiary and Aquatic Warfare in China*.

out into the city but Chao similarly had ditches dug within the fortifications that cut across and pierced them. Day and night they attacked and resisted each other in this fashion for more than twenty days.

Ts'ao Chen dispatched general Fei Yao and others to rescue him. The emperor summoned Chang Ho from Fang-ch'eng and deputed him to attack Liang. The emperor personally traveled to Ho-nai-ch'eng to send Ho off with a ritual wine ceremony. At that time he inquired of him, "When you, general, arrive will Liang have already captured Ch'en-ts'ang or not?"

Ho knew that Liang had penetrated deeply into their territory without [adequate] grain supplies and after calculating on his fingers said, "By the time your minister arrives Liang will have already departed." He advanced along the road both day and night but before he arrived Liang's provisions had already been exhausted and he had withdrawn. General Wang Shuang pursued him but Liang suddenly attacked and slew Shuang. [The Wei emperor] summoned and made Chao "Lord of Kuan-nei."

Despite having acted judiciously, Wei's forces equally failed to exploit the tactical situation as it was commonly understood and would be described in the *Hundred Unorthodox Strategies* under the rubric of "The Sated in Warfare":

> Whenever an enemy comes from afar, their supplies and provisions will not be continuous. If the enemy is hungry while you are full, you can make your walls solid and not engage in battle, maintaining your stance for a prolonged period in order to enervate them while severing their supply routes. When they withdraw, you can secretly dispatch

> unorthodox troops to intercept them along their route of retreat, and release troops to pursue and suddenly attack them. Then their destruction will be certain. A tactical principle from the *Art of War* states: "With the well-fed await the hungry."

No doubt conscious of the horrendous losses that might be experienced, and probably fearing that the vital provisions stored in Ch'en-ts'ang might be destroyed, Chu-ko Liang had also resorted to psychological measures by having one of Chao's fellow villagers, someone presumably more convincing in outlining Chao's best interest than an unknown emissary, try to persuade him to surrender:[94]

> In the twelfth month Liang led the soldiers forth through San Pass and besieged Ch'en-ts'ang. However, Ch'en-ts'ang had already prepared and Liang was unable to conquer them. Liang therefore had Hao Chao's fellow villager Chin Hsiang speak to him from a distance.
>
> From atop a tower Chao replied: "You are practiced in the laws of Wei and you also know my character. I have been well-favored by the state and my retainers are numerous. There is nothing that you can say while I must die. Please return and thank Chu-ko Liang and renew the attack."
>
> When Hsiang reported Chao's words Chu-ko Liang again had Chin seriously speak with him, saying, "Neither your men nor weapons are a match for us, you are pointlessly destroying yourself." Chao then said to Chin, "My former words stand. I recognize you but my arrows will not." Chin Hsiang then departed.

---

94 *Tzu-chih T'ung-chien, chüan* 71, "Wei-chi, 3," Ming-ti T'ai-ho 2nd year.

In evaluating the second campaign commentators have tended to emphasize the unified spirit that characterized Chao's troops and the strategic advantages enjoyed by their fortifications. Although Chu-ko Liang employed several of the standard assault measures available to commanders in his era, including overlook ladders, assault wagons, and mining, they were all adroitly countered by Chao's ingenuity and timely responses. (Somewhat puzzlingly, he appears to have avoided using incendiary arrows, presumably in order to avoid destroying the provisions.)

Even though only a portion of his fifty thousand troops could have been employed on target at one time, this sort of numerical discrepancy should still have allowed them to prevail within a few days through heroic, if expensive, assaults or the simultaneous (rather than sequential) employment of all their attack techniques. But he allowed his forces to become bogged down and they exhausted all their supplies, compelling their retreat back into Shu with their single objective pathetically unaccomplished.

Even more inexplicable is Liang's failure to modify his tactics when the defenders' courage and skills became apparent. As the tomb text edition of the *Art of War* implies, cities can be isolated or quarantined and then bypassed so that they will not pose a threat at the rear. Chu-ko Liang might also have employed Ch'en-ts'ang as an entanglement (as he initially indicated) and then ambushed the troops mobilized to rescue it as they hastened forward on easily anticipated routes. Since Chang Ho had been recalled from a campaign that targeted contingents near Wu, his troops had to race a thousand *li* in a remarkably short time. They would have been fatigued, disorganized, and highly vulnerable, just as the *Art of War* states: "If you abandon your armor [and heavy equipment] to race forward day and night without encamping, covering two days' normal distance at a time, marching forward a hundred *li* to contend for gain, the Three Armies' generals will be captured. The strong will be the first to arrive while the exhausted will follow. With such tactics only one in ten will reach the battle site."[95]

Alternatively, Chu-ko Liang could have deployed a secondary force that simply waited at a more interior Kuan-chung location until Wei's rescue forces sped

---

95 "Military Combat." Also included among the eight conditions specified by Wu Ch'i (in "Evaluating the Enemy," *Wu-tzu*) as so advantageous for attacking an enemy that divination need not be performed.

by before unexpectedly striking directly at Ch'ang-an, where the need to respond to external threats might have thrown the defenses into turmoil. Circumstances may have constrained the tactical options to a limited few once the assault at Ch'en-ts'ang commenced, but they were not nonexistent, particularly for the imaginative. Surprisingly, from the outset Chu-ko Liang's choice of objectives can hardly be deemed to have been innovative or strategically astute. However, far more damaging to his reputation for vision and cleverness was the transparency of his plan, well anticipated by Ts'ao Chen even though he did not immediately strengthen Ch'en-ts'ang's defenses. Ultimately, despite Shu's improved ability to withstand attack (as shown by their defeat of Wang Shuang's forces when they attempted to exploit their highly vulnerable withdrawal), the second campaign failed to accomplish anything other than wasting the state's manpower and dwindling resources.

The Third Northern Campaign

A third campaign with somewhat different objectives was launched in the spring of 229. Once again the *San-kuo Chih* account is quite succinct: "In the seventh year Liang dispatched Ch'en Shih[96] to attack Wu-tu and Yin-p'ing. Yung-chou's *Tz'u-shih*, the Wei general Kuo Huai, led his troops in an attempt to attack Shih. Liang then came forth himself as far as Chien-wei and when Huai turned about and retreated Liang pacified the two commanderies." However, it is more effusive in citing the emperor's congratulatory response, framed in an edict restoring him to the position of chancellor, already seen in the biography. (Somewhat surprisingly, the *Tzu-chih T'ung-chien* account is virtually identical.) The two commandaries that he captured, Wu-tu and Yin-p'ing, were in fact en route to the Wei River valley but south of the mountain ranges, with the second positioned at the start of a minor path into Shu. The main puzzle is why they had not been seized earlier, even though Ts'ao Ts'ao had deliberately augmented their troop strength when withdrawing from Han-chung.

Following this comparatively successful campaign, at the end of 229 Chu-ko Liang shifted his administrative headquarters up into the Han-chung area, where

---

96 Some texts have Chieh rather than Sh'ih.

he had the two fortified cities of Han-ch'eng at Mien-yang and Yüeh-ch'eng at Ch'eng-ku constructed on the plains south of Nan-shan (Mount Nan). No doubt intended to facilitate command and staging activities for future northern incursions, they also augmented Shu's defenses against possible Wei incursions.[97]

Whether because Wei had been preoccupied with internal problems or obsessed with reducing Wu, during the first three campaigns the initiative always lay with Shu. Wei opted to respond to exigencies as required rather than prepositioning forces well forward where they could have thwarted Shu's advance out of the mountains and thus yielded the choice of target and terrain to Chu-ko Liang. Following the loss of these two cities and over internal opposition, the emperor finally decided to dispatch an expeditionary force in 230 CE to invade Shu itself that is discussed in the concluding analytic sction. However, they were eventually compelled to abandon the effort because heavy rains impeded their progress and the transport of provisions.

In this year Chu-ko Liang also initiated an effort to reduce Wei's ability to derive supplies from the indigenous peoples in the contiguous area by sending Wei Yen into the region controlled by the Western Ch'iang. Eventually he engaged and severely defeated Kuo Huai, one of Ts'ao Ts'ao's best commanders, who had long proven himself adept at suppressing Yi and Ch'iang groups, and Fei Yao at Yang-ch'i. Although little is known about the course of the conflict, Wei Yen showed that he was not only courageous and resolute, but also almost certainly capable of successfully implementing the sort of unorthodox strike that he proposed prior to the first campaign.[98]

The Fourth Campaign

According to the *San-kuo Chih*: "In the ninth year [231 CE] Liang once again went out to Ch'i-shan, employing 'wooden oxen' to transport their provisions. When they were exhausted he withdrew the army but was engaged in battle by Chang Ho who was slain by archers."

---

[97] *Tzu-chih T'ung-chien*, "Wei-chi 3," Ming-ti T'ao-ho 3rd year.
[98] The episode is recorded in Liu Shan's annals and Wei Yen's biography in the *San-kuo Chih*, but not Kuo Huai's.

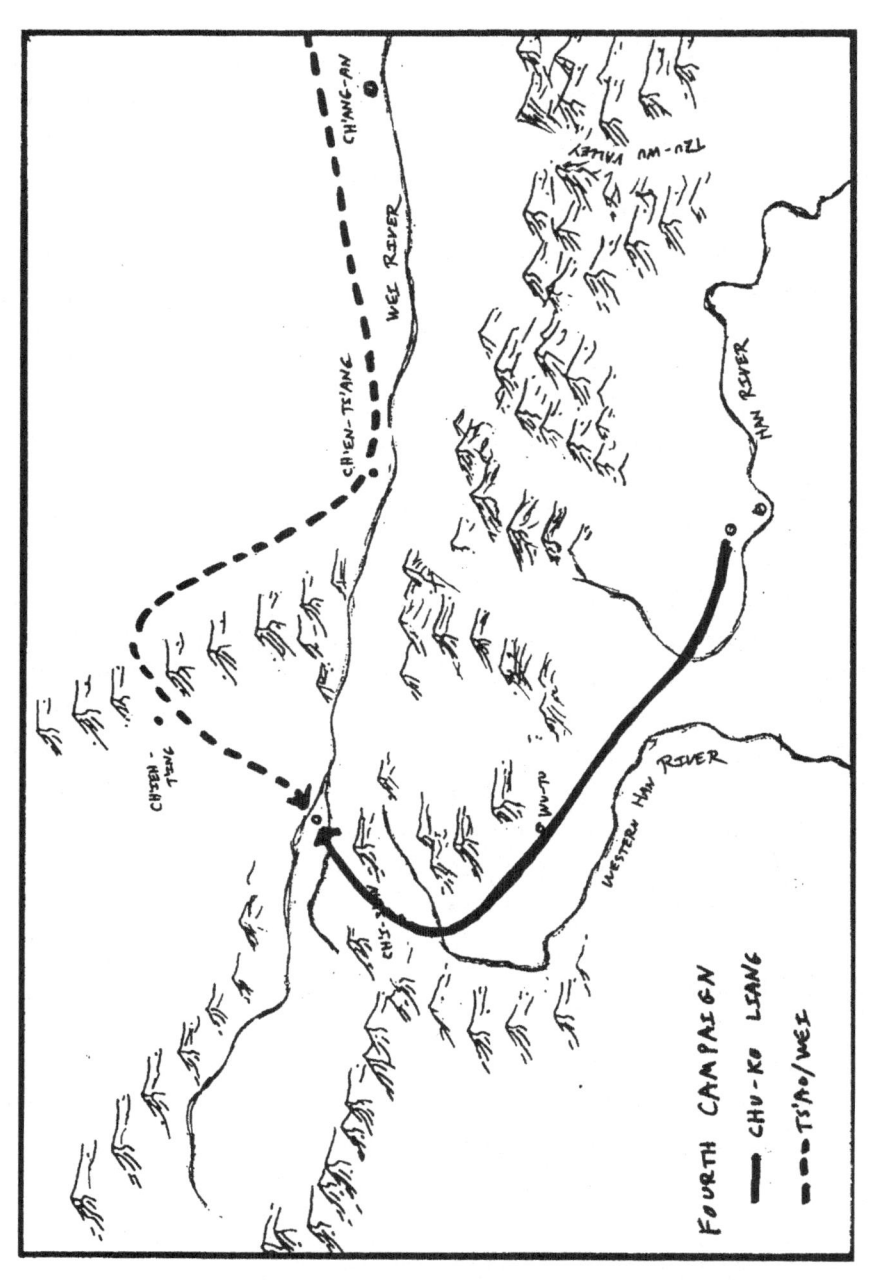

FOURTH NORTHERN CAMPAIGN

The Northern Campaigns

The *Tzu-chih T'ung-chien* begins its account by noting an apparently mundane appointment that would have serious consequences:

> In the spring, the second month, the Han chancellor Liang appointed Li Yen as *Chung-Tu-hu* to manage their administrative affairs. Li Yen changed his name to Li P'ing. Liang led the armies out to invade and besiege Ch'i-san, using wooden oxen for transport. At that time Wei's *Ta Ssu-ma*, Ts'ao Chen, had fallen ill so the emperor ordered Ssu-ma Yi to encamp at Ch'ang-an and supervise Chang Ho, Fei Yao, Tai Ling, Kuo Huai, and the other generals in repelling him. In the third month Ts'ao Chen died. From the tenth month until this month it had not rained.
>
> Ssu-ma Yi had Fei Yao and Tai Ling retain four thousand elite soldiers for the defense of Shang-kuei district but sent all the other forces west to rescue Ch'i-shan. Chang Ho wanted to temporarily deploy a portion of the soldiers to Yung and Mei districts but Yi said: "If we could anticipate that our forward army alone will be able to withstand them then what you have said, general, would be correct. But if they are unable to withstand them yet we divide into forward and rear armies, it would be how Ch'u's three armies were captured by Ch'ing Pu." He then advanced.
>
> Liang divided his soldiers, retaining some to continue the attack at Ch'i-shan while he personally countered Yi at Shang-kuei. Kuo Huai and Fei Yao intercepted Liang but Liang destroyed them and then harvested the millet from the fields before encountering Ssu-ma Yi east of Shang-kuei. Yi gathered his forces and relied upon the ravines so that the armies could not engage each other and Liang withdrew.

Yi and the other commanders maintained a pursuit at the rear as far as Lu-ch'eng. Chang Ho said: "They came from afar to counter us but were not able to get us to engage them in combat so they assume we found it advantageous not to engage in fighting and want to use a long-term plan to control them. Moreover, [the defenders at] Ch'i-shan know that our great army is already near so their emotional state will be stable. We can halt and encamp here but segment off some unorthodox troops and have them go around their rear. We should not just advance and not dare press them nor sit and disappoint the people's expectations. Right now Liang's army is isolated, their provisions are few, and they are about to depart."

Yi did not heed his advice but instead just followed Liang. When they closed with them, Yi again ascended the mountains and dug in, being unwilling to engage in battle. After Chia Hsü and Wei P'ing had repeatedly requested permission to fight, they finally said, "If you fear Shu as if fearing a tiger, will the realm not laugh at you!" Yi was troubled by [their comments] and all the generals continued to request permission to fight.

In the summer, the fifth month, on *hsin-ssu* [tenth] Yi finally had Chang Ho attack the southern defenses of Wu-tang's supervisor Ho P'ing[99] while he proceeded along the middle road toward Liang. Liang deputed Wei Yen, Kao Hsiang, and Wu Pan to counter him and Wei's forces were badly defeated in battle. The Han army slew some three thousand armored soldiers and Yi returned and defended their camp.

---

99 Some editions have Wang P'ing.

> In the sixth month Liang withdrew the army because their provisions were exhausted. Ssu-ma Yi dispatched Chang Ho to pursue them. Ho advanced to Mu-men where he engaged Liang in battle. Shu's men exploited the heights to arrange an ambush, their bows and crossbows fired randomly, and a flying arrow hit Ho's right knee and he eventually died.

This ends the account of another ultimately futile campaign, despite two early victories and the repulsion of a Wei attack. An entry for the eighth month further expands the story by explaining the lack of provisions, in spite of Liang's efforts to ensure them:

> When the Han chancellor Liang attacked Ch'i-shan, Li P'ing remained behind to supervise the transportation of supplies. It happened that unremitting rain fell, so P'ing feared that the forwarding of supplies would be interrupted. He therefore dispatched *Ts'an-chün* Hu Chung and *Tu-chün* Ch'eng Fan to convey an imperial edict calling upon Liang to return. Liang accepted it and accordingly withdrew the army.
>
> When P'ing heard that the army was withdrawing, he then feigned surprise, saying, "The army's supplies and provisions are sufficient, why are they returning?" Moreover, he wanted to kill the *Tu-yün* [supervisor of transport] Ts'en Shu in order to exculpate himself from failing in his responsibility. In addition, he presented a memorial to the emperor saying that "the army is pretending to retreat in order to lure the brigands forward." (However), when Liang compared what he had written before and after, he found discrepancies in the beginning and end. P'ing could not respond and his options were exhausted so he bowed his head and acknowledged his offense.

Naturally Chu-ko Liang reported the affair to the emperor, who removed P'ing from his post and stripped him of his title, but strangely—given Shu's draconian laws and Chu-ko Liang's emphasis in his writings about uniformly applying punishments to the noble and high ranking—did not have him executed. Meanwhile, Chu-ko Liang incomprehensibly appointed P'ing's son to the same post.[100]

Clearly, Liang had once again misread the character and reliability of people to whom he assigned crucial responsibilities because of their purported integrity and capabilities. Moreover, he had even been warned of Li P'ing's possible duplicity. According to the *Tzu-chih T'ung-chien*, he wrote a letter to Chiang Wan and Tung Yün stating, "Hsiao Ch'i previously said to me that Chang-fang [Li P'ing] had scales on his stomach and that the people from his village felt that one shouldn't be intimate with him. I assumed that he had these scales but if I did not offend him did not think that the [perfidious] affairs of Su Ch'in and Chang Yi would unexpectedly [again] arise. This can be conveyed to Hsiao Ch'i."[101]

The Fifth Campaign

Chu-ko Liang's final northern campaign was mounted in 234 CE. Prior to undertaking it, he sent a missive to Sun Ch'üan in the hope that he would launch a more or less coordinated attack on Wei so as to cause the enemy to suffer the consternation of confronting threats on two fronts and split their forces:

> The Han royal house has been unfortunate, the cords of kingship have lost their principles, and the brigand Ts'ao Ts'ao usurped power and rebelled, creating a situation that has lingered until the present time. Everyone thought of attacking and exterminating him but the objectives of our alliance have not yet been accomplished. Our illustrious emperor entrusted me with a heavy responsibility, I dare not but exert my full strength and exhaust my loyalty.

---

100 Ch'en Shou's twenty-four selections include one titled "Dismissing Liu P'ing."
101 Su Ch'in and Chang Yi were noted "persuaders" in the Warring States period who attempted to affect the alliances and fates of states.

The Northern Campaigns

> At the moment our large army has already assembled at Ch'i-shan, the maddened invaders [from Wei] are about to perish along the Wei River. I therefore hope that in accord with the righteous objectives of our alliance you will order your generals to undertake a campaign into the north so that together we can pacify the central plains and rectify the house of Han. A letter cannot fully express [my thoughts] but I earnestly hope you will reflect upon it.

Sun Ch'üan did in fact launch another major assault on Hsin-ch'eng in Honai, but it was thwarted and he timidly withdrew when confronted by superior forces.

According to the *San-kuo Chih* the fifth campaign was marked by logistical innovation:

> In the spring of the twelfth year [234 CE] Liang led all their forces out through Yeh-ku, relying on the "fluid horses" [*liu ma*] for transport. He occupied Wu-chang-yüan in Wu-kung and engaged in battle with [future] King Ssu-ma Yi south of the Wei River. On every expedition Liang had worried that their provisions would not be sustained, keeping him from fully realizing his intentions. For this reason he divided up the soldiers and had them encamp and farm in order to create a foundation for long occupation. Although these farmers were interspersed along both banks of the river and dwelled among the inhabitants, the hundred surnames remained untroubled because the soldiers did not act wantonly.
>
> After a standoff of more than a hundred days, in the eighth month of the fifth year Liang became severely ill and died in the army, being at that time fifty-four years old. When the army retired King Hsüan [Ssu-ma Yi] conducted a tour

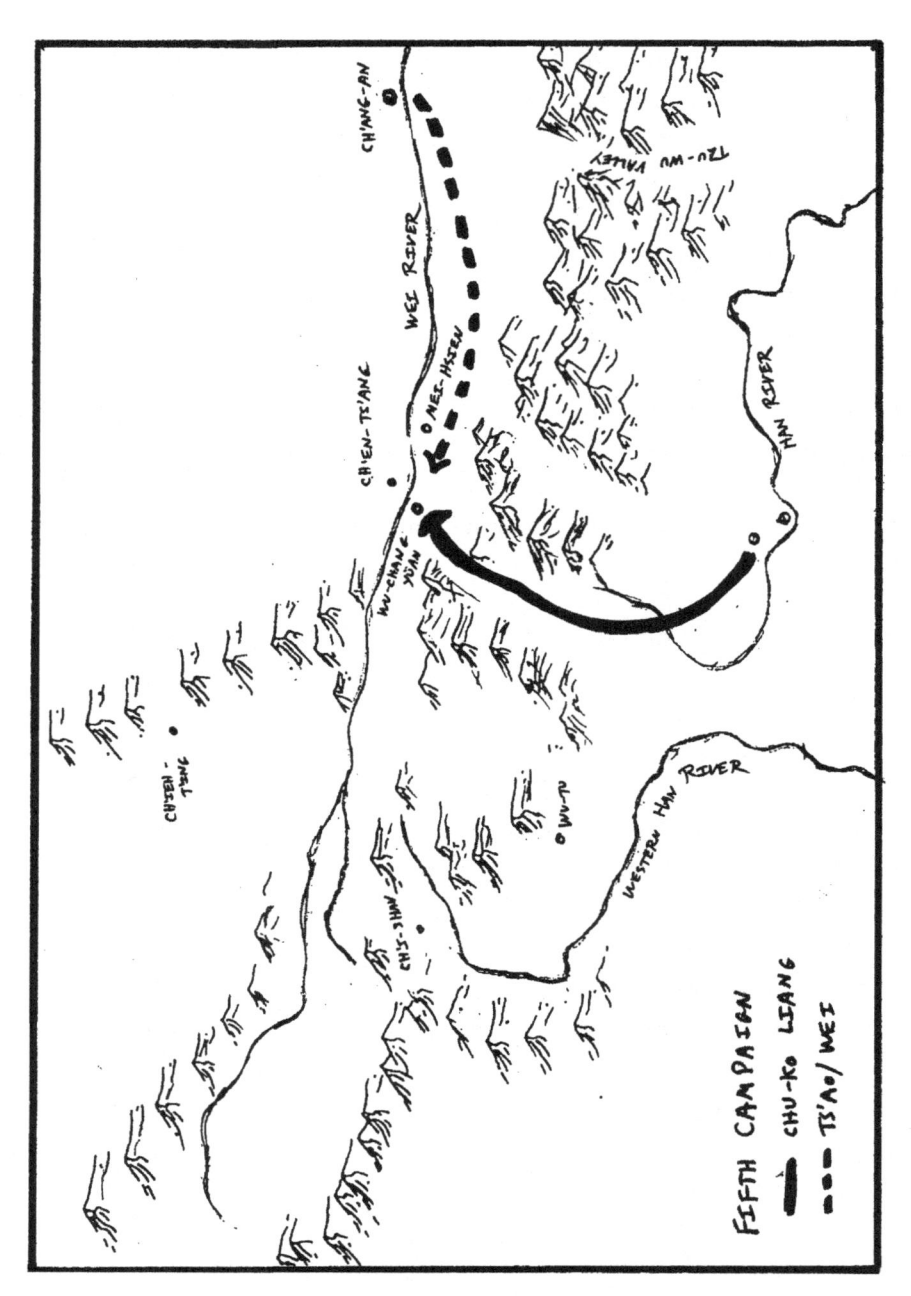

FIFTH NORTHERN CAMPAIGN

of inspection of his camps and fortifications and remarked that "he was one of the realm's unique talents."

After mentioning that a harsh Shu official had provoked unrest in the south that had to be suppressed, the *Tzu-chih T'ung-chien* adds the comment that before the campaign "Chu-ko Liang encouraged agriculture and discussed warfare, created the wooden oxen and transported rice and accumulated it at Yeh-ku-k'ou [the mouth of Yeh Valley], improving the facilities in Yeh-ku. He thus nurtured the people and rested the warriors for three years before again employing them."

After this period of recuperation and preparation, Chu-ko Liang thus once again (and highly unimaginatively) sought to invade the Wei River valley in preparation for subsequently advancing against Ch'ang-an and areas beyond the pass. According to the *Tzu-chih T'ung-chien*'s synthesized account:

> In the spring of the second year (234) of Ch'ing-lung, the second month, Liang mobilized all the troops, a total of one hundred thousand, and invaded through Yeh-ku. He simultaneously sent an emissary to Wu to conclude an agreement for undertaking an expeditionary campaign at the same time.
>
> When Chu-ko Liang reached Mei he encamped the army south of the Wei River. Ssu-ma Yi led his armies across the Wei and erected fortifications with their backs to the river to resist him.[102] He informed his generals, "If Liang comes forth at Wu-kung and moves eastward by relying on the mountains it will really be worrisome. But if he comes forth in the west above Wu-chang-yüan you will have little to do." Liang eventually encamped at Wu-chang-yüan.

---

102 Generally a deployment eschewed by the classic military writings from the *Art of War* onward, but successfully employed by Han Hsin against Chao. (For a reprisal, see Sawyer, *Tao of Deception*, 114–117.)

Zhuge Liang: Strategy, Achievements, and Writings

Yung-chou's *Tz'u-shih* Kuo Huai said to Yi, "Liang will certainly contend for the northern plains area [Pei-yüan] so it would be appropriate to occupy it first." When most of the other generals disagreed Huai said: "If Liang leaps over the Wei, ascends the plains, disperses his soldiers throughout the northern mountains, cuts off the road to Lung-yu, and manages to stir up the people and members of the Yi, it will not be to the state's advantage." Yi then had Huai encamp at Pei-yüan. Before his walls and moat had been completed a large Han force arrived. Huai immediately counterattacked and drove them back.[103]

Every time [they came forth] Liang had been troubled that a failure to sustain their provisions kept him from realizing his intentions. He therefore divided the troops into farming encampments in order to prepare a foundation for a lengthy presence. These farmers were interspersed among the inhabitants dwelling along the banks but the hundred surnames were untroubled as the army did not act wantonly.

In the sixth month the Wei emperor had the General to Extirpate Shu, the *Hu-chün* Ch'in Lang, supervise twenty thousand infantry and cavalry, and assist Ssu-ma Yi in his defense against Chu-ko Liang.[104] The emperor imposed constraints on Yi, saying: "Just solidify your fortifications and maintain a defensive posture in order to thwart their fervor. When advancing cannot realize Chu-ko Liang's intentions nor will retreating result in having us engage him in battle, if he remains long his provisions will be exhausted. When his attempts have not achieved anything he will

---

103 This discussion is employed in the historical illustration for "Contentious Terrain" in the *Hundred Unorthodox Strategies*.
104 Because of developments in the east.

The Northern Campaigns

certainly depart. If he departs and you pursue them, it will be the way to achieve a complete victory."

In the seventh month Wei's ministers thought that as Ssu-ma Yi had just entered into a mutually defensive posture with Liang that had not yet been resolved the emperor [then confronting a threat from Wu] should go west to Ch'ang-an. The emperor replied: "If Sun Ch'üan retreats Liang's courage will be destroyed and our large army will be sufficient to control him. I have no worries."

In the eighth month Ssu-ma Yi and Chu-ko Liang had maintained their mutual defensive posture for more than a hundred days. Liang repeatedly tried to provoke him into battle but Yi would not come forth. Liang then sent a woman's headdress and garments to Ssu-ma Yi. Yi angrily submitted a memorial to the emperor requesting permission to fight but the emperor [responded] by dispatching the *Wei-wei* Hsin P'i bearing orders and appointing him as the army's commander in order to control him.

The *Hu-chün* Chiang Wei said to Liang, "Hsin P'i has arrived with imperial orders so the brigands will never come forth." Liang said: "Ssu-ma Yi basically never had any intention to engage in battle so he conspicuously requested permission to fight in order to display a martial appearance to his troops. When a general is with the army there are orders of the ruler that are not accepted. If he could master me, why would he send a thousand *li* away to request permission to fight?"

Whenever Chu-ko Liang sent emissaries to Ssu-ma Yi he would ask about Liang's sleeping, eating, and handling of affairs but never about military matters. The emissaries replied, "Chu-ko Liang gets up early and sleeps late and personally scrutinizes any punishment over twenty strokes. He eats less than several bowls of grain." Yi told the others, "Chu-ko Liang eats little but is troubled by affairs, can he last long?"

When Liang's illness grew serious [the emperor] dispatched the *Shang-shu P'u-sheh* Li Fu to observe, attend [upon him], and inquire about the state's great affairs. Fu arrived, finished talking with Liang, and departed. When he returned several days later Liang said: "I knew you would think of returning. In recent days, even though our talks stretched through the day, there were things left unsaid. So you have again come to seek their resolution. What you wish to ask about is Chiang Wan's appropriateness."

Fu deferentially replied, "In our previous substantial talks I neglected to ask who can assume responsibility for great affairs a hundred years from now so I reversed my carriage and returned. I also beg to ask who can serve after Chiang Wan?" Liang replied, "Fei Yi can succeed him." He asked once more but Liang made no reply.

This month Liang died amid the army. The *Chang-shih* Yang Yi put the army into order and departed. The common people raced to tell Ssu-ma Yi and Yi pursued Shu's forces. Chiang Wei ordered Yang Yi to turn the flags about and beat the drums as if they were going to approach Ssu-ma Yi. Yi regrouped his army and retreated, not daring to press them. Thereupon Yang Yi released the formations and departed. Only after he entered the valley did he display mourning.

> The common people created a saying about the incident, "Even in death Chu-ko Liang drove away a living Ssu-ma Yi." When Yi heard it he laughed and said, "I can assess the living, I cannot fathom the dead." Yi then toured Liang's camps and fortifications, sighed and said, "He was the realm's unorthodox talent!"

Chu-ko Liang thus managed to revitalize the institution of farming encampments—a practice long exploited by Ts'ao Ts'ao and then being extensively implemented by Wu in their border regions—yet the final campaign still had a very limited objective, would have quartered troops far from their ultimate target, and once again ended dismally. Moreover, despite possibly providing a long-range solution to their chronic provisions shortages, the first crops produced by these farming encampments would have required at least ninety to a hundred days to mature once the land had been cleared. Nevertheless, if successful they would have been an essential step toward establishing garrisons that could permanently occupy the area, thereby expanding Shu's domain and reducing Wei's western territory.

The Debacle of Wei Yen

No doubt because he was the sole motivating force for these campaigns as well as the chief strategist and commander-in-chief, Chu-ko Liang's death was generally perceived (including by Liang himself) as creating an irremediable void that required the army's hasty withdrawal. It did not just end the final campaign, but also prompted severe internal strife (much as he had anticipated) that betrayed his life's very meaning. The debacle receives extensive reportage in the *Tzu-chih T'ung-chien*:[105]

> Initially the forward army commander (*Ch'ien-chün-shih*), Wei Yen's courage and fierceness surpassed other men and he excelled at nurturing officers and troops. Every time he

---
105 *Tzu-chih T'ung-chien*, chüan 72, "Wei-chi, 4," Ming-ti Ch'ing-lung 2nd year.

followed Liang in going forth [on campaign] he immediately wanted to be given ten thousand men and [after proceeding] along a different route unite with Liang at T'ung-kuan, just like the story of Han Hsin. Liang kept him under control and did not permit it. [Accordingly], Yen frequently claimed that Liang was afraid and dejectedly hated that he could not exhaust his talent.

Yang Yi was capable and sensitive and whenever Liang went forth on campaign Yi undertook responsibility for planning their arrangements and for their provisions so that without any need for further thought everything that was needed would be provided. Yi thus managed all the army's [ancillary] martial measures.

By nature Yen was arrogant and his contemporaries generally avoided him. Only Yi did not act deferentially to him, which enraged Yen, so in this way they were like water and fire. Liang deeply cherished both men's talents and could not bring himself to favor or dismiss either one.[106]

Suffering from illness, Liang planned the measures for withdrawing the army after his death with Yang Yi and others including the *Ssu-ma* Fei Yi. He ordered that Yen be made responsible for cutting off the rear and that Chiang Wei should be next. If Yen failed to follow orders the army should set off by itself.

When Liang died Yang Yi maintained the secret by not undertaking any mourning ceremonies. He also ordered Fei Yi to go ferret out Yen's intentions. Yen said, "Even though the

---

106 The *Tzu-chih T'ung-chien* ("Wei-chi, 4," Ming-ti Ch'ing-lung 2nd year) notes an incident that shows even Sun Ch'üan was aware of their differences.

The Northern Campaigns

chancellor has died I am still here. His official staff and administrative subordinates can undertake the mourning and convey the coffin back while I lead the armies in a sudden strike on the brigands. How can we abandon the realm's affairs because of one man's death? Moreover what sort of man am I to serve as Yang Yi's subordinate and act as the commander for the rear guard?"

Then with Fei Yi he planned the apportionment of the various forces that should depart or stay, ordering Fei to personally draft the orders for them to jointly sign and deliver to the subordinate generals. Fei deceived Yen by saying, "I should return and explain this to *Chang-shih* Yang Yi. *Chang-shih* is a civil office that rarely handles military affairs. He certainly will not disobey your orders." Fei departed, racing off on his horse. Shortly thereafter Yen regretted [letting him go] but he already could not be caught.

Yen dispatched people to spy on Yang Yi and the others [and found] that they were about to proceed according to Liang's instructions, each of the several encampments successively withdrawing. Just before Yi set out Yen angrily led those under his command by a bypath to return south. Wherever he passed he destroyed the planked wooden corridor with fire. Yen and Yi each reported to the emperor that the other had rebelled and within a day their feathered dispatches had arrived. When the Han ruler questioned *Shih-chung* Tung Ch'ung and *Liu-fu Chang-shih* Chiang Wan about this, they both guaranteed Yi but doubted Yen.

Yang Yi and the others hewed away at the side of the mountain to make a passage and thus traveled both day and night close upon Yen's rear. Yen arrived at Nan-ku-k'ou first, occupied it, and dispatched soldiers to launch an attack upon Yi and the others. Yi ordered General Ho P'ing to the fore to defend against Yen. Ho upbraided those who ascended first, saying, "The duke has died. How do you sort dare to do this sort of thing even before his body is cold!" Yen's officers and troops knew that the error lay with Yen so none of them were willing to obey his orders and they all scattered.

Yen fled alone with his sons into Han-chung but Yi dispatched general Ma Tai to pursue and behead him and subsequently exterminate three generations of Yen's family. Meanwhile, Chiang Wan had been leading contingents northward from the capital's encampments to contend with the difficulties but they had only proceeded several tens of *li* when news of Yen's death arrived and they turned back.

At the beginning, when Yen wanted to kill Yi and the others, he had hoped that the discussants would have had him replace Chu-ko Liang in assisting the government so he did not surrender to Wei but went south, turning back to strike Yi. He actually had no intention to rebel.

This bizarre, chaotic episode concluded Chu-ko Liang's life-defining attempts to conquer the north. Wei Yen's arrogance may have betrayed him, but his headstrong behavior probably resulted from the fundamental difference in temperament between civilian officials (including Chu-ko Liang, despite his role as commander-in-chief) and warriors such as himself and Kuan Yü. Without doubt it was further fueled by his ongoing frustration with Chu-ko Liang's excessive caution and the course of events.

Wei Yen certainly did not err in questioning their decision to abandon the campaign just because the commander-in-chief had died, particularly when they had already accomplished the tedious task of penetrating the mountains and establishing a semipermanent base that had drawn a massive response from Wei. Rather than concealing Chu-ko Liang's death, they could have blatantly publicized it and employed an intense display of conspicuous weeping and apparent confusion to induce negligence in the enemy, even prompt Wei's commanders to mount an ill-considered, supposedly unexpected attack that could be ambushed.

Meanwhile, just as he had long proposed, a smaller but lethal unorthodox force could have raced down the valley by less traveled routes to spring a surprise attack on Ch'ang-an. If nothing else, bold activity in Ssu-ma Yi's rear might have stirred consternation and compelled his withdrawal, again creating an exploitable opportunity in accord with military dictums to destabilize the enemy and compel them into motion. However, caution again prevailed, resulting in misdirected fervor rather than expended in a productive attack on Wei.

5
Strategy and Achievements

Despite extensive intelligence and astute calculations, unexpected factors such as severe weather can intervene, "luck" may unexpectedly influence the course of events, or one side simply prove to have more aggressive fighters than the other, totally skewing the projected results of the most detailed assessments. Nevertheless, the coldly succinct *San-kuo Chih* accounts make the conservative nature of Chu-ko Liang's intentions eminently visible. Irrespective of the criteria chosen, none of the five campaigns merit being termed successful, and despite several victories in the final effort only the third realized marginally positive results.

Without doubt Chu-ko Liang harbored a great ambition to restore the Han and thereby achieve a lasting name that would rival that of Chang Liang, the T'ai Kung, and other historical paragons marked by surpassing accomplishments. However, he was constrained by limited resources, impossible terrain, occasionally incompetent and obstreperous commanders, and a youthful, ignorant ruler. Perhaps his greatness and historical adulation derive from his unwavering determination to battle hopeless circumstances.

Having imposed an administrative overlay in a fundamentally inaccessible region, truly benevolent leaders would have postponed or abandoned their personal ambitions, however "righteously" conceived, rather than coerce the inhabitants to undertake futile campaigns, endure prolonged hardship, and cast away their lives. They would have followed Sun-tzu's advice to adopt a defensive position, concentrated upon nurturing the strength and prosperity of an independent kingdom, and focused upon the people's welfare, just as the Chou had more than a millennium earlier until external developments presaged certain victory.

Insofar as Chu-ko Liang appears to have been familiar with the contents of the *Six Secret Teachings* (which purports to preserve material from the Chou's ascension but was probably composed about the middle of the Warring States period), two of its fundamental pronouncements on the importance of the people's welfare merit noting. A dialogue found in the book's very first section, "King

Strategy and Achievements

Wen's Teacher," contains the T'ai Kung's reply to the essential question of "how shall we proceed to establish measures so that All under Heaven will give their allegiance?" According to the famous strategist, "All under Heaven is not one man's domain. All under Heaven means just that, *all* under Heaven. Anyone who shares profit with all the people under Heaven will gain the world. Anyone who monopolizes its profits will lose the world. Heaven has its seasons, Earth its resources. Being capable of sharing these in common with the people is true humanity. Wherever there is true humanity, All under Heaven will give their allegiance."

More concretely, this abstract pronouncement was understood to mean that "sparing the people from death, eliminating the hardships of the people, relieving the misfortunes of the people, and sustaining the people in their extremities is Virtue. Wherever there is Virtue, All under Heaven will give their allegiance. Sharing worries, pleasures, likes, and dislikes with the people constitutes righteousness. Where there is righteousness the people will go. In general people hate death and take pleasure in life. They love Virtue and incline to profit. The ability to produce profit accords with the Tao. Where the Tao resides, All under Heaven will give their allegiance."

Similarly, in reply to the question "how does one love the people?" the T'ai Kung asserted, "Profit them, do not harm them. Help them to succeed, do not defeat them. Give them life, do not slay them. Grant, do not take away. Give them pleasure, do not cause them to suffer. Make them happy, do not cause them to be angry."[107] Although Liu Pei realized that the people were the very basis of government and, in his case, the means to achieve his dream of eliminating Ts'ao Ts'ao and restoring the Han (no doubt with himself as emperor), as shown by his comments when refusing to abandon the one hundred thousand adherents he had reportedly attracted when hard-pressed by Ts'ao Ts'ao, his perspective was more utilitarian than benevolent or sympathetic.[108] After the conquest of Yi he even had to be persuaded by Chao Yün not to confiscate and distribute the

---

107 "Affairs of State."
108 *Tzu-chih T'ung-chien, chüan* 65, "Han-chi, 57," Hsien-ti Chien-an 13th year (208).

best houses and lands to his generals as a reward for their service, though more because the realm remained unsettled than the virtue of restraint.[109]

Notwithstanding his familiarity with the *Six Secret Teachings* and their own administration's reputation for improving conditions for the populace, perhaps if just because he was more oriented to a structured, law-based approach, Chu-ko Liang's attributed writings lack the usual emphasis upon the people's welfare and the preservation of life. Nevertheless, in 224 CE, with two persuasive missives, Chu-ko Liang successfully enticed the reclusive and reportedly deaf Tu Wei to participate in the government. The first cites the usual platitudes about virtuous government and the late emperor's struggles, but the second acknowledges the wisdom of simply remaining ensconced in Shu while awaiting exterior developments:[110]

> Ts'ao P'i has usurped the throne, slain [the true ruler], and set himself up as emperor. This is like dragons that have been fashioned out of dirt and dogs made of straw, they have their names alone. With our assemblage of worthies I want to take advantage of his perversity and artifice and employ the upright Tao to exterminate him. Yet you, sagacious sir, want to return to the mountains and fields without having instructed me.[111]

> Furthermore, P'i has massively mobilized and is troubling his troops to move toward [the ancient areas of] Wu and Ch'u. Now, if because of P'i's numerous activities we close our borders and encourage agriculture, nourish our people and nurture things, and in addition put our armor and weapons into good order so as to await him becoming worn-out before attacking him, we can bring it about that the realm will be settled without our troops engaging in

---
109 *Tzu-chih T'ung-chien*, *chüan* 67, "Han-chi, 59," Hsien-ti Chien-an 19th year (214).
110 The missive is found in *chüan* 42 of the *San-kuo Chih*, which contains Tu Wei's biography together with several others.
111 Chu-ko Liang had had him brought in for the interview.

> combat or our people being labored. You, sir, only need to assist the time with Virtue, I will not task you with responsibility for military affairs, so why are you so anxious to depart?

Albeit somewhat augmented by Liu Pei's armies and adherents after the conquest, it must have been an almost insurmountable burden for the indigenous population of perhaps a million to repeatedly field armies of fifty thousand to one hundred thousand men in campaigns that exhausted the state's resources, incurred casualties that required continued care, saw important manpower diverted from agriculture and other fundamental occupations, and resulted in significant loss of life with its attendant sorrows. Although none of the historical writings discuss the attitude of the people, as suggested by the fragment on Ching-chou's lack of manpower (found in the *Chün Ling*) there must have been great unhappiness and resentment, if not outright anger, over being repeatedly levied for military service. In this respect, the *Art of War*'s condemnation of prolonged warfare is particularly telling:[112]

> When employing them in battle, a victory that is long in coming will blunt their weapons and dampen their ardor. If you attack cities, their strength will be exhausted. If you expose the army to a prolonged campaign, the state's resources will be inadequate. When our weapons have grown dull and spirits depressed, when our strength has been expended and resources consumed, then the feudal lords will take advantage of our exhaustion to arise. Even though you have wise generals, they will not be able to achieve a good result. Thus in military campaigns I have heard of awkward speed but have never seen any skill in lengthy campaigns. No country has ever profited from protracted warfare.

---

112 "Waging War," somewhat abridged.

Zhuge Liang: Strategy, Achievements, and Writings

Obviously the geographic features that isolated them equally protected them, and Shu's survival could be assured if they adequately defended the mountain chokepoints where, as Wu Ch'i once pointed out, one man could defeat ten.[113] In 243 CE, nearly a decade after Liang's demise, Wei's attempt to invade Shu with a significant but insufficiently supported force would be thwarted by a determined defensive effort in the Ch'in-ling Mountains despite Shu's contingents being severely outnumbered. When Wei's supply chain failed and other factors forced them to withdraw, the southern forces managed to inflict serious damage on the retreating armies. Even though Wei would eventually vanquish Shu through a masterful concerted effort, this incident attests to the relative ease of defending Han-chung and Sichuan.

Earlier, when Chu-ko Liang initiated the first of his five northern campaigns, the oligarchs in Ts'ao/Wei had been clinging to a defensive posture to avoid becoming hopelessly entangled in invading Shu. Liang's decision to shift significant forces up to a staging ground in Han-chung finally prompted the emperor to contemplate mobilizing a large strike force to repress them. Naturally they would have been required to transit the same mountains and therefore confront the same debilitating difficulties that Shu's forces were about to experience in moving northward. Sun Tzu, a trusted cavalry commander, offered what would subsequently become a well-known analysis:[114]

> Formerly, when Wu Huang-ti [the Martial Emperor, Ts'ao Ts'ao] conducted the punitive campaign in Nan-cheng that resulted in defeating Chang Lu and achieving victory at Yang-p'ing, he was endangered and only later successful. In addition, he then went and extricated Hsia Hou Yüan's army. He repeatedly said, "Nan-cheng is simply a natural prison, in its midst the Yeh-ku road is a five-hundred-*li* rocky cave." This speaks about its deep precipitousness and reflects his happiness that Hsia Hou Yüan was able to get out. Furthermore, the Martial Emperor was highly

---

113 Which Wu Ch'i terms a "vital point of earth." (See "The Tao of the General," *Wu-tzu*.)
114 *Tzu-chih T'ung-chien, chüan* 70, "Wei-chi, 2," Ming-ti T'ai-ho 1st year (227).

Strategy and Achievements

sagacious in employing the army. Investigating, he found Shu's forces perched on the mountain cliffs;[115] observing, he saw Wu's troops lurking in Chiang-hu, and in both cases felt they would be troublesome and avoided them. Not exhausting the strength of the officers and troops nor engaging in combat because of a morning's pique can truly be said to be seeing victory and fighting, knowing difficulty and retreating.

Now, if you want to send a force through Nan-cheng to extirpate Liang the road will be constricted and narrow. If you plan to employ elite forces, defend the southern four provinces, and deflect riverine attacks you will [need to] employ some one hundred fifty thousand to one hundred sixty thousand soldiers and will certainly have to levy additional men. The realm will be thrown into turmoil and the effort will be enormous. This is what your majesty should carefully contemplate.

By adopting a defensive posture our army's strength will be tripled. Then, if we display our forces and order our high-ranking generals to occupy the important constrictions, our awesomeness will be sufficient to frighten even strong invaders and suppress and tranquilize the battlefield. Our generals and officers will then be sleeping tigers and the common people will be untroubled. In the next few years

---

115 In "Configurations of Terrain," the *Art of War* differentiates "precipitous" and "constricted" terrain. However, these lengthy valleys combined both. Sun-tzu said: "As for constricted configurations, if we occupy them first we must fully deploy throughout them in order to await the enemy. If the enemy occupies them first and fully deploys in them, do not follow them in. If they do not fully deploy in them, then follow them in. As for precipitous configurations, if we occupy them we must hold the heights and *yang* sides to await the enemy. If the enemy occupies them first, withdraw our forces and depart. Do not follow them."

Chung-kuo[116] will increasingly flourish while the two brigands, Wu and Shu, will exhaust themselves.

Apparently having forgotten this discussion, which resulted in abandoning any thought of mounting an invasion, roughly three years later Ts'ao Chen became so infuriated by Shu's three invasions that in 230 CE he demanded that Wei abandon their passivity and adopt aggressive measures:[117]

> In the summer, the sixth month, the *Ta Ssu-ma* Ts'ao Chen submitted a request to the emperor saying, "Han's forces have invaded several times. Please grant me permission to proceed through Yeh-ku Valley and attack them." The emperor approved and summoned the *Ta Chiang-chün* Ssu-ma Yi to go up the Han River and enter from Hsi-ch'eng before converging with Chen in Han-chung and ordered the other generals to proceed through Tzu-wu-ku or Wu-wei [Chienwei] and enter.
>
> The *Ssu-k'ung* [Minister of Works] remonstrated, saying, "When the *T'ai-tsu* [Ts'ao Ts'ao] previously went to Yang-p'ing to attack Chang Lu he gathered a large amount of beans and wheat in order to increase the army's provisions, yet even before Lu had been subjugated they were already short of food. Now we do not have anything [like this] to rely on and the Yeh-ku valley is obstructed and precipitous. Advancing and retreating will be difficult and the transportation of supplies certainly hampered by skirmishers and plunderers, compelling us to leave a large number of troops behind to defend the passes, thereby reducing our fighting men. This must be seriously contemplated."

---

116 Eventually the name for China, here *chung-kuo* (中國) simply means the "central state" in the north, in comparison to Wu in the southeast and Shu in the southwest.
117 *Tzu-chih T'ung-chien*, chüan 71, "Wei-chi, 3," Ming-ti T'ai-ho 4th year.

> The emperor approved his discussion. Then Ts'ao Chen again submitted a request to follow the road through Tzu-wu Valley and Ch'ün again outlined why it would not be conducive, and also spoke about the amounts required for the army's expenditures. Ch'ün's discussion was sent to Ts'ao Chen but after consulting it he still proceeded out.

By the Three Kingdoms period China already had a lengthy history of aggressively employing scouts, spies, and local informers, so it is hardly surprising that Wei's activities were known long before its armies reached the northern edge of the mountains. Chu-ko Liang reacted by moving to undertake a forward defense:

> In the eighth month, after Chu-ko Liang learned that Wei's troops had arrived, he encamped at Ch'ih-pan in Ch'eng-ku district to await them. He had Li Yen take twenty thousand men to Han-chung and appointed Yen's son Feng as Ching-chou *Tu-tu* to undertake responsibility in the rear for sustaining Yen's forces. It happened that heavy rains fell for more than thirty days and the hanging plank road was severed.
>
> Wei's *T'ai-wei* Hua Hsin submitted a memorial [to the Wei emperor] that read: "Your majesty's sagely Virtue is comparable to the glory of Kings Ch'eng and K'ang [of the early Chou] so I hope that you will first give your attention to the Tao of governing, making campaigns and attacks a subsequent affair. Those who govern a state take the people as the foundation while the people take clothes and food as their foundation. If you can bring it about that Chung-kuo does not have the misfortune of hunger and cold and the common people do not have any inclination to depart from the government, then the decimation of the two thieves [Wu and Shu] can simply be awaited."

Zhuge Liang: Strategy, Achievements, and Writings

The emperor replied: "The bandits [from Shu] are relying upon the mountains and rivers. My two ancestors labored in previous generations but still could not conquer them. How would I dare think I can accomplish more or claim that they will certainly be extinguished? But our generals think that if we don't make an attempt the enemy will not decline by themselves. For this reason we are parading our troops to see if we can detect a means to reduce them. If Heaven is not yet conducive, King Wu's reversion of the army provides a mirror from former times and I will not forget what it teaches."[118]

The *Shao-fu* Yang Fu submitted a memorial: "In antiquity, when a white fish entered King Wu's boat the ruler and ministers changed complexion. When they commenced movement they had an auspicious beginning yet they still were troubled and fearful, so how much the more so the terror when even without having engaged in battle there are baleful portents! At present neither Wu nor Shu have yet been pacified but Heaven has sent down several oddities. When our armies commenced their advance we suffered Heavenly downpours and our forces were caught in the mountainous ravines for many days. The labor of transporting provisions by stages, the misery of carrying them on their backs, is extremely wasteful, but if we do not continue we will certainly contravene our original plan. The *Tso Chuan* states, 'When an army sees it is possible and advances, knows it is difficult and retreats, it is well administered.' Causing the Six Armies to be entangled in the midst of a valley without

---

118 King Wu of the Chou aborted a massive coalition expedition just a short march away from engagement approximately two years before the final assault on the Shang that resulted in an overwhelming victory for the Chou at Mu-yeh. (For an extensive discussion and analysis, see Sawyer, *Conquest and Domination*.)

any means to advance and unable to retreat is not the Tao of a kingly army."

The *San-ch'i Ch'ang-shih* Wang Su submitted a memorial that said: "An earlier rescript states that 'When provisions are transported a thousand *li* the soldiers will have a hungry look, if they have to gather firewood before cooking the army will not sleep full.' This refers to maneuvering the army on ordinary roads, so how much more will it hold true for those who have deeply entered into obstructed narrows, who have to hew roads to advance, and whose labors must therefore be a hundredfold greater.

In addition, seasonal rains, slippery slopes and ridges, the compression of the troops, and distance and difficulty in supplying provisions are assiduously avoided by those who maneuver armies. I have heard that although Ts'ao Chen set out more than a month ago he has advanced only halfway through the valley. The work of improving the road all falls to the warriors themselves. For this reason the enemy unilaterally awaits the labored in ease, something that military thinkers have always feared.[119]

Speaking about earlier ages, when King Wu attacked King Chou of the Shang, even after he had gone beyond the pass he still returned. Speaking about contemporary events, when Emperor Wu [Ts'ao Ts'ao] and Emperor Wen [Ts'ao P'i] conducted a campaign against Sun Ch'üan they approached the Yangtze but did not cross. Isn't this what is meant by according with Heaven, knowing the time,

---

119 Commencing with the *Art of War*, the classic military writings all advocate exploiting weakness and exhaustion in the enemy to attack.

and penetrating the changes in the tactical imbalance of power![120]

The myriad people know that your majesty will allow them to rest because of the heavy rain. When, at some later date, you have an opportunity to decimate the enemy and you exploit it to employ them, it will be what is termed being pleased to contravene difficulty and the people will forget their deaths."

In the ninth month the emperor ordered Ts'ao Chen to withdraw and disband the army.

As already noted in the historical introduction, despite the undeniable defensive advantages provided by the mountains to their north, some two decades after Chu-ko Liang's death Shu's leaders decided to contract their defenses. Accordingly, they abandoned the constricted roadways and withdrew their forward deployments, opting to rely upon interior lines. However, they compounded their vulnerability by having ill-trained and ineffective troops. Once Wei's forces were assured of unfettered passage and could develop reliable staging areas, they were able to freely maneuver within the confines of Han-chung and upper Sichuan and thus increasingly isolate or compress any remnant defenses before finally reducing the capital itself.

Strategic Choices and Tactical Options

Although, as already seen, the geographic features that protected them precluded mobilizing their forces and vanquishing their enemies by simply crossing a readily accessible border, history shows that the task was not impossible, just enormously difficult. The Chou had prospered in the isolation of the Wei River valley by determinedly nurturing their people and augmenting their strength until they

---

[120] According with Heaven, Earth, and Man is not only a recurrent theme from the Warring States onward, but one also discussed and otherwise reflected in several chapters of the *Chiang Yüan*.

had become powerful enough to burst forth and vanquish the Shang in the epoch-making battle of Mu-yeh.[121] Hsiang Yü had forced Liu Pang, the Han's very progenitor, to retreat to the confines of Sichuan, where he exploited the fertility to replenish his provisions and rebuild his forces before similarly surging forth and conquering the realm, albeit in a lengthy process that required outstanding contributions from his strategists and commanders, particularly Han Hsin.

In comparison with Han Hsin, who established a lasting reputation for his innovative tactics and unorthodox measures, Chu-ko Liang was overly cautious and conservative.[122] As his critics have noted, he sought a perfect plan (*ch'uan chi* 全計) that, while including the term *ch'uan*, refers to its overall excellence rather than any attempt to accord with the *Art of War*'s behest to preserve (*ch'uan*) the enemy intact.[123] No doubt he felt compelled to preserve their limited forces while achieving the objective of defeating Wei and restoring the Han. (Ironically, success would be synonymous with condemning the realm to suffer under another useless ruler, the wastrel Liu Shan, who was already beginning to come under the influence of the eunuchs.) Accordingly, he opted for an incremental approach that would provide them with operational bases increasingly closer to the final targets of Ch'ang-an and Luo-yang.

This strategy certainly reflected his emphasis upon strict control but also inclined him to ponderousness rather than alacrity. Moreover, it was essentially self-defeating and bordered on impossibility because Wei's resources would always dwarf their own and they had strong defensive positions to fall back on, despite generally choosing to thwart incursions in Kuan-chung near the point of penetration. By adopting an attritional strategy and persistently refusing battle except on their own initiative, Wei's commanders readily realized the *Art of War*'s concept that the enemy can be continuously frustrated by determinedly assuming a defensive posture. As Sun-tzu said, "If I do not want to engage in combat, even

---

121 For a complete account, see Sawyer, *Conquest and Domination in Early China: Rise and Demise of the Western Chou*.
122 For an extensive discussion of Han Hsin's unorthodox techniques, see Sawyer, *The Tao of Deception: Unorthodox Warfare in Historic and Modern China*. It should be noted that unlike Chu-ko Liang, Han Hsin enjoyed relative freedom of maneuver in his three famous victories.
123 "Planning Offensives," the *Art of War*.

though I merely draw a line on the ground and defend it, they will not be able to engage us because we thwart their movements."[124]

Without doubt Chu-ko Liang well knew the effectiveness of this sort of attritional or withering defense because he successfully employed it against Wei's invasion of Han-chung. Moreover, in the earlier battles for control of the vital Han-chung, even after Ts'ao Ts'ao had secured Chang Lu's nominal surrender, his forces continued to suffer the severe deprivation that Sun Ts'e mentioned. When Liu Pei strove to wrest control of the area from Wei and found himself outnumbered, he too avoided battle and awaited the shortage of supplies to severely affect Wei's forces.

Chu-ko Liang must have been thoroughly familiar with history's painful lessons, the victories achieved by Sun Pin and other surpassing commanders of antiquity, and even Ts'ao Ts'ao's accomplishments in his own era. He was also well versed in the classic military teachings, ranging from the *Art of War* through the *Six Secret Teachings*, with their focus upon manipulating the enemy, rapidity, deceit, and unorthodox tactics. For example, in "Military Combat," the *Art of War* states, "The army is established by deceit, moves for advantage, and changes through segmenting and reuniting. Thus its speed is like the wind, its slowness like the forest; its invasion and plundering like a fire; unmoving, it is like the mountains. It is as difficult to know as the darkness; in movement it is like thunder." Moreover, in "Nine Terrains" it adds, "It is the nature of the army to stress speed, to take advantage of the enemy's absence, to travel unanticipated roads, and to attack when they are not alert."

Sun Pin, who both explicated and expanded Sun-tzu's teachings, similarly advised in "Those who Excel": "Those who excel in warfare can cause the enemy to roll up his armor and race far off; to travel two days' normal distance at a time; to be exhausted and sick but unable to rest; to be hungry and thirsty but unable to eat. An enemy emaciated in this way certainly will not be victorious! Sated, we await his hunger; resting in our emplacement we await his fatigue; in true tranquility we await his movement. Thus our people know about advancing but not about withdrawing. They will trample on naked blades and not turn their heels."

---

124 "Vacuity and Substance."

Strategy and Achievements

Chang Liang conceived many of the dramatic measures that allowed Liu Pang to survive, but it was Han Hsin (who Liang consciously admired) that achieved outstanding success in battling overwhelming odds by adopting bold operational measures. Yet Chu-ko Liang not only failed to initiate equally incisive tactics but actually rejected General Wei Yen's proposal to mount a direct, unorthodox strike upon Ch'ang-an prior to the initial campaign:[125]

> When Chu-ko Liang was about to initiate the invasion he made plans with his subordinates. The chancellor's *Ssu-ma*, Wei Yen, said: "I have heard the Hsia Hou Mao, the ruler's son-in-law, is timid and does not understand strategy. Now if you let me have five thousand elite soldiers together with provisions for five thousand, I will go directly forth from Pao-chung, skirt along the edges of the Ch'in-ling mountains, and move eastward before turning northward through Tzu-wu Valley. In less than ten days we can reach Ch'ang-an. When Mao hears that we have arrived by cutting across he will certainly abandon the city and flee. Within Ch'ang-an there will only be the defensive commander and the *T'ai-shou* Ching Chao.
>
> The provisions contained in the Heng-men storehouse and the grain found after the population has scattered will be sufficient to provide for all our men. In comparison, Wei will still require some twenty days to assemble their forces in the east, long enough for you to come up through Yeh-ku. In this manner all the territory west of Hsien-yang can be settled with one thrust."
>
> Chu-ko Liang viewed this as a dangerous plan, one not as good as securely proceeding through more conducive routes so that they might pacify and seize Lung-yu. This would be

---

125 *Tzu-chih T'ung-chien*, chüan 71, "Wei-chi, 3" Ming-ti T'ai-ho 2nd year.

a plan for self-preservation and conquest free of any worries so he did not use Yen's plan.

By the start of the fourth century CE, unorthodox warfare and deception, its empowering ancillary, had long characterized Chinese warfare. Some refinements had occurred since the *Art of War*'s initial articulation, but Sun-tzu's outline continued to provide the operational definition:[126]

> What enable the masses of the Three Armies to invariably withstand the enemy without being defeated are the unorthodox and orthodox. In general, one engages in battle with the orthodox and gains victory through the unorthodox. Thus one who excels at sending forth the unorthodox is as inexhaustible as Heaven and as unlimited as the Yangtze and Yellow Rivers.
>
> The notes do not exceed five but the changes of the five notes can never be fully heard. The colors do not exceed five but the changes of the five colors can never be completely seen. The flavors do not exceed five but the changes of the five flavors can never be completely tasted.
>
> In warfare the strategic configurations of power do not exceed the unorthodox and orthodox, but the changes of the unorthodox and orthodox can never be completely exhausted. The unorthodox and orthodox mutually produce each other, just like an endless cycle. Who can exhaust them?

In its tactical discussion of unorthodox warfare, the late Sung *Hundred Unorthodox Strategies* states: "In general, in warfare what is referred to as the 'unorthodox' means attacking where the enemy is not prepared and going forth when they do not expect it. When engaging an enemy, frighten them in the front

---
126 "Strategic Military Power."

and overwhelm them in the rear, penetrate the east and strike in the west, causing them never to know where to mount defensive preparations. In this fashion you will be victorious." Ironically, the historical development chosen to illustrate the astute employment of unorthodox tactics was Wei's final invasion and conquest of Shu under Teng Ai's command in 263 CE.

The Three Kingdoms period is viewed as the ultimate battleground for subtlety, imaginative stratagems, and intrigue, yet as a few of Chu-ko Liang's critics have noted, Liang suffered from trepidation. His profound sense of responsibility apparently entangled him, preventing him from opting for a bold strike, even though the number of troops required would have represented only a portion of their total strength. Wei was not expecting Shu to undertake aggressive military actions and generally regarded Wu as the more threatening adversary while Wei Yen's plan would have accorded with admonitions found in all the classic military writings to exploit flaws in enemy commanders. As a well-known Chinese aphorism states, "If you do not enter the tiger's den, how can you get a tiger cub?"

Punching through in the far west also seems to have been ill conceived because it required an additional, arduous trek up to their initial objectives and greatly lengthened the distance to the ultimate target, Ch'ang-an. Thus, except to the extent that the Wei River might be exploited to quickly float down the valley, just the way that Chin would exploit the Yangtze to finally conquer Wu, it made the task far more onerous.[127] However, a feint into the far west with a decoy force coupled with disinformation and other measures to magnify the apparent numbers might well have drawn major forces from Ch'ang-an's perimeter, thereby facilitating a rapid but still strong strike by a heavy contingent that quietly advanced through one of the other valleys, especially Tzu-wu near Ch'ang-an. Chu-ko Liang's forces would then have had the option of either assaulting the defensive response proceeding outward or directly attacking Ch'ang-an once they had passed by.

Tactics such as these would have thus cohered well with measures advocated in the *Art of War* and all the subsequent military writings. However, rather than deploying forces in ambush or attempting to manipulate or deceive the enemy

---

127 However, presumably because they lacked the nautical technology, the Chou never exploited the Wei and then the Yellow River to achieve its conquest of the Shang.

(other than with a single decoy force in the first campaign), no longer being able to implement the coordinated strike from Ching-chou that he had initially conceived in his original geostrategic analysis, Chu-ko Liang continued solely with the western component but even then simply went forth and stopped.[128] In addition, he failed to rapidly consolidate control over the three commandaries that early on had rebelled against Wei, either by annexing them or at least stationing defensive forces on their perimeters, and they were quickly lost.

Rather than mobile and dynamic, even Liang's solution to their chronic shortage of provisions could not have been more ponderous. By tying the troops to the land and committing them to a long-term farming effort he conspicuously signaled, however inadvertently, his decision to abandon energetic thrusts and his virtual resignation to never being able to advance down the valley. Furthermore, as his analysis of the futility of Han efforts against the northern steppe peoples concluded,[129] deploying men into farming encampments would require the soldiers to both farm and fight, and thus impose onerous physical burdens that had historically resulted in the erosion of their martial spirit and skills and in being too fatigued for battle.

Even allowing for a recognized propensity in works ranging from the *San-kuo Chih* through the *Tzu-chih T'ung-chien* to exaggerate the use of wisdom in historical military clashes, there is no question that military knowledge was highly esteemed and the classic military writings intensively studied in the Three Kingdoms period. Furthermore, it was not just Ts'ao Ts'ao and the other northern commanders such as Ssu-ma Yi who exploited maneuver, deception, and the unorthodox, but also Sun Ch'üan and the strategists in Wu. (Both Ts'ao Ts'ao and Ssu-ma Yi's biographies contains references to "deception being the Tao of warfare.") Their defeat of Ts'ao Hsiu, who held the exalted position of *Ta Ssu-ma* in Wei, provides an example of the sort of assessments and tactical acumen that are simply never recorded for Shu under Chu-ko Liang's aegis. (As already noted, Liang claimed that Ts'ao Hsiu's defeat had created an unmatchable opportunity for them to undertake aggressive action and therefore cited it when

---

128 Recall that he had said, "When the realm's situation changes you could order a high-ranking general to lead Ching-chou's armies in advancing into Wan [Nan-yang in Henan] and Luo [Luo-yang in Henan] while you personally lead Yi's troops out along Ch'in's rivers."
129 In "Pei Ti," found in the *Chiang Yüan*.

justifying the precipitous launch of the second invasion in the "Hou Ch'u-shih Piao.") According to the *Tzu-chih T'ung-chien*:[130]

> In the fifth month [of 228], the king of Wu had the *T'ai-shou* of Po-yang Commandary, Chou Fang, secretly seek out a distinguished commander well-known in the north among the minority peoples [in the intervening area] and have him deceptively inveigle the *Mu* of Yang-chou, Ts'ao Hsiu. However, Fang said, "The leaders of these peoples are only minor figures and are unreliable. If the affair should leak out we would not be able to bring Hsiu in. I beg to send one of my relatives with a missive in order to entice Hsiu, saying that I have been reprimanded and fear execution and so want to surrender to the north with my commandery and therefore seek soldiers to accept it." The king of Wu acceded.

> At that time the king had high officials visit Chou several times to question him about various affairs. Chou then personally went out to the gate of the administrative offices and shaved his head in apology. When Ts'ao Hsiu heard about it he led one hundred thousand infantry and cavalry toward Wan-ch'eng in order to respond to Fang.[131] The emperor also dispatched Ssu-ma Yi toward Chiang-ling and Chia K'uei toward Tung-kuan, having them advance along three routes.

> In autumn, the eighth month, the king of Wu reached Wan-ch'eng and appointed Lu Hsün as *Ta-tu-tu*, bestowing a [symbolic] yellow battle-axe upon him[132] but personally grasped the whip of supervision. He appointed Chu Huan

---

130 *Tzu-chih T'ung-chien*, chüan 71, "Wei-chi, 3," Ming-ti T'ai-ho 2nd year.
131 Ts'ao Hsiu's ability to learn about these relatively minor manifestations coincidentally shows the extensiveness and efficacy of spying efforts in the Three Kingdoms period.
132 Presumably somewhat as described in "Sending the Army Forth" in the *Chiang Yüan*.

and Ch'uan Ts'ung as supervisors of the left and right and had each of them oversee thirty thousand men in a strike upon Hsiu. Hsiu realized that he had been deceived but relying upon his massive forces still wanted to engage Wu in combat.

Chu Huan said to the king of Wu, "Hsiu has been entrusted with responsibility because he is an imperial relative, not because he is a well-known, wise, and courageous general. He will certainly be defeated in this conflict and when he is defeated will flee. If he flees it will be through Chia-shih and Kua-ch'e. These two routes are precipitous and constricted so if we have ten thousand troops set wooden barriers out on the roads their troops can be completely defeated and Hsiu captured alive. Please allow me to use my soldiers to sever the roads. If, through the benefit of Heaven's awesomeness, we manage to gain Hsiu's submission, we can then take advantage of the victory to race far, to advance and seize Shou-ch'un and then, by cutting off Huai-nan [the area south of the Huai], can look out toward Hsü-ch'ang and Luo-yang. This is a moment in a myriad, it cannot be lost!"

Sun Ch'üan consulted Lu Hsün about these tactics but as he did not believe that they were feasible the king desisted."[133]

The *Shang Shu* Chiang Chi submitted a memorial to the Emperor of Wei that said: "Hsiu has deeply advanced into the enemy's terrain where he is being opposed by Ch'üan's elite soldiers. Meanwhile, Chu Jan and the others are above him on the river, following in his rear. I do not see any advantage in this."

---

133 A surprisingly conservative judgment from the usually innovative Lu that virtually mirrors Chu-ko Liang's trepidation in rejecting Wei Yen's proposal!

The general for the forward army [*Ch'ien-chiang-chün*] Man Ch'ung then submitted a memorial: "Although Ts'ao Hsiu is intelligent and decisive he has rarely employed military forces. The route he is presently following keeps the lake at his back and the Yangtze to his side. It is easy to advance but difficult to withdraw. This is what strategists refer to as 'suspended terrain.'[134] If he enters Wu-chiang-k'ou it would be appropriate to make serious preparations."

Even before Ch'ung's memorial had received a reply, Hsiu and Lu Sun had clashed at Shih-t'ing. Sun acted as the central force and ordered Chu Huan and Ch'uan Ch'ung to be the right and left flanks. They simultaneously advanced along three routes, pummeled Hsiu's contingents lying in ambush, drove them off, and pursued the defeated troops northward through side roads to Chia-shih [where they engaged the main force], eventually slaying and capturing more than ten thousand men as well as ten thousand oxen, horses, mules, donkeys, and wagons. All the army's equipment and implements were lost.[135]

Initially, when Hsiu's memorial sought to mount a deep penetration in order to respond to Chou Fang, the emperor ordered Chia K'uei to draw his troops eastward to unite with Hsiu. K'uei said: "The brigands [Wu] have not made

---

134 Chinese military science early on developed the concept of terrain types and correlated them with tactics that would exploit the advantages and avoid the disadvantages that they entailed. In "Configurations of Terrain," the *Art of War* defines six categories, with that for suspended terrain being as follows: "If we can go forth but it will be difficult to return it is termed 'suspended.' In a suspended configuration, if they are unprepared go forth and conquer them. If the enemy is prepared and we sally forth without being victorious, it will be difficult to turn back and is not advantageous." No doubt Man Ch'ung had this passage in mind when making his assessment.

135 In theory, according to the *Art of War*, they would have found themselves on fatal terrain and the commander should have been able to elicit a death-defying effort from the troops, just as Han Hsin had previously when battling in Chao during the Han's establishment. (Deep, unsupported penetrations invariably brought the army onto "heavy terrain." The definitive discussion of the concept of "fatal terrain" and its exploitation is found in the *Art of War*'s "Nine Terrains.")

any preparations at Tung-kuan so they must be uniting their armies at Wan. If Hsiu penetrates far into their territory and engages them in battle he will certainly be defeated." Then he dispatched several generals to advance both by water and land. When they had progressed two hundred *li* they captured some men from Wu who informed them that Hsiu had already been defeated in battle and that Wu had sent an army to sever Chia-shih.

The generals did not know what to do and some wanted to wait for their own rear army. K'uei said, "Hsiu's armies were defeated outside [the state] and the route back to the interior is severed. If he advances he cannot engage in battle, if he retreats he cannot return. The moment for survival or extinction is today. The brigands assume that there are no forces following up so they have come here. If we now urgently advance and go forth where they do not expect it, it will be what is referred to as 'those who precede others seize their minds.' When the brigands see our soldiers they will certainly flee. If we wait for our rear army the brigands will have severed the ravines, so even if our soldiers are numerous, of what advantage will they be?"

He then advanced his troops along both routes, setting out numerous flags and pennants in order to create "doubtful" troops. When Wu's forces saw K'uei's army in the distance they fled in fright. Hsiu was thus able to return.

Being familiar with the *Six Secret Teachings* attributed to the T'ai Kung, Chu-ko Liang must have also been aware of the subversive methods advanced in its two infamous chapters, "Three Doubts" and "Civil Offensive."[136] However, perhaps consonant with Liu Pei's avowed emphasis upon righteousness, he never

---

136 For translations, see Sawyer, *Six Secret Teachings*, in *The Seven Military Classics of Ancient China*.

employed any of them and appears to have made only one or two attempts to persuade important individuals to defect, including Meng Ta, who had formerly been a general in Shu but had joined Wei after being attacked by another commander with whom he had differences.

An experienced leader and eventual administrator of the broad area of Hsi-ch'eng in Hubei, Meng subsequently became disaffected with the new emperor (late in 227). Unfortunately, Meng's intentions were betrayed, and rather than acting rapidly to secure his bastion, as he intended, he dithered and hesitated. Ssu-ma Yi first allayed his doubts with a conciliatory missive and then raced forth, covering the twelve hundred *li* in eight days, to unexpectedly arrive and prevent the loss of an important city. Wu and Shu had both dispatched rescue contingents, but Meng was defeated in the first month of the next year and executed.

In comparison with the historical reportage of Ts'ao/Wei and Wu's activities in the two chief sources, accounts of Shu's campaign efforts are thus astonishingly bereft of discussions of innovative strategies, the unorthodox, maneuver, or tactical options, even though Liu Pei resorted to ambushes, lures, feigned retreats, and incendiary attacks against such enemies as Yü Chin and Hsia Hou Yüan. Even the *Art of War*'s adage that "war is the Tao of deception," a virtual watchword by the Three Kingdoms period, frequently cited by discussants in Wei and Wu, never appears in Shu's accounts and is essentially absent from Chu-ko Liang's writings, except as it and the concept of the unorthodox receive incidental recognition.

In contrast, the *Art of War*'s importance in this era is evident in Ts'ao Ts'ao's commentary, his court and battlefield discussions, supposed editorship of the text, and his visible application of its fundamental concepts and tactical principles.[137] Chu-ko Liang's own commanders, men such as Liu Hui and Chao Yün, are also noted as having formulated innovative tactics, displaying great courage, and being successful in clashes with the enemy, showing that not all his subordinates were unimaginative, mediocre, or incompetent, contrary to the claims of Liang's apologists. For example, although the inception of the empty city ploy has

---

137 For some examples, see Sawyer, *Tao of Deception*.

been universally attributed to Chu-ko Liang, Chao Yün actually employed it years earlier (in 219 CE) amid efforts to resist Ts'ao Ts'ao's invasion of Han-chung:[138]

> Ts'ao Ts'ao had rice transported to the base of the northern mountains. Huang Chung led his forces out in order to seize them but did not return by the appointed time. Chao Yün led several dozen cavalry out of their encampment to reconnoiter the situation but suddenly encountered a major mobilization of Ts'ao Ts'ao's forces. Chao attacked, penetrating their formation, then conducted a fighting retreat. After scattering, Wei's troops regrouped and pursued them to outside their encampment. Yün entered the encampment, opened the gates even wider, furled their flags, and silenced the drums. Wei's soldiers suspected Yün had prepared an ambush so they withdrew. Yün beat the drums so that they shook the heavens and had his strong crossbows shoot at the rear of Wei's soldiers. Wei's startled and frightened troops trampled each other and many fell into the Han River and drowned.

The Flawed Campaigns

Because they kept Wei on the defensive, a few analysts have praised Chu-ko Liang's five campaigns as having been strategically conceived and have claimed that only an "active" defense of this sort could have prevented Shu's annihilation, just as Chu-ko Liang argued. Since clashes were inevitable, Liang preferred to fight on the exterior, keeping the conflict and the enemy's forces as distant as possible, at what he calculated to be comparable costs, rather than risk any

---

138 *Tzu-chih T'ung-chien, chüan* 68, "Han-chi 60," Hsien-ti Chien-an 24th year. However, Li Kuang, a Han dynasty cavalry commander, was probably the first to use conspicuous nonchalance to cause doubt in the enemy. Chao's attack on the befuddled enemy troops was instrumental in causing the disorder and eventual defeat that prompted Wei to withdraw their forces. (For a discussion of the empty city ploy's history, see Sawyer, *Tao of Deception*, 362–371.)

inroads that would make the interior vulnerable (as well as result in extensive destruction).

But in their early years, even when Shu had not yet fully recovered from their horrendous losses in Ching and the debacle in Wu, Chu-ko Liang fervently maintained their avowed objective of reconquering the north. Meanwhile, being preoccupied with Wu, Wei was disinclined to risk an invasion through the mountains and thus did not pose a vigorous threat. A small number of stalwart units strategically ensconced in the intervening terrain could have thwarted any incoming thrust, whereas his aggressive policies, possibly with unprepared and decrepit forces (as he noted), debilitated the state, particularly as the first expedition resulted in a severe defeat, even though he had adroitly employed collateral measures, including specious troop deployments and a feint.

Despite changing commanders, none of the next three efforts achieved more than minor victories, and even the last campaign—undertaken by an almost unimaginable one hundred thousand men, despite their limited population, in the futile expectation that Wu would provide effective coalition support—was again forced to withdraw without any accomplishment.[139] The futility of Chiang Wei's subsequent, similarly structured attempts offers further confirmation that in the context of their situation this strategy was inherently flawed.

In 247 CE, the energetic Chiang Wei initiated the first of nine northern thrusts generally undertaken with limited troop strength that would end in 262 and thus stretch over sixteen years. Initially prompted by what Shu's leaders perceived as internal turmoil in Wei after Ssu-ma Yi seized power and intended to exploit the entanglement of the numerous Wei forces that had responded to Wu's massive attack on Ho-fei, they merely resulted in minor clashes that at best achieved localized victories. Furthermore, even these advances were quickly reversed when Chiang Wei similarly had to withdraw his forces under the duress of inadequate numbers and supplies.

Although Wu also mounted a number of significant strikes into the southern Huai region that coincided with Chu-ko Liang's tenure as commander-in-chief

---

139 It should be noted that numbers of this type are almost certainly unreliable, and rather than arguing about how significantly they should be discounted—30 percent or 50 percent—should be understood simply as indicating a massive force of several army-sized contingents. Thus, probably sixty thousand or slightly more, and therefore an enormous burden on the small state.

from 226 to 234, they were rarely initiated as part of a two-front policy or otherwise coordinated with Shu's efforts. After fending off three punitive expeditions out of Ts'ao/Wei from 221 to 225, as already seen, Sun Ch'üan attempted to entrap Ts'ao Hsiu and he later attacked Ho-fei again in 233. In 234, in a failed attempt that was actually timed to coincide with Chu-ko Liang's final campaign, they mounted another three-pronged effort against Ho-fei with more than one hundred thousand men that ended ignominiously when Sun Ch'üan timidly withdrew to avoid a decisive battle with the enemy's forces. In the face of Wei's potential five hundred thousand troops, better synchronization of these aggressive efforts with Shu would certainly have been advisable. However, Sun Ch'üan's emphasis of Wu's interests, lack of any desire to empower Shu or restore the Han, and a mixture of suspicion and antagonism thwarted further cooperation.

A serious detrimental factor was probably a fundamental lack of contemporary support for Liu Pei's vision or, in terms that Chu-ko Liang's writings employ, absence of the strategic advantages of Man. Not only had they not received—or more correctly, claimed to have received—a mandate from Heaven, the pathetic drama that ensued after Chu-ko Liang's death indicates that, apart from Wei Yen, Shu's commanders lacked either the will or the ambition to continue his aggressive efforts. Perhaps repeated failure had subverted their confidence; perhaps they simply failed to embrace the task of restoring Han rule throughout the realm, or their loyalty had been personal, to Liu Pei and then Chu-ko Liang, and thus their motivation ended with the demise of their heroes. Whatever the reason or combination of causes, quiescence prevailed for nearly a decade until Chiang Wei managed to motivate them for another strike.

Liu Pei had attracted adherents from less charismatic leaders such as Liu Piao at the outset, and Ts'ao Ts'ao thought he was a serious threat,[140] but the world at large seems to have been far less enthusiastic than Chu-ko Liang, who (rather naively) believed that Liu Pei would be universally welcomed because he was "a hero for our age whom the troops and officers think of and respect the way the water [in rivers] returns to the sea." Furthermore, before they seized Shu, Liang

---

140 As did Wu's great commander Chou Yü, who suggested that they employ a variant of the ploy of beautiful women to distract Liu Pei and cause him to be estranged from Chu-ko Liang (much in the way Ch'i subverted Confucius in the state of Lu during the Spring and Autumn period). (See *Tzu-chih T'ung-chien*, *chüan* 58, Hsien-ti Chien-an 15th year.)

had claimed that Liu Chang's "wise and capable officers long for an enlightened ruler," yet many fought determinedly against Liu Pei's forces, and many more people seem to have condemned Liu Chang's displacement than embraced it. (Their initial period of occupation was apparently marked by such noticeable and continued unrest that it gained Ssu-ma Yi's attention in Wei.)

The local populace never greeted Chu-ko Liang's ventures into Kuan-chung with the sort of supportive uprisings that Liu Pang had engendered (and the great hero Yüeh Fei would prompt) or with the voluntary offerings of foodstuffs that Chu-ko Liang had envisioned. Although it cannot be denied that a few important commanders such as Ma Chao and Chiang Wei defected to their side, there was no onrush such as witnessed when the Chou reportedly garnered the allegiance of two-thirds of the realm before embarking on the final campaign. Nor was there any repeat of the phenomena witnessed at the epoch-making battle of Mu-yeh, where Shang's massive forces reportedly offered little opposition to the Chou's onrush because of their reluctance to fight the righteous King Wu. Instead, just a thousand men held out against fifty thousand at Ch'en-ts'ang rather than simply surrender to what must have seemed inevitable defeat.

Chu-ko Liang had allowed himself to be persuaded that Ts'ao Ts'ao's increasing usurpation of the Liu family's authority was causing great consternation and significant anger among the people. However, an old Chinese adage holds that "Heaven is high and the emperor is far." Except when the state's presence in their lives proved unusually harsh (such as had been experienced under Ch'in's heavy impositions and draconian punishments), the populace rarely knew anything of their government beyond rumors, official announcements, and the often onerous and inequitable actions of local officials. While heroic deeds tend to become widely known (and quickly exaggerated) because people have a natural propensity to spread stories, more mundane activities such as imposing restraint in government, opening lands, digging irrigation channels, and other positive measures intended to improve the people's welfare and the state's prosperity might not be discerned until discrepancies with conditions in contiguous states become conspicuous.

Moreover, despite displaying tactically imaginative leadership a few times in limited engagements, Liu Pei had never been a particularly effective or charismatic commander whose battlefield accomplishments could inspire confidence. Instead, he had been severely defeated by Ts'ao Ts'ao when he misjudged the situation and assumed Yüan Shao would be the primary target, had only occupied territory through Liu Piao's and then Sun Ch'üan's tolerance, expanded into the western portion of Ching-chou through Kuan Yü's efforts subsequent to Ch'ih-pi rather than his own, and wrested control of Han-chung more through the enemy's errors and shortcomings than strategic brilliance. His victory over Liu Chang after a yearlong siege at Luo-ch'eng and the seizure of Ch'eng-tu through Chang's humanitarian surrender represented the conquest of an ally, not an enemy, while his impetuous advance into Wu, however righteously motivated, and the resulting debacle provided clear evidence of his lack of strategic acumen and command ability.

Having been licentious, weak, incompetent, and generally self-obsessed, the last few Han rulers had hardly been positive figures capable of attracting the people's admiration or official emulation. In contrast, Ts'ao Ts'ao was energetic, intelligent, decisive, and conscious of the need to ameliorate the realm's misery. Some might vilify him for being brutal and perverse, but he fostered the people's welfare and implemented many positive measures that attracted enthusiastic adherents. Moreover, he controlled an entrenched, comparatively effective administrative apparatus that, despite the realm's turmoil and fissures in its integrity, retained considerable authority and entangled many in its structure, whereas Liu Pei was compelled to constantly grapple with the problems of administration and control as he wandered about. Just as Sun Ch'üan in the east (who also enjoyed great support among the populace), Ts'ao Ts'ao attracted and employed many astute, highly motivated commanders (such as Kuo Huai and Chang Ho) and strategists, not the stooges and incompetents that people traditionally assume.[141]

Attempts to portray the conflict between Ts'ao Ts'ao and Liu Pei as simply a clash of good and evil thus belied the internal dynamics of their opposition and almost certainly lacked the popular appeal that Liu Pei and Chu-ko Liang

---

141 His coercion of Hsü Shu (which of course also deprived Liu Pei of his services) exemplifies his determination to acquire the best strategists possible. Somewhat surprisingly, he seems to have made no effort to induce Chu-ko Liang to join him, perhaps because he was still completely unknown. Whether Liang's own (clearly lesser) commitment to righteousness would have allowed him to accept an advisory post is perhaps an interesting question.

had envisioned. Although the actual attitude of the ordinary people remains unknown, it is extremely doubtful that the populace would have been persuaded to willingly upend their lives just to witness an exchange in masters, particularly once the ineffectual Liu Shan assumed the mantle of power in Shu.

Another negative aspect was the dubious nature of Liu Pei's purported righteousness and the extent to which the common people (who would furnish most of the fighters) ever heard of it, believed in it, or cared. Liu Pei consistently proclaimed his commitment to righteousness, just as the Chou had previously (and successfully) stressed their Virtue in marked contrast with the Shang, but Pei's behavior visibly and persistently betrayed it. Ts'ao Ts'ao accused him of being deceitful and unrighteous, as did Sun Ch'üan, Chou Yü, and other leaders in Wu, and even many of Shu's aristocrats.

First, he was charged with having been disloyal in abandoning Ts'ao Ts'ao shortly after having thrown in with him, a particularly egregious act since he changed his allegiance to Ts'ao's nemesis, Yüan Shao, and led an unsuccessful attack on Shao's behalf against Ts'ao's forces. In addition, claiming to possess a secret missive from the Han emperor that would supposedly justify his actions, he had even conspired to assassinate Ts'ao Ts'ao, the protector he had voluntarily sought out and had openly (if reluctantly) acknowledged as his commander and ruler.

Second, he refused to return the Ching-chou commandaries that Sun Ch'üan had allowed Pei to temporarily occupy so that he could augment Wu's perimeter defenses against Ts'ao Ts'ao's still potent forces, despite the debilitating impact of the defeat at Red Cliffs. Having been a virtual beggar when Chu-ko Liang originally approached Wu on his behalf, Liu Pei's duplicity drew Sun's repeated condemnation and eventually prompted the furtive attack that ended in Kuan Yü's death.

Third, Sun Ch'üan had felt a campaign to displace the weakling Liu Chang had become imperative if Ts'ao Ts'ao were to be prevented from conquering Shu to their strategic disadvantage. Furthermore, he had actually begun to initiate it before Liu Pei impeded him by asserting that it would be unrighteous to remove another member of the Han royal family, one with the surname Liu, from an official position. Yet, after moving his forces down into Shu's periphery at

Liu Chang's request, to supposedly protect them from the consequences of Ts'ao Ts'ao's imminent elimination of Chang Lu, Liu Pei still seized it after two years of posturing, despite vehement criticism but well in accord with Chu-ko Liang's initial analysis. Naturally these developments prompted Sun to accuse Liu Pei of having been deliberately deceptive from the outset.

Perhaps unintentionally, the *Tzu-chih T'ung-chien* account conveys (however incorrectly) a sense that Fa Cheng and P'ang T'ung seduced Liu Pei from the path of righteousness by persuading him at the end of 211 of the necessity to act against Liu Chang if all hope of restoring the Han were not to be abandoned:[142]

> When Fa Cheng reached Ching, he secretly presented a strategy to Liu Pei: "Enlightened general, with your courage and talent, if you take advantage of Liu *Mu's* (Liu Chang) trepidation and weakness and with Chang Sung, the pillar of Yi, responding from within, taking Yi will be as easy turning over your palm."
>
> Pei was doubtful and indecisive. P'ang T'ung then said to Liu Pei: "Ching has become a wasteland, the people are exhausted, and its materials depleted. In the east you have the cavalry general Sun Ch'üan and in the north Ts'ao Ts'ao so it will be difficult to achieve your ambition. Presently Yi has a population of a million, the land is fertile and its wealth abundant. If you really use it as your resource, great affairs can be accomplished."
>
> Liu Pei replied: "Ts'ao Ts'ao and I are like fire and water. Ts'ao Ts'ao is urgent so I am genial, he is brutal while I am benevolent. He is deceitful, I am loyal. Only by being the opposite of Ts'ao Ts'ao in every way can I be successful.[143]

---

142 *Chüan* 66, "Han-chi 58."

143 Obviously narrow-minded and overstated because not all of Ts'ao Ts'ao's behaviors and traits would be situationally inappropriate or even contrary to the ideals then being espoused.

What will happen if I lose my good faith and righteousness throughout the realm for the sake of a minor advantage?"

P'ang T'ung replied: "This is a time of chaos and separation, there certainly is not just one way to settle it. Moreover, uniting the weak and attacking the benighted, opposing the contrary and preserving the conducive is what the ancients valued. After affairs are settled if you enfeoff [Liu Chang] with a large state, how will you have betrayed your good faith? If you do not take Yi today, in the end it will be to the advantage of others."

Liu Pei's protestations of being committed to righteousness and fidelity or good faith (hsin 信), just as dramatically exemplified by commanders in the Spring and Autumn period[144] and prominently advocated by Confucius and his disciples, may have reflected a degree of real consternation. However, according to this dialogue and the thrust of Chu-ko Liang's initial strategic analysis, from the outset Liu Pei ventured to Yi for the sole purpose of annexing it, not defending it against Chang Lu or Ts'ao Ts'ao. His hypocrisy is thus revealed not just by his readiness to be convinced by their arguments but also deliberately having chosen opposing values in order to distinguish himself from Ts'ao Ts'ao, almost as if their actual nature were irrelevant. If Liu Pei's betrayal and subjugation of Liu Chang can be deemed righteous in the context of the greater good or some transcendent matrix of virtue, so should Ts'ao Ts'ao's attempts to rescue the kingdom from the irremediable chaos spawned by ineffectual and debauched Han rule and widespread rebellion.

---

144 And even Chu-ko Liang himself, in allowing troops whose period of service had expired to return home, despite facing an overwhelmingly strong foe. Surprisingly, none of Chu-ko Liang's writings ever refer to Confucian discussions of *hsin*. (For a concise reprisal of the attitude toward trust, see "Trust" in the *Hundred Unorthodox Strategies*. Duke Wen of Chin was a particularly famous Spring and Autumn exemplar.)

The Conquest of Yi

Although some, perhaps many, members of the aristocracy had become disaffected with Liu Chang, prompting Chang Sung and Fa Cheng to subvert the state by first encouraging Liu Pei to subjugate it and then supplying internal intelligence about military dispositions, as already noted others strongly opposed Liu Pei's intercession. For example, early on in Yi's invasion, Chang Fei's forces attacked and seized Pa Commandery and captured the *T'ai-shou*, Yen Yen, whom Chang Fei reviled for his stupidity in not discerning and acquiescing in the flux of events. Chang said, "After our great army arrived, why did you not surrender but instead dared wage a war of resistance against us?" However, the *T'ai-shou* replied, "You have rudely invaded and seized our province. In our province we have generals who are willing to die but none who are willing to surrender." This of course angered Fei, who condemned him to death, but ultimately relented and spared him when Yen remained unfazed by the sentence. Quite perspicaciously, Yen had been dismayed when Liu Chang had initially allowed Liu Pei to come into the area and greeted him with generous gifts and supplies. Reportedly he sighed and said, "This is like sitting alone in the deep mountains and releasing a tiger for self-protection."[145]

The conquest of Yi required more than a year even after Liu Pei had idly held his forces along the border for longer than two years, as if poised to undertake aggressive actions in Han-chung, during which he presumably courted support within Shu. Feigning anger at Liu Chang's failure to adequately sustain his efforts to support Sun Ch'üan, who was purportedly being threatened by an attack from the north, he duplicitously initiated actions against Yi.[146] About the fourth month of 214, Kuan Yü was entrusted with defending their holdings in Ching, Chu-ko Liang was appointed to military command for the first time and ordered to direct Chang Fei and Chao Yün in a splinter campaign that targeted Pa-tung, and Liu Pei went northward with a strong force.

Although a few commanders surrendered without a fight and Liu Pei appears to have been warmly embraced by part of the population, Shu's subjugation

---

145 *Tzu-chih T'ung-chien*, chüan 66, "Han-chi 58," Hsien-ti Chien-an 16th year.
146 Certainly an inexplicable development if Wu had really been threatened! (Liu Chang only offered three thousand men, rather than the ten thousand requested, and just one-third of the provisions.)

essentially proceeded through the application of military power, not persuasive words or virtuous posturing. Not many fortified cities or towns welcomed the invaders, and Liu Pei's forces had to besiege Luo-ch'eng for more than a year before it fell. (Pei's important strategist, P'ang T'ung, even died there from arrow wounds.)[147]

When, after Ch'eng-tu had been besieged for several weeks and Liu Pei dispatched an emissary to persuade Liu Chang to surrender, it was said that "at that time there were still thirty thousand elite troops, enough food and silks to sustain them for a year, and that the officials and people all wanted to fight to the death." Shortly after the conquest, finding the harshness of the laws unendurable, the aristocrats complained about their supposedly perverse treatment to Fa Cheng (as evidenced by Chu-ko Liang's response in the section on writings and beliefs below). Even if the new legal system had been equitable, the people clearly did not welcome its forceful imposition and implementation.

Sun Ch'üan's several military campaigns into Ts'ao/Wei had been basically unsuccessful, yet in 229 CE he usurped the title of emperor, posthumously conferred it upon his father, Sun Chien, as well, changed the reign period, and initiated other actions normally identified with the ascension of a new ruler, such as revising the administrative offices. This incensed the (Han) officials in Shu who wanted to conspicuously sever their alliance with Wu, as they not only believed it to be useless but also justified their reaction in terms of uprightness and the correctness of names, a possible echo of the Confucian doctrine of the rectification of names (正名).

Had he not died, Liu Pei probably would have reacted similarly, whether because he would have regarded it as a fundamental affront or because it would have challenged his claim to sole legitimacy and thus undermined their propaganda efforts. However, Chu-ko Liang clung to his original vision and realistically opted for equivocation in order to preserve the strategic necessity of a tripartite division:[148]

---

147 If P'ang T'ung had lived, much of Shu's subsequent military history might have been changed and he would have continued to be a strong rival for Chu-ko Liang.
148 Liang's reported retort is cited from the *Han-Chin Ch'un-ch'iu*, in the commentary to his biography in the *San-kuo Chih*, as well as integrated into the *Tzu-chih T'ung-chien* account. ("Wei-chi 3," Ming-ti T'ai-ho 2nd year.)

Ch'üan has long harbored contrary intentions but I have tolerated his perfidious behavior because we are seeking his support in making pincer strikes [against Wei]. Now if we conspicuously sever [relations] with him his enmity will be deep and we will have to shift troops to defend the east. If we engage in a battle of strength with them, we will have to annex their territory before we can discuss [acting against] the central plains [Wei]. They still have numerous worthies and talented people who act harmoniously so Wu cannot be pacified in a single morning. Deploying forces into a mutual defensive posture, sitting idly until they grow old and thereby allowing the northern brigands to achieve their aims is not a superior plan.

Formerly Emperor Hsiao Wen spoke deferentially toward the Hsiung-nu and the late emperor perspicaciously concluded an alliance with Wu. In both cases they responded to the current tactical imbalance of power in order to penetrate changes that had occurred and pondered deeply about future advantage rather than becoming annoyed like ordinary fellows. Today you all believe that Sun Ch'üan finds it advantageous to be one of the three feet of a cauldron and that he is incapable of uniting his forces with ours. His ambition is already satisfied so he has no desire to ascend the northern cliffs.[149]

Thinking along these lines seems correct but is actually erroneous. Why is this? Sun Ch'üan's strength does not match his wisdom so he is willing to preserve himself south of the Yangtze. His inability to cross the Yangtze is like the brigands in Wei being unable to cross the Han River. It's

---

149 On the other side of the Yangtze River when invading Wei.

not that they do not have more than enough strength but that it is advantageous not to choose that strategy.

If our great army undertakes a punitive expedition they will think of plans to break off some of Wei's territory [and annex it] or at least encroach upon Wei's populace and expand their borders, manifesting their martialness within the state rather than just sitting about. Even if they remain inactive and simply observe us, we will not have any obvious worries in the east if we should mount an invasion northward. Meanwhile, the masses south of the Yellow River [in Wei] will not be able to fully shift westward [to counter us]. This will be advantageous and also profound."

Although Chu-ko Liang remained confident that Wu was committed to preserving the tripartite geostrategic division of the realm, he seems to have deliberately overlooked Wu's actions in periodically undertaking large expeditions against the north, campaigns that would have been highly unnecessary if Sun had been content to simply remain ensconced in their southeastern bastion. In addition, while he acknowledges the competence of Wu's officials and commanders, perhaps because he remained committed to their own (ineffectual) northern expeditionary efforts, Chu-ko Liang seems to have naively believed that Sun would not exploit a power void to attack Shu itself and thus expand his southern base into a highly protected area.

Sun Ch'üan clearly subscribed to the belief that the entire realm should be ruled by a single power—himself—and was therefore not willing to battle Wei just to become subservient to the minor Han emperor in Shu. (Ironically, after Chin reunified the realm China would still suffer two centuries of fragmentation before the Sui arose.) An interview with Teng Chih that reportedly occurred in the spring of 224, after Shu's alliance with Wu had been restored, indicates his intransigence:[150]

---

150 *Tzu-chih T'ung-chien*, *chüan* 70, "Wei-chi 2."

Han again dispatched Teng Chih on an official visit to Wu where the king asked him, "If the realm achieves great tranquility and we two rulers divide it up and control it, will that not be joyous!"

Chih replied, "Heaven does not have two suns, earth does not have two rulers. If, after we have annexed Wei, your majesty still has not profoundly recognized the mandate of Heaven the result will be that each ruler will flourish his virtue, the ministers will exhaust their loyalty, the generals will raise their drumsticks over the drums, and war will commence!"

Laughing, the king of Wu said, "What an accurate appraisal!"

Perhaps Chu-ko Liang felt that circumstances dictated ignoring Liu Pei's hypocrisy, or perhaps he simply thought that the need to restore Han rule obviated any concern with conventional interpretations of righteousness. In either case, these Han pretenders lacked the realm's enthusiastic support and were therefore consigned to recreating their vision of virtuous government in Sichuan's fertile but limited terrain. By bending himself to the task of government Chu-ko Liang imposed order and nurtured prosperity, difficult tasks even without the financial and material demands of nearly incessant warfare.

Without doubt Chu-ko Liang's great contribution was therefore ensuring the survival of an ineffectual, erstwhile leader amid a turbulent martial sea. Lacking partisans of measurable strength and battered about in a troubled realm, Liu Pei would have faced imminent extinction without Chu-ko Liang's vital insight into the geostrategic possibilities, however limited and virtually transparent they may have been. Liang then adroitly persuaded (or, more correctly, conned) Sun Ch'üan into believing that Wu's best interest lay in availing himself, however temporarily, of Liu Pei's limited strength at Ch'ih-pi and then as a lateral defensive bulwark in Ching. For Liu Pei (and thus Chu-ko Liang), the trick lay in being nominally rather than actually submissive, in maintaining the fiction of an independent existence and a claim to realistic prospects as the one person who could resolve the world's woes.

Contrary to their conspicuously paraded claims of righteousness, Chu-ko Liang was a realist who deceived Sun Ch'üan from the very beginning, just as he clearly planned to subvert Liu Chang (as his famous proposal indicates) despite Chang's imperial heritage. Oddly, he rarely resorted to employing deception in his subsequent direction of political and military affairs (when it might have benefitted them considerably) and spoke about the importance of credibility in his missives, well after Liu Pei can be said to have abandoned his.

Despite his legendary reputation for tactical cleverness and the eight formations, it is therefore in articulating the original geostrategic vision and implementing these essential measures that his greatness lies, not in formulating strategy and exercising military command. Thus Ch'en Shou's approbation, previously noted, seems remarkably accurate, as does Ch'en's appraisal of his ambition and martial expertise in his final years:

> At this time Chu-ko Liang manifested his intentions. In advancing he wanted to be like a dragon soaring and a tiger [fiercely] staring, encompassing the four seas. In retreating he wanted to overstep the border and shake up the state. Moreover, he thought that when he was no longer alive there would not be anyone who could stomp across the central plains and resist the upper state across the land. For this reason he unceasingly employed the army and frequently flourished his martial [plans].
>
> However, Chu-ko Liang's talent lay in putting the army into order, his shortcoming was in making unorthodox (*ch'i*) plans. His ability to govern the people was vastly superior to his strategizing as a general. All the enemies that Shu opposed had valiant supporters and Shu was never a match for the enemy's strength while attacking and defending

have different natures. Thus, even though he mobilized the masses year after year, he was never able to conquer Wei.

As he separately noted, "He mobilized the troops for years in succession but was never able to achieve success, probably because formulating military strategy in response to changes was not his strongpoint."[151]

---

151 Although Ssu-ma Kuang frequently quotes and otherwise extensively appropriates Ch'en Shou's analyses and comments, the *Tzu-chih T'ung-chien* omits this statement. It might be noted that Chu-ko Liang's first military responsibility was commanding the rear guard during Liu Pei's flight from Ts'ao Ts'ao, a task in which he failed miserably.

II
Military Writings

6
Beliefs and Martial Writings

Early in life Chu-ko Liang apparently developed an immense desire to achieve lasting historical fame. Because the realm's disintegrating circumstances severely constrained the possibilities for anyone who lacked a power base or a dedicated body of adherents, he chose to emulate the great strategic advisers of antiquity. The sagely paragons mentioned in his writings and memorials include Yi Yin, who aided King T'ang in subverting the tyrannical Hsia and establishing the Shang; the T'ai Kung, who enabled the Chou's progenitors to overthrow the brutal and debauched Shang before founding their own great dynasty; and Kuan Chung, who crafted Duke Huan's emergence as hegemon over the realm when the Chou's legitimacy faded in the Spring and Autumn period.

Chu-ko Liang conspicuously revered China's great wisdom tradition and embraced its vision of surpassing knowledge, however esoteric, being crucial to worldly achievement and epoch-making accomplishments. Equally crucial was its fundamental orientation to wresting surpassing victories through contemplation and planning rather than force; through assessing and manipulating the enemy by utilizing a wide variety of means, including enticements and deceit. However, Liang rarely employed most of the key concepts, including the unorthodox and tactical imbalance of power.

Several individuals and their military writings had long been prominent by the onset of the Three Kingdoms period. These included Sun Wu, best known as the Sun-tzu of *Art of War* fame; Sun Pin, whose *Military Methods* (ping-fa 兵法) had perhaps already been lost and was only recently recovered a few decades ago;[152] the T'ai Kung, with whom the *Liu-t'ao* (六韜) has traditionally (though speciously) been associated; Chang Liang, who achieved fame as Liu

---

[152] There are numerous translations of the *Art of War*, including our own (which includes a lengthy historical and analytical introduction). Sun Pin's reconstructed *Military Methods* is also available in our similarly configured, highly annotated translation. (Authorship of the *Art of War* has become a matter of contentious debate in recent decades and it has clearly undergone extensive editing, but throughout our work, in the absence of definitive evidence to the contrary, we assume Sun Wu to have been the progenitor, even if not the actual author of every statement.)

Pang's strategist and reportedly transmitted the *San-lüeh* (三略) or *Three Secret Strategies* attributed to the reclusive Huang-shih Kung (Duke of Yellow Rock); and the legendary[153] Kuei-ku Tzu (鬼谷子) or Master of Ghost Valley, supposedly Sun Pin and P'ang Ch'üan's teacher, to whom a fragmentary synthetic work has also been attributed.

Attaining wisdom was thought to require fervent desire, total commitment, and treading an arduous path characterized by unremitting effort.[154] Although much teaching was oral (and therefore required a superlative master), reading remained basic. Furthermore, "reading" was not a leisurely pursuit, but instead had to be focused upon gaining a thorough grasp of essential knowledge, the very foundation for the perceptiveness needed to penetrate difficult situations and the means for conceiving measures to master them.

This sort of surpassing wisdom could only be achieved through directed contemplation, through pondering what had been learned from historical records, previous achievements and failures, and the thoughts of the ancients. It would be a lifelong process that required grinding dedication, at a time when books still consisted of comparatively succinct writings on bamboo strips that were held together with thin cords and just a few volumes in their rolled-up form would easily fill a wheelbarrow. Memorization was essential, the words themselves rather than just the crux necessarily being recalled whenever a problem or occasion demanded.

Chu-ko Liang's "Letter of Admonishment to his Son" expresses his understanding of the process and reflects his sober-minded attitude:

> In his conduct the perfected man (*chün-tzu*) is tranquil in order to cultivate himself and frugal in order to nurture his Virtue. Apart from calm equanimity he has no way to make his will enlightened, apart from quiet tranquility no means to achieve distant [objectives].

---

153 But apparently unfamiliar to Chu-ko Liang.
154 For example, as expressed by the famous Warring States Confucian "realist" known as Hsün-tzu in his essay "Encouraging Learning." (Surprisingly, Chu-ko Liang never mentions Hsün-tzu, even though there are many commonalities in perspective and substance.)

> Now study requires tranquility and talent requires study. Without study there is no way to broaden talent, without will no way to complete study. If you are licentious and dilatory you will not be able to forge the essence, if you are hasty and rash you will not be able to control your nature. The years will race away with the time, thoughts will go with the days, and you will become a withered tree that has lost its fruit. Having little intercourse with the world and mournfully cleaving to an impoverished hut, how will you then revert?

Despite having an admonitory tone, the final lines betray Chu-ko Liang's dismay that time had passed too quickly and possibilities remained elusive.

Liang's biography indicates that he was primarily concerned with the problems of administration except when he directed the five missions after Liu Pei's demise. Without doubt he based his approach on the methods espoused by the "Legalist" school (*fa-chia* 法家), whose beliefs were defined by Shang Yang, Han Fei-tzu, Shen Pu-hai, and Kuan-tzu, as well as reflected in such classic military writings as the *Six Secret Teachings* and the last half of the *Wei Liao-tzu*.[155] In fact, according to Liu Pei's final missive to his children, Chu-ko Liang had prepared précis of the *Shen Pu-hai*, *Han Fei-tzu*, *Kuan-tzu*, and *Liu-t'ao*, which they had yet to receive, and in his bequeathed instructions (drafted by Chu-ko Liang) he further advised them to read the *Han Shu*, *Li Chi*, *Six Secret Teachings*, and Shang Yang's *Shang-chün Shu* to increase their wisdom.[156]

As the name implies, adherents of the Legalist (or "realist") school believed that a strong, well-ordered state marked by internal prosperity and a powerful army could only be achieved through strict laws and highly regularized rewards and punishments. Although they disagreed about the particulars—some thinkers emphasized keeping rewards minimal and inflicting harsh punishments even for minor offenses, while others hoped to exploit the motivating incentive

---

155 Complete translations (with historical introductions and textual notes) of the *Liu-t'ao* (*Six Secret Teachings*) and *Wei Liao-tzu* may be found in our *Seven Military Classics of Ancient China*.
156 Based upon the contents of the *Chiang Yüan* and *Pien Yi*, Chu-ko Liang was also thoroughly familiar with the *Ssu-ma Fa*, *Wu-tzu*, and *San-lüeh* (*Three Strategies*), even though he never mentions the last two by name.

associated with large rewards—they all stressed that no exceptions should ever be permitted. Especially when imposing punishments everyone should be treated equally, including the rich, favored, and high ranking. Furthermore, the rewards bestowed for various achievements and the punishments meted out for defined offenses must always be equitable.

His probable writings, especially the materials encompassed in the compilations known as the *Pien Yi* and *Chiang Yüan*,[157] confirm that Chu-ko Liang determinedly embraced a Legalist perspective rather than the political philosophy of Confucianism, despite the latter's emphasis upon righteousness and Virtue. His commitment is particularly visible from his strong rejection of amnesties or pardons because they distort the system and undermine the deterrent effect of punishments. According to a memorial directed to the young emperor known as the "Reply on Compassionate Pardons":

> You should govern the realm with great Virtue, not with minor acts of beneficence. Thus K'uang Heng and Wu Han were not willing to have pardons granted. The late emperor similarly said, "I formerly associated with Ch'en Yüan-fang and Cheng K'ang-ch'eng. Whenever I read their illuminating missives arraying everything about the Tao of governing disorder I found they never spoke about pardons. Year after year men such as Liu Ching-sheng (Liu Piao) and Chi Yü (Liu Chang), father and son, granted pardons and amnesties but of what use were they to the task of governing?

Although the others were never more than minor historical figures, the mention of Liu Piao's demise is particularly telling.

---

157 Finding a felicitous English translation for *pien yi* proved somewhat elusive. *Pien* can have the meaning of what is convenient and thus conducive, what facilitates something, while *yi* indicates what is right or appropriate, especially within a moral context. The two are thus somewhat opposed, the former being what is convenient rather than correct, but as a later compound the term conveys the idea of utility. However, based upon the contents, perhaps the best rendering would be *Facilitation and Appropriateness*. In contrast, the title *Chiang Yüan* simply means a compilation of sayings on generalship, consistent with much of the contents, as in the famous Han dynasty's *Shuo Yüan*. Therefore, it can be termed *Compilation on Generalship*.

A second letter addressed to the *T'ai-shou* Fa Cheng offers further confirmation of Chu-ko Liang's dedication to the rule of law. Having been a powerful official in Shu prior to Liu Chang's displacement and instrumental in persuading Liu Pei to subjugate Shu, Cheng was chosen by the local aristocracy to protest the newly imposed draconian regulations. They argued that when he founded the Han, the first emperor (Liu Pang) had conspicuously suspended Ch'in's harsh constraints and implemented a benign policy that included reducing the numerous, highly onerous laws to just three. In response Chu-ko Liang, who had found the nobility rather perverse and corrupt when they initially occupied Shu, drafted the following letter to Fa Cheng:

> Sir, you understand part but not all of it. Ch'in was bereft of the Tao, the government was harsh and the people resentful. The common people protested loudly and throughout the realm the government had collapsed. Therefore Emperor Kao-tsu adopted a congenial policy that proved effective.
>
> Liu Chang and his father Liu Yen were ignorant and weak. For two generations they granted beneficence to the people while their civil and punitive regulations significantly contradicted each other. Ordinances were promulgated but they did not implement Virtuous government and their awesome punishments were not strictly [imposed]. Shu's inhabitants and officers monopolized authority and indulged themselves, the Tao of rulers and subjects gradually verged on ruin. Favored with office, they became contemptible as their positions reached the pinnacle. Accorded beneficence, they become dilatory when it was exhausted. The people's fatigue stems from this.
>
> I am now overawing them with laws and once the laws have been implemented they will recognize beneficence. I am constraining them with ranks and once the ranks have been

have been implemented they will know prominence. When beneficence and prominence are practiced in unison, the upper and lower ranks will be constrained. The essence of rule lies in just this.

Finding himself compelled to execute Ma Su, Chu-ko Liang was severely distressed and even wept, but he still rejected suggestions that a knowledgeable strategist such as Ma Su should be spared and employed because the realm had not yet been settled. However, Chu-ko Liang replied, "Sun-tzu and Wu-tzu were able to be victorious throughout the realm because their employment of the laws was clear. Now when the land within the four seas is sundered and the armies are just beginning to clash, if we again abandon the laws, how will we be able to conduct punitive expeditions against the brigands?"[158]

Other than letters such as these and the memorials preserved in the *Chronicle of the Three Kingdoms*, just what Chu-ko Liang wrote remains uncertain. According to Ch'en's appended comments, he selected a number of pieces from among the memorials, missives, and other jottings preserved in the imperial libraries that he deemed particularly worthy of preservation and arrayed them into twenty-four sections. (Whether the sections encompassed several items, were of equal length, or consisted of single pieces are all unknown.) As recorded in Chu-ko Liang's *San-kuo Chih* biography, there are just eighteen categories because some titles have two or three parts:[159]

開府作牧　　*K'ai-fu Tsuo-Mu* "The Administrative Office of Provincial Governor"
權制　　　　*Ch'üan Chih* "Authoritative Governing"[160]
南征　　　　*Nan Cheng* "Southern Expeditionary Campaign"
北出　　　　*Pei Ch'u* "Going Northward"
計算　　　　*Chi Suan* "Assessments and Calculations"
訓厲　　　　*Shun Li* "Instructing and Disciplining"

---

158 *Tzu-chih T'ung-chien*, chüan 71, "Wei-chi, 3," Ming-ti T'ai-ho 2nd year. Others commonly said that they were successful because of their tactics and strategies.
159 Lacking the contents, the section titles are somewhat tentative.
160 If this were a purely military title it might well mean "Controlling [the enemy] through the Tactical Imbalance of Power."

綜覈上下　*Tsung Ho, Shang* and *Hsia* "General Investigations"
雜言上下　*Tsa Yen, Shang* and *Hsia* "Miscellaneous Words"
貴和　　　*Kuei Ho* "Esteeming Harmony"
兵要　　　*Ping Yao* "Military Essentials"
傳運　　　*Ch'uan Yün* "Communication and Transportation"
與孫權書　*Yü Sun Ch'üan Shu* "Missive to Sun Ch'üan"[161]
與諸葛瑾書 *Yü Chu-ko Chin Shu* "Missive to Chu-ko Chin"
與孟達書　*Yü Meng Ta Shu* "Missive to Meng Ta"
廢李平　　*Fei Li P'ing* "Dismissing Li P'ing"
法檢上下　*Fa Chien, Shang* and *Hsia* "Judicial Investigation"
科令上下　*K'o Ling, Shang* and *Hsia* "Categorized Orders"
軍令上中下 *Chün Ling, Shang, Chung,* and *Hsia* "Army Orders"

Whether or not Ch'en Shou's posthumous compilation included Liang's thoughts on strategy, his work was either lost by the Sung or possibly obscured by a name change. Although several of the topics focus on military affairs, only a few of the titles can even be marginally correlated with any of the chapters that now appear in the two collections generally attributed to him, the *Chiang Yüan* and *Pien Yi*. Furthermore, even when one of Ch'en's titles seems to cohere with a selection's name, questions remain as to the nature of the materials. However, a couple of sections found in the following translations, the "*Ping Yao*" and "*Chün Ling*," appear to represent recovered portions.

The titles *Chiang Yüan* and *Pien Yi* both appear in the *Sui Shu's* bibliographic treatise, suggesting that they continued to exist as discrete works at least into the Sui. However, the *Chiang Yüan* may have become confused with another book in fifty chapters known as the *Hsin Shu* (心書), a title that literally means *Book of Mind* (but really mental techniques) and is therefore at least consistent with Liang's traditional reputation for having employed a psychological approach to warfare. It supposedly integrated considerable material from the *Art of War*, certainly a focal text for Chu-ko Liang and his era, even though he rarely referred to it by name, but was also said to suffer from rustic language and an intermixture of trivial materials. (However, in response to this sort of criticism, Ch'en's comment that Liang was writing for effect and deliberately kept the language simple

---

161 Presumably the one already quoted, intended to restore their alliance after Liu Pei's death.

Zhuge Liang: Strategy, Achievements, and Writings

so that it would be comprehensible to often illiterate men of action should be noted.) Apart from a few minor variations in characters, all the texts currently circulating under the *Hsin Shu* name are identical with the *Chiang Yüan*.

The *Pien Yi Shih-liu Ts'e, shih-liu ts'e* (十六策) meaning sixteen strategies, is sometimes thought to have been derived from Ch'en Shou's twenty-four chapters, but also said to have been compiled from material that he excised. As with the *Chiang Yüan*, opinion as to the authenticity of the contents varies from zealous assertion to skepticism and outright rejection. The passages included in the translation from the *T'ai-p'ing Yü-lan* are similarly viewed, direct attribution to Chu-ko Liang having been deemed proof of authenticity formerly but no longer.

A brief manual of deployments known as the *Book of Eight Formations* (八陣書) has traditionally been associated with Chu-ko Liang and stone models of the eight that he supposedly erected credited with magical properties. The famous T'ang Dynasty commander Li Ching even claimed to have based his formations upon Chu-ko Liang's eight,[162] and the *Wu-ching Tsung-yao*, a Sung dynasty military compendium, contains a subsection titled "Methods for the Eight Deployments" ("Pa-chen Fa" 八 陣 法), but as discussed in the introduction, no such work presently exists. Furthermore, formations and deployments only receive minimal mention in the *Chiang Yüan*, *Ping Yao*, and *Chün Ling*.

The *"Ping Yao"* ("Military Essentials" 兵要) and *"Chün Ling"* (軍令 "Army Orders"), two titles found in Ch'en's list, have themselves been cobbled together from numerous sentences and short passages culled from works that quote Chu-ko Liang, as well as from compendia such as the *T'ai-p'ing Yu-lan* that contain pronouncements on various categorical topics. Even though their contents are quite similar, *"Ping Yao"* tends to focus on the army's movements and activities in the field before adding a few comments regarding the commander's nature. *"Chün Ling"* primarily discusses order and discipline but also includes a few tactical observations, including a few rare fragments on riverine combat, a topic little discussed in the military writings.

---

162 According to his statement Book III of the *Questions and Replies between T'ang T'ai-tsung and Li Wei-kung*. (For the complete passage, see Sawyer, *Seven Military Classics*, 339.)

7
Collected Military Passages

"Military Methods"
Ping Fa
兵 法

One who understands what should be strongly loved and what is not worth loving can employ the military. Thus surpassing generals have always used what is not worth loving to nurture what is truly loved. Not every warrior can be skilled, not all the horses can be excellent, and not all the implements can be sturdy and solid. It all rests in how they are employed.

Armies can be ranked as superior, middling, and inferior, for which reason there are three possible tactical imbalances of power (*ch'üan* 權). Sun Pin [said to the ruler], "You should pit your inferior team of horses against their superior team, your superior team against their middling team, and your middling team against their inferior team." This is a military discussion, not a discussion about horses. The most inferior [forces] are not capable of competing with the [enemy's] superior [forces], but since I already know it I abandon them. Their middle [forces] are incapable of competing with our superior [forces], their inferior incapable of contending with our middling, so haven't I already won twice? Because I gain more than I sacrifice I choose this option. This is the superior of three tactical possibilities. Through these three tactical imbalances, with one effort I gain victory. Kuan-tzu said, "If you attack the sturdy [points] the insubstantial become sturdy; if you attack the insubstantial [points] then the sturdy become insubstantial." If you don't target anything for attack, all under Heaven will become sturdy enemies.[163]

---

[163] Source: *Chu-ko Liang Chung-wu Hou Wen-chi* citing the *Yü-hai*. (Throughout the original, the sources of the various selections will be indicated.)

Comment: Even those who knew nothing about Sun Pin were familiar with this story, which is now preserved in the *Shih Chi*. However, this apparently inconsequential display of cleverness actually encompasses the harsh realization that battlefield victories can often be achieved only by deliberately sacrificing part of the forces. As the author points out, success becomes a question of the tactical imbalance of power (*chüan*), a crucial concept from the *Art of War* that Chu-ko Liang rarely discusses.

Collected Military Passages

"Military Essentials"
Ping Yao
兵 要

When the army approaches the enemy, roving scouts are normally first sent out at first light to [reconnoiter] all the terrain within ten *li* to the front of the army. They should also investigate the minor roads off to the left and right within this range of ten *li*. Five men should compose a squad and each man should carry a white flag. They should ascend the heights and look about and carefully investigate dark and desolate locations. As the army arrives they should turn and investigate the high ground in front of them. When the first squad sees the enemy they should verbally transmit the information back to the second squad. The second should then inform the commander. Whenever the scouts see less than a hundred enemy troops they should just raise their flags to indicate [the enemy's position], but if they see more than a hundred they should raise their flags and shout loudly. The commander should then dispatch fleet horses to go and investigate.[164]

> Comment: The classic military writings, including the *Six Secret Teachings*, emphasize the need for forward observers and scouts, while the contents of the passage are quite close to the tactical discussion found in the late Sung dynasty's *Hundred Unorthodox Strategies* under the topic of "Observers," showing that it continued to circulate.

Whenever an army in the field is about to encamp or occupy a bastion it is necessary to first have trusted staff members and local guides proceed ahead and carefully observe the situation in order to fully understand it. Separately order scouts and lictors to go there in advance, determine the camp's boundaries, establish how the army's numbers are to be apportioned, set up observation and control points at the four corners, and only thereafter shift the camp.

In addition, first have some roving cavalry scouts go forth carrying five different colored flags. When they see ditches and hillocks they should raise a yellow

---

164 Originally found in *T'ai-p'ing Yü-lan*, *chüan* 331.

flag; at intersections raise a white flag; where there are rivers and streams raise a black one; for forests and destitute areas raise a green one; and for wildfires raise a red one. In every case respond to the situation with appropriate drumming. By employing both flags and drums the orders [they convey] will be both heard and seen.

If you are about to ford rivers or pass through mountains, deep gorges, or forested marshes, [dispatch] your swiftest horses and [most] courageous cavalrymen to sweep the area for several *li* to ensure that there is no sound anywhere about and no evidence of others. Dispatch men to the top of high mountains and trees, ordering them to look far out, and at the critical points have elite soldiers defend against all four directions. Thereafter divide the troops into forward and rear [contingents] in order to occupy and open the roads. Then order the heavy baggage wagons and old and young to [proceed], next the infantry, and finally the cavalry, all well regulated and strict in order to defend against the enemy's [unexpected] arrival. Neither the men nor horses should make a sound nor should they lose the order of the ranks.

In constricted areas and along decrepit paths you should sequentially arrange your contingents like fish scales. Sometimes it is necessary to turn about, to take the rear as the front or the left as the right. Then, if you are in movement, cluster together like fish scales, but if stationary then deploy in awl formations.

When you reach the designated halting place to the fore, have roving cavalry and elite [warriors] disperse in all four directions and set out markers. Then everyone should encamp in accord with their original quarters. Every man requires one [square] pace, but irrespective of the numbers you should always lay out the twelve [earthly] stems. Flags of two *chang* eight feet should mark out *tzu*, *wu*, *mao*, and *ch'iu*, do not let them get displaced. Use a vermillion sparrow flag to establish *wu* [the southern sector], a white tiger flag to set out *ch'iu* [the western sector], a dank colored martial flag to set out *tzu* [the northern sector], a green dragon to establish *mao* [the eastern sector], and a command flag for the central sector. Cooking food, feeding animals, drinking, and eating are not permitted outside the boundaries.[165]

---

165 *T'ai-p'ing Yü-lan*, *chüan* 331.

> Comment: These procedures were obviously formulated to ensure the orderly establishment of camps and mitigate the numerous problems posed by moving myriads of troops as well as prevent being decimated by a surprise attack when the troops were engaged in the physical tasks and therefore mentally distracted and highly vulnerable. Surprisingly, apart from a chapter found in the *Wei Liao-tzu* titled "Orders for Segmenting and Blocking Off Terrain," they were little discussed in the classic military writings.[166]

Loyalty in men is like fish in the depths. When fish are taken out of water they die, when men lack loyalty it is baleful. Thus superlative generals preserve it, their wills are established and their fame spreads.[167]

> Comment: The classic military writings all esteemed the fundamental virtues of wisdom, loyalty, courage, credibility, and benevolence.

Rather than loving a jade disc one foot in diameter, instead love [the moment of time] indicated by an inch of *yin* [on the sundial]. [Opportune] times are difficult to encounter but easily lost. Thus when surpassing generals pursue the moment they do not loosen the belts on their clothes, their feet do not tread on the ground, nor do they pause to retrieve a lost boot.[168]

> Comment: Timeliness, recognizing and exploiting the moment, was a crucial concept not just in the early military writings but also the *Tao Te Ching* and *Yi Ching*. Found especially in "Preserving the State's Territory" in the *Six Secret Teachings*, it pervades the *Chiang Yüan* as well.

---

166 This concern with surprise attack also explains the item in "Army's Orders" below: "When the army is arranging the camp the infantry, cavalry, and everyone from the officers down should wear their helmets."
167 *T'ai-p'ing Yü-lan, chüan* 273.
168 *T'ai-p'ing Yü-lan, chüan* 273.

Honored [with rank] he does not become arrogant, entrusted with power he does not become dictatorial, assisted he does not become dependent; endangered he does not become fearful. Thus the movements of surpassing generals are like jade disks in remaining uncontaminated.[169]

> Comment: For comparison see the *Chiang Yüan*'s chapters on the necessary traits of generals, especially "Talents of Generals."

In their practice of government superlative generals have men select others [for office], they do not nominate them themselves. They employ the laws to measure achievements, they do not determine it themselves. Thus the capable cannot remain undistinguished, the incompetent cannot adorn themselves, and the speciously praised cannot advance.[170]

> Comment: The Legalistic emphasis upon law as an impartial and necessary basis for determining rewards and punishments not only underlies Chu-ko Liang's thinking but also underpinned his administrative measures.

Their speech and actions do not cohere; they establish their own interests and corrupt the public; externally they join with slanderers, internally they join with caustic critics and the vituperative. When they are not eliminated it is termed being defeated by chaos.[171]

> Comment: This and the following passage are clearly fragments from discussions warning of the dangers posed by the "worms" that can affect the court. Because their presence was generally seen as symptomatic of a state in decline, similar passages are found in the classic military writings,

---

169 *T'ai-p'ing Yü-lan*, chüan 273.
170 *T'ai-p'ing Yü-lan*, chüan 273.
171 *Pei-t'ang Shu-ch'ao*, chüan 113.

including "Superior Strategy" in the *Three Strategies* and in several *Chiang Yüan* sections such as "Banishing Evil."

The branches are strong and the leaves large, different ranks have the same power, and people collude with their cliques and parties and compete to advance the crafty. If they are not eliminated, they can be termed signs of defeat.[172]

A disciplined army commanded by an incompetent general cannot be defeated but an undisciplined army commanded by a competent general cannot be victorious.[173]

> Comment: A possibility much and vehemently debated in the context of discipline and generalship over the centuries, but not viewed as particularly consequential except when undertaking prebattle assessments.

From the commanding general down all should have their own pennants. At the time the army sets out whomever's pennants point toward Heaven will be victorious.[174]

> Comment: The military writings vary in their approach to prognostications and omens. Many of them (such as the *Wei Liao-tzu*) warn against the pernicious effects of omens and admonish commanders not to undertake divination, but others include extensive material on *ch'i* phenomena and other indications, as well as their interpretation.[175] Chu-ko Liang had a reputation for being an esoteric practitioner and the *Chiang Yüan* includes some material on rituals, so perhaps this sort of "observation" coheres with his thinking.

---

172 *Pei-t'ang Shu-ch'ao*, chüan 113.
173 *Chu-ko Liang Chung-wu Hou Wen-chi*.
174 *Pei-t'ang Shu-ch'ao*, chüan 112.
175 For a discussion of the paradox of simultaneous practice and condemnation, see Sawyer, "Paradoxical Coexistence of Prognostication and Warfare," *Sino-Platonic Papers* #157.

If someone can unite the strength of three men his power will rival that of a horse, a skilled lacquerer can make arrows that will be like flying wasps. You certainly should favor and reward them.[176]

> Comment: The military writers mainly focused on generals and the responsibilities of commanders; only a few chapters (such as the *Wu-tzu*'s "Planning for the State") noted the importance of men with superior physical qualifications or motivation. Craft or technical skills were rarely mentioned, despite their importance.

---

176 Apparently from the *T'ai-p'ing Yü-lan*.

Collected Military Passages

"Army Orders"
Chün Ling
軍 令

When the thundering of the drums is heard, raise the white pennants and red flags. The large and small boats should then all advance into combat. Those that do not advance should be executed. When the sound of the gongs is heard, raise white flags and the boats should return. If the brigands are nearby, return slowly; if they are distant, then swiftly.[177]

> Comment: This is one of the rare passages on riverine warfare found in pre-Sung military writings.

When the sound of the drums is heard, raise rectangular flags to signal the three-sided formation.[178]

The connected pummeling formation seems narrow but it is thick so as to be sharp. Order the cavalry not to stray far from the main body, but if they are tasked with protecting the flanks they can venture somewhat further off.[179]

> Comment: Among the classic military writers only Sun Pin discussed formations and their utility in "Offices, I" and "Ten Deployments."

When the enemy advances rely on deer horn barriers [*chevaux-de-frise*] and have all the troops retreat behind, forming linked transverse formations. When the enemy is in close proximity the soldiers within the deer horn barriers can only move about in a crouched position to stab at them with their spears and spear-tipped

---

177 *T'ai-p'ing Yü-lan, chüan* 340.
178 *Pei-t'ang Shu-ch'ao, chüan* 117.
179 *Pei-t'ang Shu-ch'ao, chüan* 117.

dagger-axes. They cannot stand up because it would interfere with the crossbows [shooting from behind].[180]

> Comment: The fabrication and employment of *chevaux-de-frise* is discussed in several chapters of *Six Secret Teachings*.

When [the army] first proceeds out of the encampment they should carry their spears and spear-tipped dagger-axes (*chi*) upright, unfurl the banners and flags, beat the drums and blow the horns. When they have traveled three *li* have them lower their spears and spear-tipped dagger-axes, furl up the banners and flags, and silence the drums and horns. When you are not yet three *li* from the [next] encampment again carry the spears and spear-tipped dagger-axes upright, unfurl the banners and flags, and beat the drums and blow the horns. When you reach the encampment once again furl up the banners and flags, stop the drumming and silence the horns. Those who disobey these orders should have their heads shaved [as punishment].[181]

In times of combat everyone [on board] the boats should take the spare sails and any pieces of cloth, soak them in water, and then gather them together in order to employ them to assist when using water to suppress fires. Then if the brigands employ torches or flaming arrows you can use them to smother and extinguish them. Those who disobey this order should have their heads shaved and ears severed.[182]

> Comment: This passage, which describes basic preparations for extinguishing incendiary arrows, reflects the simultaneous growth of riverine combat and the employment of incendiary measures in the Three Kingdoms period to

---

180 This passage, which appears in the *T'ai-p'ing Yü-lan* section (*chüan* 337) on "deer horns," is subject to varying interpretation. (Here we read *tai* (待) for *ch'ih* (持), as it is improbable that an advancing enemy would be conveying the ultimate defensive device of *chevaux-de-frise* in front of them.)
181 *T'ai-p'ing Yü-lan, chüan* 339.
182 *T'ai-p'ing Yü-lan, chüan* 699.

achieve dramatic results, as illustrated by Ts'ao Ts'ao's defeat at Ch'ih-pi.[183]

When the troops are deploying for combat there should not be any shouting or clamoring so that they can clearly hear the sound of the drums. The troops should carefully watch the banners and signal flags. When forward is indicated they should advance, when movement to the rear is indicated then move to the rear, left when directed and right when indicated. Those who do not obey these orders but instead wantonly advance, retreat, or go left or right should be executed.[184]

> Comment: Flags and drums being the only means for a commander to order changes in deployments or tactics both prior to and during battle, regulations were promulgated to ensure they were not obscured or that other distractions were permitted. (Both flags and drums are extensively discussed from the *Art of War* onward, including in several sections of the *Chiang Yüan* where further comments will be found.)

When advancing into combat in a pincer formation [the troops] should look to the flags for their indications. When they hear the gongs being sounded with a triple beat they should halt and when they hear a double beat of the gongs they should return.[185]

Those around the command flag and the soldiers on the right flank should all carry large shields.[186]

It is not the case that Ching-chou is short of people but that those enrolled on the registers are few. If military impositions are applied during peacetime the people will not be happy. But if we speak about conducting a campaign of

---

183 For the history of incendiary warfare in China, see Sawyer, *Fire and Water: The Art of Incendiary and Aquatic Warfare in China*.
184 *T'ai-p'ing Yü-lan*, *chüan* 341.
185 *T'ai-p'ing Yü-lan*, *chüan* 341.
186 *T'ai-p'ing Yü-lan*, *chüan* 357.

rectification in the south and compel all the migrant households within the state to enroll themselves, it should be possible to increase the number of troops based upon the records."[187]

> Comment: This seems to be a fragment from a discussion on how to resolve manpower problems while Liu Pei was still ensconced in Ching-chou and thus limited in potential resources.

Normally on *chi-ch'ou* sacrifice is offered to the ancestral spirits of oxen and horses. The litany states, "on a certain month, date of *chi-ch'ou*, such and such a person dares to make a proclamation to the ancestral spirits of oxen and horses. Horses are the very Tao of the army's employment, oxen are used by the army and farmers. I have prepared and respectfully make an offering of sacrificial victims, millet, and superlative wine."[188]

When an advancing army must ford a river the ritual master should always first sink a white jade disc [into the river]. The litany reads, "a certain commanding general has ordered me to dare announce to you that a certain rebellious minister is fomenting chaos. The son of Heaven has ordered our commander to lead the troops in fording the river and conducting a punitive campaign against the miscreants. Therefore I have sunk a disc in the hope that you, the spirit of the river, will sustain [our army in crossing]."[189]

On the first day of autumn sacrifice should be offered to the [spirits of] the gongs, drums, banners, pennants, *lung* chariots, and *heng* chariots. A day before the sacrifice the ritual master requests the litany and his commander provides it. If the army has been victorious while on campaign and they have captured prisoners, they should also offer sacrifice. When sacrificing in front of an enemy the blood should be [smeared] on the bells and drums. The autumnal sacrifice and those following victory in battle are only rites, no blood is smeared on the bells or drums. The litany states, "A certain official has ordered me, such and such a

---

187 *San-kuo Chih*, "Wei Lüeh," and also found in the *T'ung Tien*.
188 *T'ai-p'ing Yü-lan, chüan* 526.
189 *T'ai-p'ing Yü-lan, chüan* 526.

person, to dare make an announcement to [the guardian spirits of] the *lung* and *heng* chariots, bells, drums, pennants, and banners. The army is a martial implement, the means to rectify the unrighteous and eliminate harm on behalf of the people. Thus, on this first day of autumn I have prepared and reverently offer these sacrificial victims, millet, and superlative wine.[190]

When the army is arranging the camp the infantry, cavalry, and everyone from the officers down should wear their helmets.[191]

When the army is on the march each man carries one *tou* of dry food. They are not permitted to carry cooking equipment or tenting which should be transported in the extra large wagons. Their equipment should glisten in the sun, especially when they meet others.[192]

> Comment: This concludes the cluster loosely grouped under the topic of *Chün Ling*. Overall these passages are concerned with maintaining order within the army, a topic that will be frequently revisited in the *Chiang Yüan*. However, the materials on riverine warfare and some basic rituals are unusual and noteworthy.

---

190 *T'ai-p'ing Yü-lan, chüan* 526.
191 *T'ai-p'ing Yü-lan, chüan* 526.
192 *Pei-t'ang Shu-ch'ao, chüan* 132.

8
Chiang Yüan
將苑

1	兵權	Military Authority
2	逐惡	Banishing Evil
3	知人性	Knowing Human Nature
4	將材	The General's Talents
5	將器	The General's Capabilities
6	將弊	The General's Corruption
7	將志	The General's Intentions
8	將善	The General's Superlative Aspects
9	將剛	The General's Firmness
10	將驕吝	Arrogance and Parsimony in Generals
11	將彊	The General's Strengths
12	出師	Sending the Army Forth
13	擇材	Selecting Talent
14	智用	Wise Employment
15	不陳	Not Deploying
16	將誠	The General's Constraints
17	戎備	Martial Preparations
18	習練	Practice and Training
19	軍蠹	The Army's Worms
20	腹心	Critical Staff
21	謹候	Cautious Observers
22	機形	Momentary Shape
23	重刑	Heavy Punishments
24	善將	Superlative Generals
25	審因	Investigating Factors
26	兵勢	Military Power

27	勝敗	Victory and Defeat
28	假權	Bestowing Authority
29	哀死	Grieving for the Dead
30	三賓	Three Guests
31	後應	Later Response
32	便利	Employing Advantage
33	應機	Responding to the Moment
34	揣能	Assessing Ability
35	輕戰	Slighting Warfare
36	地勢	Strategic Power of Terrain
37	情勢	Nature of Strategic Power
38	擊勢	Power of Sudden Strikes
39	整師	The Well-Ordered Army
40	厲士	Encouraging the Officers
41	自勉	Self-Encouragement
42	戰道	The Tao of War
43	和人	Harmonizing Men
44	察情	Investigating True Nature
45	將情	The General's Nature
46	威令	Awesome Commands
47	東夷	Eastern Yi
48	南蠻	Southern Man
49	西戎	Western Jung
50	北狄	Northern Ti

1
兵 權
Military Authority

Military authority is Master of Fate for the Three Armies and the commanding general's awesome power. A general who can take hold of military authority and grasp the army's essential power, thereby controlling all those below him, may be compared to a fierce tiger to whom is added feathered wings that allow him to soar above the four seas and apply [his power] to whomever he encounters. Generals who lose their authority or fail to grasp power are like a fish or dragons cast out from the rivers and lakes. Even if they want to seek the power to swim about in the ocean, race in the billowing swells, and play in the waves, how will it be possible?

> Comment: Legalist and early military thought stressed the absolute need to control rewards and punishments, the so-called handles of power and very foundation of awesomeness and authority. The concept of a nebulous spiritual entity known as the Master of Fate appears as early as the *Art of War*, which states that "a general who understand warfare is Master of Fate for the people, ruler of the state's security or endangerment."

2
逐 惡
Banishing Evil

There are five factors that cause distress in the army and state. The first is that cliques conspire together to contume the worthy and slander the good. Second, they make their clothes extravagant and their caps and belts outlandish. Third, they vacuously boast about [being capable of] magical methods and they deceitfully speak about the Tao (way) of spirits. Fourth, they monopolize investigations of right and wrong and move the masses for personal interest. Fifth, they assess [the prospects for] gain and loss and secretly collude with enemy personnel. Men of this sort, men who might be termed conniving, artificial, and perverse, should be kept at a distance and not brought close.

> Comment: In describing the behavior that characterizes five different types of inimical people this section revisits a topic already briefly raised in the *Ping Yao*. Some collude for power; others deliberately manifest specious appearances in order to garner attention and influence. The ones noted here are among those detailed in "Honoring the Worthy" in the *Six Secret Teachings* and found in "Superior Strategy" of the *Three Strategies*.

3
知 人 性
Knowing Human Nature

In knowing human nature nothing is more difficult than conducting investigations. Beauty and ugliness are distinctly different, emotions and their expression are not [necessarily] unified. There are those who appear congenial and good yet they are deceptive within, those who are externally respectful but internally deceitful, those who are externally courageous but fearful within, and those who exhaust their strength but are not loyal. Even so, there are seven methods for knowing men:

First, query them about right and wrong and observe their intentions.

Second, confound them through verbal disputation and observe how they change.

Third, query them about plans and strategy and observe their knowledge.

Fourth, inform them about misfortune and difficulty and observe their courage.

Fifth, get them drunk with wine to observe their character.

Sixth, entice them with profits to observe their scrupulousness.

Seventh, entrust them with affairs to observe their fidelity.

Comment: The crucial need to assess ability and fathom character before entrusting people with responsibility commanded great attention in antiquity. Apart from the tradition of "knowing men"—instantly recognizing great talent in otherwise undistinguished individuals—considerable contemplation was devoted to the means and methods that might be employed by both political thinkers (especially Han Fei-tzu) and the military writers, resulting in tests such as those outlined in this chapter.[193] They are primarily found in "Six Preservations" in the *Six Secret Teachings*, in the "Offices of King Wen" in the *Yi Chou-shu*, and in "Techniques for Probing the Mind" and "Mirroring Talent" in the T'ang dynasty *T'ai-pai Yin-ching*.

4
將 材
The General's Talents

Generals have nine categories of talent.

Those who lead [their troops] with Virtue and unify them through the *li*, who know their hunger and cold and investigate their labor and suffering, are termed benevolent generals.

In their management of affairs they do not seek to escape [difficulty], they are not enticed by advantage, and prefer the glory of certain death to the disgrace of life. They are termed righteous generals.

Honored, they do not become arrogant; victorious, they do not become lax. They are worthy yet able to be deferential to those below, firm yet able to be tolerant. They are termed generals of *li* [proper form].

None can fathom their unorthodox methods and changes while their actions and reactions have numerous ends. They can change misfortune into good

---

193 For a discussion of the practice and import of "knowing men," see the similarly named section in our *Tao of Spycraft*.

fortune and achieve victory when confronted by danger. They are termed wise generals.

For advancing [they grant] generous rewards, for retreating [impose] severe punishments. Rewards are not delayed past the appropriate time, punishments do not spare the high ranking. They are termed trustworthy generals.

They have the nimble feet of martial horses, their *ch'i* exceeds that of a thousand fellows, they excel at solidifying the battlefield, and are skilled at wielding swords and dagger-axes. They are termed infantry generals.

They ascend the heights, tread constricted narrows, and shoot arrows from racing horses just as if they were flying. When [the army] advances they are in the forefront, when it retreats they are in the rear guard. They are termed cavalry generals.

Their *ch'i* can shame the Three Armies, their will slights strong enemies. They are circumspect in minor battles but courageous against large enemies. They are termed fierce generals.

When they see worthies they act as if they cannot gain them and they react to remonstrance as if according with the current's flow. They are congenial but can be firm, are courageous and can formulate numerous strategic plans. They are termed commanding generals.

> Comment: This is the first of a series of sections in the *Chiang Yüan* on the immensely important topic of generals. Although this chapter is unusual, the subject matter ranges from descriptions of recognizable gestalts through ideal traits and fatal flaws. As usual, the *Art of War* commenced the discussion by listing a few necessary components and asserting that "the general is the supporting pillar of the state. If his talents are all encompassing the state will invariably be strong. If the supporting pillar is marked by fissures, the state will inevitably grow weak."[194] Virtually all of the classic military writings then touched upon the subject to a greater or lesser degree, and the *T'ai-pai Yin-ching* includes a chapter

---

194 "Planning Offensives."

on "Generals of Wisdom and Strategy." However, the most detailed consideration appears in two chapters of the *Six Secret Teachings*: "A Discussion of Generals" and "Selecting Generals," and four chapters of Sun Pin's *Military Methods*: "The General's Righteousness," "The General's Virtue," "The General's Defeats," and "The General's Losses."

5
將器
The General's Capabilities

The ways in which the capabilities of generals are employed, great and small, differ. Those who can ferret out the crafty, foresee misfortune, and cause the troops to submit are commanders for ten fellows. Those who rise early and sleep late, whose words and speech are precise and thorough, are commanders for a hundred fellows. Those who are straightforward but can ponder [affairs], who are courageous and can fight, are generals for a thousand fellows. Those whose appearance is severe and martial and are loyal and ardent within, who know men's efforts and labors and are fully aware of their hunger and cold, are generals for ten thousand fellows. Those who advance the Worthy and capable, who are always cautious in their daily undertakings, sincere and trustworthy, generous and encompassing, and are experienced in governing chaos, are generals for one hundred thousand men. Those whose benevolence and love penetrate below, whose credibility and righteousness bring about the submission of neighboring states, who comprehend the patterns of Heaven above, investigate human affairs in the middle, and recognize the patterns of earth below, who view all within the four seas like their family, are generals for All under Heaven.

6
將弊
The General's Corruption

For those who act as generals there are eight points of corruption. The first is termed being rapacious without satiation; the second being envious of the worthy and jealous of the capable; the third is listening to slander and loving sycophants; the fourth is assessing others but not themselves; the fifth is hesitating and being indecisive; the sixth is being dissolute in wine and licentious in sex; the seventh is being treacherous and deceitful yet also fearful; the eighth is speaking cleverly and not following the proper forms of behavior.[195]

7
將 志
The General's Intentions

Weapons are baleful instruments and the post of general a dangerous responsibility. For this reason, if their temperament is firm they will suffer deficiencies and if their responsibilities are heavy they will be endangered. Thus those who excel at being generals do not rely on strength nor do they rely on power.[196] Even if highly favored they are not happy, if insulted they are not afraid. Thus when they see profits they are not greedy and when they see beauty are not licentious. They sacrifice themselves for the state, being dedicated throughout.

8
將 善
The General's Superlative Aspects

Generals have five superlative aspects and four desires. What are considered "excellences" include excelling at knowing the enemy's disposition of power; excelling at knowing the routes for advancing and retreating; excelling at knowing a state's vacuity and substance; excelling at knowing Heaven, the seasons (timeliness), and human affairs; and excelling at knowing the mountains, rivers, constricted spaces, and obstructions. What are termed the four desires are wanting to employ the unorthodox in battle, wanting to be secretive in plans, wanting to keep the troops tranquil, and wanting to be unified in mind.

---

195 For comparison, note "The General's Defects" in *Sun Pin Military Methods* and "The Tao of the General" in the *Wu-tzu*.

196 A remarkable statement in the context of the traditional military writings, explainable only in terms of wisdom being foremost.

9
將 剛
The General's Firmness

The firmness of those who excel in generalship cannot be broken nor can their softness be compressed; therefore, they can employ weakness to control the strong and softness to control the hard. Pure softness or pure weakness will inevitably result in their strategic power being dissipated; pure firmness or pure hardness will certainly result in their strategic power being lost. Being neither soft nor firm is the normal way of according with the Tao.

> Comment: The idea that softness, especially as epitomized by water, can overcome hardness receives its most expressive elucidation in the *Tao Te Ching*:
>
> Human life is pliancy and weakness,
>
> Death is stiffness and strength.
>
> Thus the firm and the strong are disciples of death,
>
> The pliant and weak are disciples of life.
>
> For this reason strong armies will not be victorious.[197]
>
> However, the later classic military writers such as Huang-shih Kung well recognized that hardness and softness had particular qualities or "virtues" that made them useful in diverse realms and sought to balance and employ them appropriately. *The Three Strategies* thus cites a widely acknowledged saying: "The state of someone who can be soft and

---

[197] For a martial translation of the entire verse, see Sawyer, *Tao of War: The Martial Tao Te Ching*, chapter 76, "Life of the People."

can be hard will be increasingly glorious. The state of someone who can be weak and strong will be increasingly illustrious. The state of someone who is purely soft and purely weak will inevitably decline. The state of someone who is purely hard and purely strong will inevitably be destroyed."

10
將 驕 悋
Arrogance and Parsimony in Generals

Generals cannot be arrogant. If they are arrogant they will neglect the proper forms of behavior; when they neglect the proper forms of behavior people will depart; and when people depart the masses will rebel.

Generals cannot be parsimonious, for if they are parsimonious rewards will not be given out. When rewards are not given out warriors will not risk their lives. When warriors are unwilling to risk their lives the army will lack achievement, and when it lacks achievement the state will be vacuous. When the state is vacuous invaders will surely arrive.

Confucius said, "Even given the attractiveness of the Duke of Chou's talents, if he had been arrogant or parsimonious the rest would not be worth noticing."[198]

> Comment: Arrogance was identified as early as *Art of War* as an exploitable trait, but here the emphasis is on the untoward effects it has upon people in general. However, all the classic military writers emphasized the motivational effect of rewards.

11
將 彊
The General's Strengths

Generals have five strengths and eight perversities. Those with high principles can shape customs; those who are filial and respectful to their inferiors can achieve

---
198 Found in the first section of "T'ai Po" in the *Analects*, item VIIIA12.

great names; those who have credibility and are righteous can form friendships; those who ponder deeply can encompass the masses, and those who act forcefully can establish achievements. These are the five strengths of generals.

In formulating strategy they are unable to determine right or wrong; in their practice of the *li* they are unable to entrust responsibility to the worthy and the good; in their administration of government they are unable to be upright in imposing punishments and laws; when wealthy they are unable to aid the impoverished and those in hardship; their wisdom is inadequate for preparing against what has not yet taken shape; their contemplations are incapable of anticipating minute developments and secret [affairs]; when successful they are not able to raise up those they know; and in defeat they cannot avoid rancor or criticizing others. These are termed the eight perversities.

12
出 師
Sending the Army Forth

In antiquity, when states were endangered or in difficulty, the ruler would select the worthy and capable and entrust them with responsibility. He would observe a vegetarian fast for three days, enter the grand temple and stand facing to the south. The general would face north and the *T'ai Shih* would advance, bringing the great axe to the ruler. Grasping the handle of the great axe, the ruler would give it to the general and say, "General, you will control from this to the army." Thereafter he would again order, "When you see vacuity you should advance, when you see substantiality retreat. Do not slight others because of your high rank and do not think you are strong and therefore keep the masses far-off. Do not rely on [your own] achievements and capability, do not lose the loyal and faithful.

When your officers are not yet seated, do not sit; when your officers have not yet eaten, do not eat. If you share cold and heat, labor and ease, and sweetness and bitterness, and are united with them in danger and disaster, the officers will certainly fight to the death and the enemy will invariably be destroyed." After accepting these words the general forcefully exits through the "baleful gate" and leads the army forth in departing. The ruler sends him off by kneeling and pushing the hubcap of his [chariot] wheel, saying "Advancing and retreating should be appropriate to the time, within the army affairs should not follow the ruler's orders but should all proceed from the general."

In this way there is no heaven above, no earth below, no enemy to the fore, and no ruler to the rear. For this reason the wise contemplate on his behalf and the courageous fight for him. Thus he can be victorious in battle outside the state while the achievement is completed within. His name is raised for later generations and the blessings flow down to his children and grandchildren.

> Comment: The potential political implications of formally empowering someone with military authority meant that the ceremony was never a psychologically simple affair, particularly when the general was about to command the majority of a state's forces. (In the Three Kingdoms period both Ts'ao Ts'ao and Ssu-ma Yi wrested rulership of the remnants of the Later Han through their acquisition and exercise of military power, Ts'ao Ts'ao ironically but futilely having warned his descendants to beware of Ssu-ma Yi.)
>
> Chapters with similar contents that describe the commissioning ceremony are found in the *Six Secret Teachings* ("Appointing the General") and *T'ai-pai Yin-ching* ("Bestowing the *Yüeh* Ax"), with the former being the original. In every case they strongly express the idea already seen in the historical incidents of the general's necessary independence when conducting military operations in the field. First articulated in the *Art of War*, dating to the transition period when rulers no longer led in person and the complexity of command and maneuver required professional (or at least experienced) military officers, it received unequivocal formulation in "Appointing the General" that probably dates to the middle Warring States

period and, of course, great currency among field leaders thereafter.

13
擇 材
Selecting Talent

When the army is on campaign there are those who love to fight and take pleasure in battle, who seize strong enemies by themselves. They should be gathered into an infantry contingent and called "warriors who requite the state." Those whose courage exceeds that of the Three Armies, who have talent, strength, courage, and nimbleness, should be assembled into a contingent and termed "warriors who suddenly penetrate formations." Those who are nimble of foot and excel in running, who can race like fleet horses, should be assembled into a contingent and termed "warriors who can grasp the enemy's flag." Cavalrymen who can shoot as if they are flying and whose every shot hits the mark should be assembled into a contingent and called "warriors who can battle at the front." Those whose shots are invariably accurate and their targets always perish should be assembled into a contingent and termed "warriors who can overturn the [enemy's] front." These six are the army's superlative warriors, they should all be employed in accord with their abilities.

> Comment: Because military conflict demands the ultimate in physical skills, every culture, including China's, esteemed them. However, until the growth of larger armies, the increased mobility provided by both chariots and cavalry, and the advent of weapons with longer shafts that were more difficult to wield, military preparation and organization in early China did not particularly emphasize the capabilities of the fighting troops. The changes witnessed toward the end of the Spring and Autumn period (722–481) necessitated a greater emphasis upon physical qualifications and made the creation of more lethal and adroit contingents essential.

Several Warring States chapters contain essentially the same contents, including "Selecting Talent" and "Planning for the State" in the *Wu-tzu* and "Selecting Warriors" in the *Six Secret Teachings*. Furthermore, the T'ang dynasty *T'ai-pai Yin-ching* replicates much of the latter within a somewhat broader context, showing the continuity of martial thought.

14
智 用
Wise Employment

Those who undertake the responsibility of generalship must follow Heaven, accord with the time, and rely upon men in order to establish victory. Thus when Heaven and men are conducive but the time is not it is termed "contravening the time." When time and men are conducive but Heaven is not it is termed "contravening Heaven." When Heaven and time are in accord but men are not, this is termed "contravening man." The wise do not contravene Heaven nor do they go contrary to the time or men.

> Comment: The idea that major affairs must accord with Heaven, Earth, and Man already enjoyed great currency in the Warring States period, prompting Mencius to stress that the advantages provided by the first two are not as important as human harmony. Proposals for major political innovation or military action came to be justified as cohering with the three in various ways and commanders ignored them in formulating plans at their peril. However, even though Heaven was often associated with the weather (or, as in the Chou, the Mandate of Heaven) and Man with harmony or the promise of beneficial results, the exact correlates were never precisely defined, explaining the discussion in the upcoming chapter "Military Power."[199]

---

199 Also see "Administering the State" in the *Pien Yi*.

15
不 陳
Not Deploying

The ancients who excelled in ordering affairs did not [create] armies; those who excelled in military affairs did not deploy [into formations]; those who excelled at deployments did not engage in battle; those who excelled in battle were not defeated; and those who excelled at defeat did not perish. In their management of affairs the early sages rested in their dwellings, took pleasure in their tasks, and throughout their lives never attacked each other. This is what is meant by those who excelled in ordering affairs did not [create] armies.

When Shun rectified the canons and punishments Chiu [Hao] Yao acted as commander of the officers. The people did not violate the orders and there was no place that punishment could be imposed. This can be said to refer to "those who excelled in military affairs did not deploy." Yü attacked the Yu Miao, Shun performed martial and civil dances [with staves and feathers], and the Miao submitted. This can be termed "those who excelled in deployments did not engage in battle." Duke Huan of Ch'i subjugated strong Ch'u in the south and the Shan Jung in the north. This can be termed "those who excel in battle were not defeated." In cases such as the Duke Chao of Ch'u suffering disaster [from Wu's invasions], he was finally able to return to his state by fleeing to Ch'in and requesting aid. This can be termed "those who excel at defeat did not perish."

> Comment: Although these passages echo the spirit and perspective of the *Tao Te Ching*'s teachings, they more nearly integrate the early Chinese belief that the devolution from Virtue required increasingly harsh and militaristic measures to maintain social order and even survive.[200]

---

[200] For a brief discussion of the devolution idea, see the extensive commentary to "Preparation of Strategic Power" in my *Sun Pin Military Methods*; for the *Tao Te Ching*'s military concepts, see the introduction and chapter commentaries to our *Tao of War: The Martial Tao Te Ching*.

16
將誡
The General's Constraints

The *Book of Documents* states, "Those who are overly familiar with or insult perfected men (*chün-tzu*) will lack the means to exhaust men's minds. Those who are overly familiar with and insult common men will lack the means to exhaust men's strength." Thus the essence of employing the military [lies in] the general focusing upon taking hold of the minds of heroes, being strict in judging rewards and punishments, unifying the Tao of the civil and martial, grasping the techniques of the hard and soft, taking pleasure in the rites and music, esteeming the *Book of Odes* and *Book of Documents*, placing benevolence and righteousness first and wisdom and courage thereafter.

In tranquility the commander should be like a fish in the depths, in movement like a racing otter. He should disperse the enemy's unity and break their strength. He should dazzle the [troops] with flags and pennants and raise their martial [spirit] with gongs and drums. His retreats should be like a mountain shifting, his advancing like the windblown rain. His shattering attacks should be like tipping [something] over, he should engage in combat like a tiger.

He should press and engulf [the enemy] and [display] profits to entice them. He should [feign] disorder and seize them, be deferential to make them arrogant. If they are unified he should separate them; if they are strong, he should weaken them. He should give security to those who are endangered, calm those who are frightened, embrace those who rebel, and explicate the claims of the wronged. He should repress those who have strength and support those who have weakness. He should bring those who have plans close, overturn flatterers, and give wealth to those who seek to acquire it.

He does not double his strength to attack the weak nor slight the enemy because of his masses. He does not become arrogant because of his surpassing talent nor flaunt his awesomeness when heavily favored [by the ruler].

He plans before moving and knows he can be victorious before initiating battle. When he acquires riches and silks he does not keep them as his personal treasure, when he acquires children and female [prisoners] he does not employ them himself. When a general can behave in this fashion, make his mandates strict, and express his orders so that the men will be willing to fight, then when the weapons clash and the blades intersect the men will take pleasure in dying.

> Comment: Two of the several varied practices discussed in this section are particularly noteworthy: the unusual mention of swiftness, innovative tactics, manipulation, and deceit in the second and third paragraphs—all absent in Chu-ko Liang's own command style—and the need to plan before acting. Although the *Chiang Yüan* contains a chapter that discusses the process of assessment—"Assessing Ability"—quite surprisingly none of the sections ever address the crucial topic of planning. In marked contrast, the *Art of War* not only stressed the need for assessment and strategic planning but also for calculating the possibilities of victory before mobilizing for action. Since these determinations were undertaken in the state temple before the ancestral spirits to ensure their acceptance, Li Ch'üan even titled his similarly heterogeneous *T'ai-pai Yin-ching* chapter "Victory in the Temple."

17
戎 備
Martial Preparations[201]

Among the state's great affairs nothing takes precedence over martial preparations. Even if the deficiency is a matter of millimeters, the difference [will be] like a thousand *li* for it will result in the army being overturned and the general slain. Since these strategic developments happen within a breath, are they not fearful?

When [a state] confronts disaster and difficulty, neither the ruler nor his ministers eat until late at night because they are formulating their strategy and

---

201 Some editions append the title 戒 備, substituting *chieh/chiai* (戒), meaning "to take precautions against" for 戎, *jung*, meaning "martial," and repeat the difference in the first sentence. Given the chapter's contents and conclusion, *jung* seems more appropriate.

selecting the worthy and entrusting them with responsibility. Therefore, neither contemplating danger while dwelling in security nor knowing to be afraid when invaders approach might be likened to a swallow making a nest atop a screen or fish swimming in a cauldron, their demise is a matter of moments!

The *Tso Chuan* states, "Those who do not prepare against the unforeseen cannot [direct] military affairs." It also says, "Anciently, those who prepared against the unforeseen excelled in governing." Moreover, if wasps and scorpions are poisonous, how much more are states? Without preparations even large masses of troops cannot be relied upon. Thus it is said that "those who prepare will be free from disaster." Accordingly the activities of the Three Armies must be prepared.

> Comment: All the classic military writings contain admonishments to contemplate perversity and disaster during times of tranquility and good fortune. However, the most articulate expression is found in the late Sung *Hundred Unorthodox Strategies*, which cites the early *Ssu-ma Fa*: "The Sage remains conscientiously alert not to forget danger when secure nor chaos when well-ordered. Even when the realm is free from military affairs the martial cannot be neglected. If every aspect isn't pondered, you will lack the means to defend against the violent. It is necessary to internally cultivate culture and virtue while externally making strict martial preparations. When embracing and being conciliatory toward distant peoples, guard against the unanticipated. Throughout the four seasons one must practice the martial rites in order to show that the state has not forgotten warfare. One who has not forgotten warfare teaches the people not to neglect their military training. A principle from the *Ssu-ma Fa* states: 'Even though the realm is at peace those who forget warfare will inevitably be overturned.'"[202]

---

[202] It should be noted that in "Benevolence the Foundation," the *Ssu-ma Fa* equally advised against the opposite: "Even though a state may be vast those who love warfare will inevitably perish."

18
習 練
Practice and Training

When the army lacks training and practice a hundred will not be able to oppose one [of the enemy], but if they are trained and then employed, one can oppose a hundred. Thus Confucius said, "Engaging in warfare with an uninstructed populace is referred to as discarding them."[203] He also said, "When a good man teaches the people, in seven years they can also undertake martial affairs."[204]

Thus to make them martial they must be taught. Teach them the rites and righteousness, imbue them with loyalty and fidelity, constrain them with laws and punishments, and overawe them with rewards and punishments. Only after the people have been admonished can they be trained. Have them deploy and divide, kneel [stand down] and arise, move and halt, go forward and then reverse, separate and reunite, disperse and reassemble. One man can teach ten men, ten men can teach a hundred men, a hundred men can teach a thousand, a thousand teach ten thousand, and ten thousand can teach the [entire body of] the Three Armies. Only after they are instructed and trained instruction can victory be achieved over the enemy.

> Comment: One of the great puzzles of Chinese history is how Confucianism became so identified with antimilitarism when the founder, Confucius, was a warrior known to have been accomplished in chariot driving and shooting with a bow, the surpassing weapon in the Spring and Autumn period.[205] Of particular interest here is Confucius's belief that people had to be educated in the basic virtues before they could assume a military role.

---

203 *Analects* XIII:30.
204 *Analects* XIII:29.
205 Being a complex topic, it requires a book-length discussion rather than a few words. However, Mencius (who vehemently opposed military activities) reoriented the thrust of the original emphasis upon righteousness and other virtues.

Several of the classic military writings discuss not just the need for training but also the methods, with the most complete exposition being found in "Teaching Combat" in the *Six Secret Teachings*. More concisely, Wu Ch'i said: "Now men constantly perish from their inabilities and are defeated by the unfamiliar. Thus among the methods for using the military, training and causing them to be alert are first. One man who has been trained in warfare can instruct ten men. Ten men who have studied warfare can train a hundred men. And a hundred such men can train a thousand. A thousand, ten thousand; and ten thousand who have been trained in warfare can train the entire body of the Three Armies."[206] He also noted, "It is not forming a battle array that is difficult; it is reaching the point that the men can be ordered into formation that is hard."[207]

19
軍蠹
The Army's Worms

When the army is on campaign, if the reconnaissance is not thorough, the warning beacons lose their sequence, the soldiers arrive late and contravene orders, do not respond at the appointed time, obstruct and cause disorder in the army and infantry, sometimes going to the front, sometimes to the rear, and do not obey the drums and gongs; if the upper ranks do not have compassion for the lower ones and appropriate expenses without measure; if they encamp in sumptuous fashion but have no compassion for the hungry and cold; if their words are negative and their speech full of prodigies, they wantonly predict misfortune and fortune; if they clamor and dissemble without basis, startling and misleading the generals and officers; if they are courageous but do not

---

206 "Controlling the Army," also cited as the historical illustration for "Instructions" in the *Hundred Unorthodox Strategies*. In general, the military writings conceded that the people had to be educated and have a sense of shame before they could embark on teaching them military skills.
207 "Strict Positions," *Wu-tzu*.

accept control; if they act willfully and contume their superiors and they appropriate the contents of the storehouses and warehouses, utilizing them to increase their own wealth. These nine are the army's worms. Those who have them will certainly be defeated.

> Comment: This is a rather unique concatenation of perversities, one significantly dissimilar from the sort of negative aspects outlined in the classic military writings. However, several of the early thinkers were especially concerned with the adverse impact of omens and prodigies, just as noted here, and therefore advised instituting vigorous measures to forbid them and counteract the pernicious effects.

20
腹心
Critical Staff

Those who act as generals must have "stomachs and hearts" [critical staff], "ears and eyes," and "claws and teeth." Lacking "stomachs and hearts" may be likened to a man traveling about at night without anywhere to place his hands and feet. Being without "ears and eyes" is like dwelling in a mist and not knowing how to move about. Being without claws and teeth may be compared to a hungry person eating something poisonous, death is certain! Thus superlative generals must have men of wide learning and expansive wisdom as their "stomachs and hearts," men who deeply investigate and are circumspect about details as their "ears and eyes," and those who are courageous and good at fighting as their "claws and teeth."

> Comment: This general assertion and some of the terms are doubtlessly based upon an extensive chapter in the *Six Secret Teachings*, "The King's Wings," which details eighteen categories of essential talent, many of which are expected to serve as the commander's critical staff.

21
謹侯
Cautious Observers

The defeat of armies and the loss of regiments have always resulted from slighting the enemy and thereby bringing about disaster. Thus, when the army goes forth it must be according to the standing orders. If it fails to adhere to them it will be baleful. There are fifteen standing orders:

First, pondering: the spies and agents are enlightened.

Second, verbal examination: closely questioning the scouts so that they are attentive.

Third, courage: even when the enemy is numerous the [army] is not discomforted.

Fourth, scrupulousness: when they see profit they think of righteousness.

Fifth, equitable: rewards and punishments are equitable.

Sixth, resilience: excelling at enduring shame.

Seventh, congeniality: able to encompass the masses.

Eighth, credibility: stressing what was promised.

Ninth, respect: treating Worthies and the capable according to the *li*.

Tenth, enlightened: [the commander] does not accept slander.

Eleventh, circumspect: they do not contravene the *li*.

Twelfth, benevolent: [the commander] excels at nurturing officers and troops.

Thirteenth, loyal: they are willing to sacrifice their bodies for the state.

Fourteenth, discriminating: they know where to halt their feet.

Fifteenth, strategy: they assess themselves and know others.

> Comment: Although the terms and correlations in this section are somewhat problematic and the chapter purports to be framed in terms of so-called "standing orders," the fifteen items actually refer to the commander's character and actions, not any aspect of the army's performance. In this sense it represents another contribution to the general

discussion of command qualifications and traits found earlier in the *Chiang Yüan*.

22
機 形
Momentary Shape

When the stupid conquer the wise it is contrary [to the natural order of things]; when the wise conquer the stupid, it accords [with the natural order]; when the wise conquer the wise, it is a question of opportunity. The factors are three: the first is called affairs, the second strategic power, and the third emotional nature. When the moment [to undertake] affairs arises if [the commander] is incapable of responding he is not wise. When the moment that strategic power changes if [the commander] is unable to control it, he is not a Worthy. At the moment the enemy's situation becomes exposed if [the commander] is not able to act, he is not courageous. Those who excel at generalship invariably rely on the moment to establish victory.

> Comment: Although the chapter arrays three crucial elements—affairs, strategic power, and emotional nature—it is merely to give concrete form to the underlying issue, the critical importance of acting at the opportune moment. Previously seen in the *Ping Yao* passage referring to a sundial, it receives additional emphasis in the *Chiang Yüan*'s "Responding to the Moment." Early on the *Six Secret Teachings* had already asserted that "one who excels in warfare will not lose an advantage when he perceives it or be doubtful when he meets the moment. One who loses an advantage or lags behind the time for action will, on the contrary, suffer from disaster."[208]

---

208 "The Army's Strategic Power."

23
重 刑
Heavy Punishments

Wu Ch'i said, "The large and small drums, gongs, and bells are the means to overawe the ears; flags and pennants the means to overawe the eyes; and prohibitions and orders, punishments and fines the means to overawe the heart. Ears that are overawed by sound are invariably clear; eyes that are overawed by appearance are invariably perceptive; minds that are overawed by punishments are invariably strict. If these three are not established the officers may become indolent. Thus it is said that wherever the commander indicates with the tail of his whip, there are none whose minds do not shift there; wherever the general points, there are none that do not advance into death."[209]

> Comment: The role of the flags and drums is raised in the *Chün Ling*, but this section is unique in simply being a direct quotation from the *Wu-tzu*, a Warring States military work. However, the primary discussion appears in the *Art of War*'s "Military Combat": "Because they could not hear each other they made gongs and drums; because they could not see each other they made pennants and flags. Gongs, drums, pennants, and flags are the means to unify the men's ears and eyes. When the men have been unified the courageous will not be able to advance alone, the fearful will not be able to retreat alone."

24
善 將
Superlative Generals

In antiquity there were four kinds of superlative generals: Those who instructed the men in advancing and retreating so that the men knew the limits; those who

---
[209] The passage is found in "The Tao of the General."

led them with benevolence and righteousness so that the men knew the rites; those that impressed right and wrong upon them so that men knew the admonitions; and those that made them decisive through rewards and punishments so that the men knew credibility. Prohibitions, the rites, admonitions, and credibility are the army's great cords. Now when the main cords [in a net] are straight, the openings are never distorted. Therefore they were able to achieve certain victory when they fought and capture [the enemy] when they attacked.

Ordinary generals are not like this. When the army retreats they are unable to make them halt, when it advances they cannot make them stop so they perish with the army. Without admonitions and constraints rewards and punishments lose their measure and the men will not know what is credible. Then the Worthy and good will withdraw and submerge themselves while wastrels and panderers will ascend and be used. For this reason if the army engages in battle it will certainly be defeated and scatter.

25
審 因
Investigating Factors

Even the Yellow Emperor could not have contended in awesomeness with someone who attacks the evil through relying on the strategic power of men. Even Kings T'ang and Wu would not have been able to contend for [greater] achievement with someone who engages in warfare by relying on the strength of men to decide victory. If you are able to investigate these factors and augment it with awesome victories, you will be able to make plans with heroic generals who command ten thousand men and the valiant will accept your control.

> Comment: Strategic power or *shih* (勢), one of the core concepts of traditional Chinese military science, was first discussed in the *Art of War*. Sun-tzu likened its effects to the power of a mountain torrent that had been suddenly released or a whetstone dropped on an egg. However, here the concept is somewhat different because the chapter focuses

on the men who create it rather than on strategic power itself. Moreover, in clear contradiction Sun-tzu said: "One who excels at warfare seeks victory through strategic power, not from reliance upon men" and "one who employs strategic power commands men in battle as if he were rolling logs and stones."[210]

26
兵 勢
Military Power

In utilizing the army's strategic power there are three [critical factors]: The first is called Heaven, the second Earth, and the third Man. Heaven's strategic power [is conducive] when the sun and moon are clear and bright; the five stars [planets] are in their appropriate locations; comets do not portend disaster; and the wind and atmospheric vapors (*ch'i*) are mixed harmoniously. Earth's strategic power [is conducive] when the city walls are imposing, multiple, and steep; the river waves extend a thousand *li*; the stone gateways are dark and deep; and [the routes of approach] wind about like a sheep's intestines. Human strategic power [is conducive] when the ruler is sagacious and the ministers worthy; the Three Armies proceed according to ritual; the officers and troops follow orders and their provisions are prepared and armor sturdy.

If those who excel as generals rely upon the moments of Heaven, exploit the strategic power of Earth, and depend upon the strength of men, wherever they go no enemy will be able to contend with them and they will always be successful whomever they strike.

> Comment: The second of two consecutive entries to discuss strategic power (*shih*), it provides the clearest definition in terms of the focal concept of harmonizing with Heaven, Earth, and Man previously encountered in "Wise Employment."

---
[210] "Strategic Military Power."

27
勝 敗
Victory and Defeat

When the worthy and capable occupy the upper ranks and the morally inferior occupy inferior positions; the Three Armies take pleasure in their tasks; and the officers and troops respectfully submit, persuade each other to be courageous and fight, look to each other expectantly for awesomeness and martialness, and exhort each other with rewards and punishments, these are evidence of certain victory. However, if the Three Armies have been repeatedly frightened; the officers and troops are lazy and dilatory; those in the lower ranks lack ritual and credibility; the men do not respect the laws, frighten each other about the enemy, speak with each other about profit, enjoin each other with disaster and good fortune, and delude each other with prodigal sayings, these are evidence of certain defeat.

> Comment: Reflecting a realization that numbers and weapons are not the sole determinants of an enemy's strength, attempts to characterize the morale, readiness, and capabilities of opposing armies from their behavior and actions were initiated as early as "Military Combat" in the *Art of War*. Although the commander's character could not be disregarded, the *ch'i* (氣 spirit or morale) and cohesiveness of the line officers and ordinary troops were also considered important.[211] The paragraph succinctly notes several important manifestations of both (including the adverse emotional effects of fear visible in a concern with omens and prodigies), thereby providing a brief profile of vigorous and so-called "old" armies.

---

211 For an extensive discussion of *ch'i* in China, see Sawyer, "Martial Qi in China: Courage and Spirit in Thought and Military Practice," *Journal of Military and Strategic Studies*, Winter 2008/2009, www.jmss.org.

Chiang Yüan

28
假 權
Bestowing Authority

Generals are the very fate of the army, what determines success or defeat, and what good fortune and misfortune stem from. But if the ruler does not bestow [the authority] to grant rewards and impose punishments upon them it will be like binding a chimpanzee's paws and expecting him to adroitly jump about and cavort or gluing Li Lou's eyes shut and having him try to discriminate blue and yellow. It would be impossible.

If [the authority to make] rewards is shifted to the powerful minsters while punishments do not proceed from the commanding general, the people will connive for profit so who will have a heart for fighting? Even with the strategies of Yi Yin and the T'ai Kung or the achievements of Han Hsin and Pai Ch'i no one would be able to be preserve himself. Thus Sun Wu (Sun-tzu) said, "When the general goes forth there are orders of the ruler that are not accepted." Ya-fu said, "Within the army the commanding general's orders are obeyed, summons from the emperor are not heeded."

> Comment: The importance of rewards in motivating men, previously raised in "Arrogance and Parsimony of Generals," was well noted not just by all the classic military writers but also the early Legalists, including Shang Yang and Han Fei-tzu. As already mentioned, punishments were considered equally important to establishing and enforcing authority and the loss of these twin "handles" deemed disastrous. Thus the *Six Secret Teachings* warns: "Do not loan the handles of state to other men. If you loan the handles of state to other men you will lose your authority."[212] (The historical figures Chu-ko Liang obviously esteemed should be noted together with the reiteration of the commander's

---
[212] "Preserving the State's Territory."

necessary independence in the field, hardly integral to the section's topic yet cobbled on for emphasis.)

29
哀 死
Grieving for the Dead

Those who excelled as generals in antiquity nurtured men as if raising their own children. In difficulty they preceded them, in achievement they deferred to them. They wept for the wounded and comforted them, grieved for the dead and buried them. They provided their own food to the hungry and gave their cloaks to clothe the cold. They treated the wise according to the *li* and gave them salaries, they rewarded the courageous and exhorted them. Generals like this are invariably victorious wherever they go.

> Comment: The idea that successful commanders can gain the fervent allegiance of their men through being solicitous of their well-being and sharing difficulty and hardship with them pervades the military writings and appears in the *Chiang Yüan*'s "Sending the Army Forth" and "The General's Nature." *The Six Secret Teachings* contains a focal chapter titled "Encouraging the Army," and several of the classic works not only discuss the necessity of gaining the troops' allegiance through these measures but also cite Wu Ch'i's exemplary behavior in this regard because of the great success his armies enjoyed in disadvantageous circumstances. However, as discussions from the *Art of War* onward show, the issue is highly complex because solicitude can lead to softness and intractability, yet an overly harsh approach to rebelliousness.[213] However, generals had to avoid allowing overfamiliarity to undermine the awesomeness necessary to authority.

---

213 See especially "Configurations of Terrain" in the *Art of War*.

30
三賓
Three Guests

When the Three Armies are employed they must have honored guests who can hold discussions about gain and loss and thereby provide information for the general's use. Those whose speech is as fluid as flowing water can formulate unfathomable unorthodox plans, have heard widely and seen extensively, and have numerous skills and multiple talents that attract the admiration of the masses can be brought in as top-ranked guests. Those who are as fierce as bears and tigers, as nimble as cavorting monkeys, as hard as iron rocks, and as sharp as [the sword] Lung Ch'uan are heroes for a season so they can be included as middle-ranking guests. Those whose extensive talk sometimes hits the mark, who have limited skills and little talent, are men of ordinary ability so they can be brought in as the lowest rank of guests.

> Comment: In the Spring and Autumn period it was realized that the state could benefit from employing not just astute strategic advisers but also others with unique talents. Although some of their skills proved to be highly specialized and even normally undesirable—such as those of assassins—the thrust was toward men with encompassing talents, sagacious wisdom, or surpassing moral character, the latter two being known as "sages" and "worthies." The military writings, including the *Chiang Yüan*, repeatedly note the need for wise strategists and moral exemplars in the government, and as shown by Ts'ao Ts'ao's coercion of Hsü Shu and Liu Pei's three visits to Chu-ko Liang, the great leaders of the Three Kingdoms period certainly concurred. Worthies of course ranked the highest as passages, even chapters, in the *Six Secret Teachings* and the *T'ai-pai Yin-ching* show.

31
後 應
Later Response

Planning for difficult affairs while they are still easy, undertaking great affairs while they are still slender, moving first and afterward employing [the army], and imposing punishment in the formless[214] constitutes wisdom in employing the army. When the regiments and lines have already formed ranks, the martial horses are racing about and intersecting, the strong crossbows have just engaged, and the short weapons are also clashing, if [the commander] exploits their awesomeness and establishes his credibility, prompting the enemy to acknowledge the extremity of their situation, this constitutes capability in employing the army. Bodies enduring the onslaught of the enemy's arrows and stones, [troops] fighting for victory in a moment with success and defeat not being distinguishable, suffering casualties while the enemy dies, constitutes the lowest form of employing the military.

> Comment: The idea of preparation, of anticipating the unseen, previously seen in "Martial Preparations," and of acting while affairs are still minute and therefore easily managed pervades the military writings and is also found in the *Tao Te Ching*.[215] The section title suggests that a tardy response is synonymous with extemporaneous, purely military measures that require the ultimate in effort from the men rather than exploiting wisdom and tactics to shape and control the battlefield and lever power, verging on the ideal of victory without combat, and the concluding lines certainly confirm it.

---

214 An alternate text has "using rewards first and punishment afterward."
215 For a discussion of the *Tao Te Ching*'s emphasis upon early action, at the incipient moment, see the introduction to our *Tao of War*.

Chiang Yüan

32
使 利
Employing Advantage[216]

Grasslands and terrain with densely clumped shrubs are advantageous for maneuvering and escaping. Multiple passes and mountain forests are advantageous for being unexpected. Forests free of hidden spots to the front are advantageous for concealing ambushes. Sunset is advantageous for a small number to attack a massive [force] but early morning is advantageous for a massive force to strike a small one. Strong crossbows and long weapons are advantageous for defending camps. Deeps pools that require crossing, intervening rivers, and wind, fire, and darkness are advantageous for pressing enemies at the front and striking their rear.

> Comment: By the end of the Spring and Autumn period experienced commanders had realized that topographical variations could dramatically affect operations and that certain features or configurations of terrain could be exploited to advantage. As the *Chiang Yüan*'s "Strategic Power of Terrain" asserts, "the strategic power associated with terrain assists the army." Commencing with the *Art of War*, in which a dozen different types of terrain are identified and their characteristics correlated with operational implications, discerning, and then employing the features of terrain while avoiding inimical ground formed a crucial part of Chinese military science. Although the *Wu-tzu* contains a number of tactical correlations, the most extensive realization is found in several chapters of the *Six Secret Teachings*, including "Forest Warfare" and "Divided Valleys."

---

216 Some texts have 便 利, "Facilitating Advantage."

33
應 機
Responding to the Moment

The techniques for certain victory and the dispositions for uniting and changing lie in the moment. Other than the wise, who can perceive the moment and act? In the Tao for discerning the moment nothing takes precedence over being unexpected. Thus when fierce animals lose [the protection of] ravines even young men wielding spear-tipped dagger-axes pursue them and when scorpions expel their poison (even) stout fellows are flustered and lose their complexion because these misfortunes arise outside expectation and the changes are not anticipated.

> Comment: Although the selection continues the idea first expressed in "Momentary Shape," this is the clearest expression of the realization that the battlefield is not static, that commanders must be sensitive to and respond to momentary changes.

34
揣 能
Assessing Ability

In antiquity those who excelled in employing the military assessed their ability and calculated [the possibilities] of victory and defeat by asking:
Whose ruler is more sagacious?
Whose generals are more worthy?
Whose officials are more capable?
Whose provisions and foodstuffs are more bountiful?
Whose officers and troops are [better] trained?
Whose components are more ordered?
Whose martial horses [cavalry] are more rested?
Whose strategic configuration of power has [more] constrictions?

Whose guests and retainers are wiser?
Whose neighbors are more afraid?
Whose wealth and materials are greater?
Whose hundred surnames are more settled?

Observing it from this perspective, the shape of strength and weakness can be determined.

>   Comment: One of the *Art of War*'s many contributions to Chinese military science was its assertion that warfare is not just a life-defining activity for the state, but also that it should be conducted on a sound, rational basis rather than prompted by desire or emotions. Planning and calculation had to precede any engagement, with the process of net assessment being based on a number of identifiable factors: "Warfare is the greatest affair of state, the basis of life and death, the Way (Tao) to survival or extinction. It must be thoroughly pondered and analyzed. Therefore, structure it according to [the following] five factors, evaluate it comparatively through estimations, and seek out its true nature. The first is termed the Tao, the second Heaven, the third Earth, the fourth generals, and the fifth the laws [for military organization and discipline]."
>
>   Although some forty or more criteria are actually enumerated in the body of the extant text, the crucial list (upon which this chapter is clearly based) simply states: "Thus when making a comparative evaluation through estimations, seeking out its true nature, ask: Which ruler has the Tao? Which general has greater ability? Who has gained [the advantages of] Heaven and Earth? Whose laws and orders are more thoroughly implemented? Whose forces are stronger? Whose officers and troops are better trained?

Whose rewards and punishments are clearer? From these I will know victory and defeat!"[217]

35
輕 戰
Slighting Warfare

The stingers of poisonous insects carry their poison while warriors are able to be courageous by relying on preparedness. So when the edges [of their weapons] are sharp and their armor solid, the men will regard combat lightly, but if their armor is not sturdy and dense it will be the same as if they exposed their flesh. If the archers are unable to hit the target, it is the same as being out of arrows. If the arrows hit but do not penetrate, it will be the same as if they had no arrowheads. If the observers and scouts are not attentive, then it will be the same as if they had no eyes. If the generals lack courage it will be the same as being without generals.

Comment: A reiteration of the ideas already expressed in "Cautious Observers" and "Martial Preparations."

36
地 勢
Strategic Power of Terrain

The strategic power associated with terrain assists the army. No one who was ignorant of the battlefield ever [successfully] sought victory. Mountain forests, earthen slopes, dirt tumuli, and large rivers are terrain for the infantry. Terrain with high mounds of soil, narrow mountains, and lush vegetation is suitable for cavalry. Terrain where they can rely upon mountains and array themselves among caves, where there are tall forests and deep valleys, is suitable for bows and crossbows. Where the grass is low and land level, where one can move forward or to the rear, this is terrain for [employing] long-handled spear-tipped dagger-axes

---

217 These are the first words from the first chapter, "Initial Estimations."

[*chi*]. Where reeds and marsh grass are intermixed and bamboo and trees only allow glimmers of sunlight is terrain for lances and spears.

> Comment: This section revisits the concept of the strategic advantage of terrain previously seen in "Employing Advantage" by describing a few concrete realizations and embodiments. However, although mountain and forest warfare are extensively discussed in the *Six Secret Teachings*, the last part is unique in the context of the classic military writings because it correlates specific weapons with characteristics of terrain.

37
情 勢
Nature of Strategic Power

Among generals there are those who are courageous and regard death lightly, who are hasty with quick minds, who are greedy and love profit, who are benevolent but lack resilience, who are wise but mentally fearful, who excel at strategy but are by nature slow. Those who are courageous and regard death lightly can be brutalized; who are hasty with quick minds can be [defeated] through persistence; those who are greedy and love profit can be sent gifts; those who are benevolent but lack resilience can be labored; who are wise but mentally fearful can be distressed; who excel at strategy but are by nature slow can be suddenly attacked.

> Comment: Another of the sections devoted to exploitable flaws in commanders, one that thus continues the tradition initiated by the *Art of War*, Sun Pin's chapter "The General's Losses," and "A Discussion of Generals" in the *Six Secret Teachings*. Although Sun Pin's *Military Methods* greatly expands the list of flaws and points out measures that might be advantageously employed, the most famous

passage appears in the *Art of War*'s "Nine Changes," where five dangerous character traits are outlined:

One committed to dying can be slain.

One committed to living can be captured.

One [easily] angered and hasty [to act] can be insulted.

One obsessed with being scrupulous and untainted can be shamed.

One who loves the people can be troubled.

The text then concludes, "Now these five dangerous traits are excesses in a general, potential disaster for employing the army. The army's destruction and the general's death will invariably stem from these five, so they must be investigated."

38
擊 勢
Power of Sudden Strikes[218]

Those who excelled in combat in antiquity invariably investigated the enemy's nature before formulating their plans. When the army is "old" and their provisions exhausted, when the hundred surnames are troubled and annoyed, when the army's orders are not effected, the implements and weapons not kept in good repair, plans are not first established, rescue does not come from without, the generals and officials are abrasive and oppressive, rewards and punishments are arbitrarily and negligently imposed, the camps are disordered, or they are arrogant after a victory, they can be attacked.

---

218 The selection's title is rather puzzling, as it discusses neither sudden strikes nor surprise attacks.

If they employ the Worthy and give [responsibility] to the capable, their provisions and foodstuffs are plentiful, armor sturdy and weapons sharp, four neighbors harmonious and well-disposed, or powerful states respond with support, they should be planned for but avoided.

> Comment: Previously mentioned in the commentary to "Victory and Defeat," the concept of an "old" army first appeared in the Warring States period. According to the *Three Strategies*: "A disordered general cannot be employed to preserve an army while a rebellious mass cannot be used to attack an enemy. If this sort of general attacks a city it cannot be taken, if this type of army lays siege to a town it will not fall. If both are unsuccessful then the officers' strength will be exhausted. If it is exhausted then the general will be alone and the masses will be rebellious. If they try to hold defensive positions they will not be secure, while if they engage in battle they will turn and run. They are referred to as an 'old army.'"
>
> Most of the military classic writings identify various factors that were deemed indicative of defeat, but the most extensive list appears in the *Wu-tzu*'s "Evaluating the Enemy," victory being so certain that an attack can be mounted without performing divination. (The *Art of War*'s "Configurations of Terrain" lists six categories of disordered armies: "running off," "lax," "sinking," "crumbling," "chaotic," and "routed.")

39
整 師
The Well-Ordered Army

Whenever sending regiments forth or maneuvering the army on campaign, good order brings victory. If the rewards and punishments are not clear, the laws and orders not trusted, and they do not halt to the sound of the gongs nor advance to the sound of the drums, even an army of a million men would be useless. A "well-ordered army" means that when at rest they observe the *li* and when in movement they are awesome. Their advance cannot be opposed, their retreat cannot be pressed. Their front and rear actively connect, the left and right flanks respond to the [command] flags. They can be joined with in peace but they cannot be endangered. Their masses can be united but cannot be separated, they can be employed but not exhausted.

> Comment: Among the classic military writings, the *Ssu-ma Fa* and *Wu-tzu* particularly discussed the need to organize the men into effective, responsive contingents and offered methods for resolving the difficulties that might be encountered. (The selection is basically abstracted from *Wu-tzu*'s "Controlling the Army.") However, achieving unity was an objective that was emphasized by all the writers from Sun-tzu onward because it was viewed as the very foundation of military activities. (The *Ssu-ma Fa* states that "when the Three Armies are united as one man they will conquer.") Achievable only through extensive training and the consistent enforcement of discipline, it required unremitting effort and years of instruction.

40
厉 士
Encouraging the Officers

The Tao for employing the military [consists of] honoring [the soldiers] with ranks and supplying them with wealth, for then all the officers will come. If you treat them according to the *li* and incite them with good faith, all the officers will be willing to die. If you are untiring in granting of beneficence and are consistent in applying the laws, all the officers will submit. If you lead in person and have the men follow, all the officers will be courageous. Small points of excellence must be recorded, minor achievements must be rewarded, for then all the officers will be stimulated.

> Comment: The question of motivation loomed large in the classic military writings and even in previous chapters of the *Chiang Yüan*, where the importance of rewards has been mentioned. The *Wu-tzu* even contains a chapter titled "Stimulating the Officers" that discusses how to structure a ritual feast so that it will stimulate courage and resolve as well as camaraderie among the officers, although this point is not explicitly raised. Conjoined with this is the idea that officers should lead in person. However, in stressing that the nature of command is to direct the battle, Wu Ch'i berated those who thought the commander should fight in the forefront.[219]

41
自 勉
Self-Encouragement

Sages model on Heaven, Worthies take their measure from Earth, and the wise follow antiquity. The arrogant bring disaster upon themselves and the foolish nurture misfortune. Those who speak a lot have little credibility, those who promote themselves have little grace. When rewards are made to those without achievement there is disaffection and when punishments are imposed on the innocent there is rancor. One whose happiness and anger are inappropriate will suffer extinction.

---

[219] In its "Martial Plans," the *Wei Liao-tzu* cites the Wu Ch'i incident. However, its "Combat Awesomeness" asserts the need to lead in person, well illustrating the contradictory nature of material sometimes encompassed by the classic military writings, as would be expected for compilations that evolved over time and underwent repeated losses, accretions, and editing.

42
戰 道
The Tao of War

According to the Tao of forest warfare, flags and pennants should be broadly set out in the morning and the gongs and drums should be made numerous at night. It is advantageous to employ short weapons and skillful to set out ambushes, some attacking the front, others the rear.

According to the Tao of warfare for terrain with heavy shrubbery, it is advantageous to use swords and shields. The general should plan for it, first measuring the routes, then expecting one battle every ten *li* and one active response every five. Furl and conceal the flags and pennants, being especially strict about the gongs and drums in order to keep the enemy from having anywhere to place their hands and feet.

According to the Tao for valley warfare, ambushes must be skillfully set out. It will be advantageous to courageously fight, to have those with nimble feet ascend the heights and have death-defying warriors protect the rear. Array your strong crossbows and pummel them, follow up with those who wield short weapons. Then they will not be able to advance, but neither will you be able to go [forward].

According to the Tao for riverine warfare, it is advantageous to employ boats and oars and train the officers and troops that man them.[220] Set out numerous pennants and streamers in order to mislead [the enemy], maintain strict order when having the bows and crossbows fire to strike them, wield short weapons to ward them off, and set out sturdy palisades for protection. Follow the current and strike them.

According to the Tao for night warfare, advantage lies in alacrity and secrecy. Perhaps you will use a concealed regiment to assault them, going forth where they do not expect it; perhaps multiply the fires and drums in order to confuse their eyes and ears before attacking them for then you can be victorious.

---

[220] It might seem overly obvious that boats would be needed for river combat, but most battles had previously been along the banks, on land.

Chiang Yüan

Comment: The third *Chiang Yüan* selection to discuss tactics felt to be particularly appropriate to various types of terrain, much in the tradition of the *Six Secret Teachings*. The measure of multiplying the flags in the daytime and fires at night, initially advanced in the *Art of War*, became a fundamental technique thereafter.

43
和 人
Harmonizing Men

The Tao for employing the military lies in human harmony. When harmony is attained they will [willingly] fight without being exhorted. But if the commanders and officials are suspicious of each other, the officers and troops unsubmissive, loyal strategists go unemployed, clusters of subordinates hold vituperative discussions, and slander, idleness, and perversity spawn each other, then even with T'ang and Wu's acumen victory could not be achieved over an ordinary fellow, much less a mass of men.

Comment: The need for harmony, also termed "unification in the Tao" (according to the *Art of War*), was well recognized by the classic military writers, Chu-ko Liang, and subsequently Li Ch'üan, whose *T'ai-pai Yin-ching* contains a chapter titled "Esteeming Harmony" (貴 和), a title identical to the one included in Ch'en Shou's twenty-four. Whether this brief selection is a fragment from the latter or whether the *T'ai-pai Yin-ching* preserves it remains unknown.

Wu-tzu's "Planning for the State" has the clearest explanation of the need for harmony: "There are four disharmonies. If there is disharmony in the state you cannot put the army into the field. If there is disharmony within the army, you cannot deploy into formations. If you lack harmony within the formations, you cannot advance into battle. If you lack cohesion during the conduct of the battle, you cannot score a decisive victory. For this reason when a ruler who has comprehended the Tao is about to employ his people he will first bring them into harmony and only thereafter embark on great affairs."

44
察 情
Investigating True Nature

When troops that have been mobilized are quiet, they are relying upon ravines; when they press forward and provoke combat they want others to advance. When masses of trees move, chariots are coming. When the dust is low and expansive, infantry are coming. One who speaks boldly and advances wants to retreat; one who half advances and half retreats is trying to inveigle you. If they lean on their staffs as they move about, they are hungry. If they see advantage but do not advance, they are labored. Where birds gather it is empty. Those who cry out at night are afraid. If the army is unsettled the general is not respected. Those whose flags and pennants move about are in chaos. Those whose officials are angry are tired. Those who frequently make rewards are distressed, who frequently impose punishments are in difficulty. Those whose emissaries make specious apologies want to rest, who offer generous gifts and employ honeyed words are enticing you.

> Comment: Drawing conclusions from observable phenomena was a crucial part of the assessment process in traditional Chinese military science. Although discrete pronouncements of this sort are found throughout the military writings, most of these have their origin in "Maneuvering the Army" in the *Art of War*.[221]

---

[221] An extensive discussion of these practices and the use of deception in creating false impressions Chinese military science may be found in our *Tao of Spycraft*.

45
將 情
The General's Nature

The Tao of the general is that when the army's wells have not yet provided water, the general does not speak about thirst; when the army's food has not yet been cooked, the general does not speak about hunger; when the army's fires have not yet been lit, the general does not speak about being cold; and when the army's tents have not yet been set up, the general does not speak about being fatigued. In the summer he does not use a fan, in the winter does not wear a cloak, and in the rain does not use an umbrella, being the same as the troops.

> Comment: This is the classic enunciation of the practices felt to facilitate gaining the allegiance of the troops, essentially as found in "Encouraging the Army" in the *Six Secret Teachings*, "Combat Awesomeness" in the *Wei Liao-tzu*, and "Superior Strategy" in the *Three Strategies*, as well as embedded in the *Chiang Yüan*.

46
威 令
Awesome Commands

If one single man [can cause] a mass of a million to put their shoulders together, to hold their breath, and to turn about and submissively obey, no one even daring to look up, it is the laws that bring it about. Now, if upper ranks lack punishments and fines while the lower ranks lack the *li* and righteousness, even though someone might be so highly honored as to rule the realm or so rich as to possess [all within] the four seas he will still be unable to escape with his life, just as in the cases of King Chieh [of the Hsia] and King Chou [of the Shang]. But by commanding men with rewards and punishments even ordinary men like Sun Wu and Jang Chü ensured that they could not contravene their mandates. Thus orders cannot be lightly [regarded], power cannot be contravened.

Comment: Even though it mentions righteousness and the *li* (ritual and prescribed forms of social behavior), this chapter accords well with Chu-ko Liang's approach to organizing and governing. Moreover, (as raised in the section on analysis) it mentions Sun-tzu and Ssu-ma Jang-chü, both of whom resolved the problem of establishing their authority over well-established, powerful interests with dramatic punitive actions. It is not the ruler's Virtue, thought to be fundamental by most military writers throughout the centuries, but laws and punishments that impose discipline and create obedience.

47
東 夷
Eastern Yi

It is the nature of the Eastern Yi (*Tung Yi*) to have minimal rituals (*li*) and little regard for righteousness; to be fierce and rash and capable of fighting; to rely on the mountains and make a moat of the sea; and to depend upon precipitous terrain for their security. When the upper and lower ranks are harmonious and the hundred surnames settled and satisfied they cannot be planned against. However, if the upper ranks should become disordered and the lower ones disaffected, it becomes possible to dispatch spies [to promote estrangement] and when estrangement develops, gaps will be created. When gaps are created we should cultivate our Virtue in order to attract them and make our armor and weapons secure and strike them. In this way their strategic power will certainly be overcome.

Comment: Before the widespread dispersion of Chinese culture under the Chou, central state pretensions to govern the entire world were often vigorously challenged by Eastern Yi groups that populated the area from Shandong down to nearly contemporary Vietnam, frequently compelling the late Shang and early Western Chou to conduct punitive expeditions into their territory, with varying success.[222]

48
南 蠻
Southern Man

The Southern Man (*Nan Man*) consist of several groups. It is their nature not to be teachable. They combine to form cliques and parties that fight with each other when they do not gain their way. They dwell in caves and among the mountains, some gathered together, some dispersed, reaching as far as K'un-lun in the west and the ocean in the east. The ocean produces unusual goods, resulting in the people being greedy and courageous in battle. Contagious diseases are numerous in the spring and summer. Therefore, it is advantageous to quickly fight; you cannot expose the army for a prolonged period.

> Comment: The south (including the Sichuan area) always proved problematic for northern fighters and their mounts. Thus the Chou found difficulty in undertaking punitive expeditions into the area that became Ch'u and beyond, the Han incurred horrendous losses in Vietnam, and steppe invaders such as the Khitan (Liao) and Jurchens suffered heat exhaustion and disease with the onset of summer when they crossed below the Yangtze in later ages.

49
西 戎
Western Jung

It is the nature of the Western Jung (*Hsi Jung*) to be courageous, fierce, and love profit. Some dwell in cities, others occupy the wilds. They have little rice or grain

---

[222] For a discussion of these early conflicts, see Sawyer, *Ancient Chinese Warfare* and *Conquest and Domination: Rise and Demise of the Western Chou*.

but lots of metal and shells. Therefore their men are courageous in combat and difficult to defeat. From Ch'i-shih [in the K'un-lun mountain range] west the various Jung are populous. The land is expansive but characterized by precipitousness terrain. By custom they are headstrong, violent, and hateful so most of the people are not submissive. You should observe them to see if they engage in external warfare and watch them to see if internal discord arises. In these situations they can be destroyed.

> Comment: Members of the Hsi Jung were particularly active during the Western Chou, even participants in the melodramatic events that precipitated its downfall, but of course continued to evolve, splinter, and recombine over the centuries. They and the northern steppe peoples became particularly dangerous with the increased mobility that fast chariots and eventually horseback riding furnished, enabling them to essentially elude China's more ponderous defensive forces.

50
北狄
Northern Ti

The Northern Ti (*Pei Ti*) live without walls or moats but instead follow the water and grass. When their strategic power proves advantageous they mount incursions southward [into China proper], when they lose their strategic advantage they escape to the north. Their long mountain ranges and expansive deserts are sufficient for protection. When they are hungry they catch animals and drink the milk, when they are cold they sleep in leather and wear fur cloaks. They race about shooting and hunting and are focused on slaying. You cannot embrace them with the Tao and Virtue and it has never been possible to subjugate them by martial means.

There are three reasons that the Han was not successful in engaging them in battle. First, Han troops [practicing the *t'un-t'ien* system] both fought and farmed so they were fatigued and fearful while the barbarians merely herded and hunted and thus were rested and courageous. Being fatigued, they could not oppose well-rested enemies; being fearful, they could not withstand courageous enemies. This is the first reason that they could not fight with them.

Second, Han strength lay in infantry that could race a hundred *li* in a day while the barbarians' strength lay in cavalry that could traverse double that in a day. When the Han wanted to pursue a barbarian group they had to carry their provisions, shoulder their armor, and follow them. When the barbarians pursued Han [troops] they raced their fleetest cavalry and transported [their provisions]. Thus the strategic task of transport already differed greatly and the nature of their movement and pursuit was not equal. This is the second reason that they could not fight with them.

Third, the Han employed masses of infantry in warfare while the barbarians fought with numerous cavalry. When contending for terrain cavalry are swifter than infantry. The strategic advantages of swiftness and slowness being vastly different was the third reason they could not fight with them.

When there is no alternative, nothing is better than defending the border. The Tao for defending the border consists of selecting good generals and giving them responsibility while training elite warriors and entrusting them with its defense. Broaden the camps and fields and make them substantial; set up warning fires, deploy observers, and await [their signals]; watch for gaps and exploit them; and take advantage of their decline to seize them. This is what is termed eliminating invaders without any expenditure. Your men will not be fatigued but the barbarians will become malleable.

> Comment: The Han found incursions by northern (and northwestern) groups so troublesome that they frequently mounted massive expeditions into their territory. Liu Pang, the Han's progenitor, nearly lost his life when surrounded by an overwhelming force but Emperor Wu-ti, the Martial Emperor, was more successful in subjugating both contiguous groups and more distant proto-states, resulting in the creation of the passage that became the earliest realization

of the Silk Route. However, these campaigns required enormous manpower, heavy logistical support, and vast numbers of horses and oxen, and thus severely depleted the state's resources and impoverished the people. Imaginative commanders sometimes proved successful, but both political solutions such as marriage alliances and more static measures (including lengthy walls) were also tried, albeit futilely.

9
Pien Yi
便宜十六策

1	治國	Administering the State
2	君臣	Rulers and Ministers
3	視聽	Seeing and Hearing
4	納言	Adopting Words
5	察疑	Investigating the Doubtful
6	治人	Governing Men
7	舉措	Raising and Repressing
8	考黜	Investigating and Dismissing
9	治軍	Administering the Army
10	賞罰	Rewards and Punishments
11	喜怒	Happiness and Anger
12	治亂	Governing Chaos
13	教令	Teaching Orders
14	斬斷	Beheading and Severing
15	思慮	Thinking and Contemplating
16	陰察	Clandestine Investigation

1
治 國
Administering the State

Governmental measures for "administering the state" are like those for governing a family. In governing a family one concentrates upon establishing the foundation. When the foundation is established then the ends will be correct. The foundation is [synonymous] with origination, the end with harmoniously responding. The originators are Heaven and Earth, it is the myriad things that harmoniously respond. The affairs of the myriad things are not given birth apart from Heaven, do not grow apart from Earth, and are not completed without men.

The ruler's measures and actions should respond to Heaven, just the way the Pole Star acts as the master, (the star) *T'ai-fu*[223] acts as the Pole Star's minister, the various interstices of the zodiac demark the offices, and the numerous stars found within them represent the people. For this reason the pole star cannot change, *T'ai-fu* cannot lose its measure, and the positions arrayed within the zodiac cannot be erroneous. These are the images of Heaven.

Therefore [the ruler] erects observatories in order to scrutinize the patterns of Heaven, holds sacrifices to Heaven and Earth in the suburbs, and responds to changes in the atmospheric vapors (*ch'i*) in order to match their spiritual numinosity and thereby concentrate on the Heavenly foundation. Plowing and farming, the altars to the spirits of soil and grain, mountain forests, rivers, and marshes, sacrifices to the ancestors, and praying for good fortune are the means to concentrate upon the foundation. The rituals in the schools, the elegance of the eight rows of dancers [from Chou ritual], the *Ming T'ang* (Hall of Enlightenment) and schools for the nobility, and the family and state ancestral temples are the means to concentrate upon the human foundation of men.

Thus the foundation provides the laws for ordinary and constant affairs and the essence of the regulations. A round chisel cannot be fixed onto a square shaft, a lead knife cannot be used to cut and attack. These abnormal affairs cannot result in achievement, these abnormal implements cannot produce skillful [results]. Thus when Heaven loses its normalcy contrary *ch'i* is produced, when Earth loses

---

223 Found alongside.

its constancy there is decayed wood and defeat, and when men lose their constancy there is misfortune and harm. A classic states, "Without the regulations of the former kings we would not even dare get dressed."[224] This is what is meant.

> Comment: The *Pien Yi* commences with an interesting disquisition on the absolutely crucial trilogy of Heaven, Earth, and Man already separately seen in several *Chiang Yüan* selections, including "Wise Employment" and "Military Power."[225] However, the real focus falls upon Heaven, and although sacrifices have previously been mentioned, the material in the third paragraph is not only somewhat unusual but also concretely reflects the era's mindset. No matter how realistic and immersed in the enterprise of warfare, governments in antiquity could not neglect religious practices. Sun-tzu sanctified warfare as the greatest affair of state, but even before that it had been said (in the *Tso Chuan*) that ritual and warfare constituted the essence of rule.

---

224 A quote from the *Hsiao Ching*, one of the Confucian classics generally known in English as *The Classic of Filial Piety*.
225 As the *Pien Yi*'s chapters are far more discursive than the *Chiang Yüan*'s selections, are generally self-explanatory, and frequently revisit topics already commented upon, few notations are required.

2
君 臣
Rulers and Ministers

Governmental measures for "rulers and ministers" may be likened to images of Heaven and Earth. When the images of Heaven and Earth are bright the Tao of rulers and ministers is fully present. In treating his subordinates the ruler employs benevolence, in serving the ruler the ministers employ righteousness. Those with divided loyalties cannot serve a ruler but a doubtful administration cannot confer [authority] upon ministers. When the upper and lower ranks love ritual, the people will be easy to employ, when the upper and lower ranks are harmonious and in accord, the Tao of rulers and minsters will be complete. The ruler employs his ministers according to the *li* (ritual), the ministers serve the ruler with loyalty. The ruler conceives the government's strategy, the ministers plan the affairs.

Governing means "rectifying names," "affairs" mean "encouraging achievement." When the ruler encourages his government and his ministers exert themselves in their affairs, the Tao for name and achievement will be fully realized. For this reason the ruler faces south, toward *yang*, in order to make his instructions illustrious while his ministers face north, toward *yin*, in order to display their shadows. The one who utters these sounds instructs and orders, those who display their shadows attain achievements and exert themselves. When instructions and orders are appropriate achievements will be established; when achievements are established the myriad beings receive blessings.

For this reason the three cords and six relationships are characterized as upper, middle, and lower. The superior is [visible in] the relationship between the ruler and his ministers, the middle between fathers and sons, and inferior in that of husbands and wives. If each of them cultivates the [appropriate] Tao, good fortune and blessings will arrive. In the relationship of superior and inferior marking that between rulers and minsters ritual is taken as the basis; in the relationship of superior and inferior seen in fathers and sons beneficence is taken as the basis for intimacy; in the relationship of superior and inferior characterizing husbands and wives harmony is taken as the peaceful basis. Superiors must be upright, inferiors must be principled. If superiors are not upright, inferiors will be crooked. If superiors are disordered, inferiors will be contrary.

Thus the ruler focuses on governing and minsters focus on implementing affairs; therefore, when the government of an enlightened ruler is cultivated the affairs of loyal minsters will be promoted. Students hope for enlightened teachers, officials long for an enlightened ruler. Thus a variety of offices are established and ranks and salaries arrayed to enrich them. The government arrays its positions like a planchette board and establishes assistants like the *T'ai-fu*. When the personal is not allowed to disorder the public and perversity does not interfere with uprightness, the Tao for governing the state is fully complete.

> Comment: Despite Chu-ko Liang's pervasively Legalistic outlook, this chapter reflects the Confucian belief that social order must be based upon the maintenance and cultivation of a series of inherently hierarchical relationships, all to be structured in accord with the classic doctrine of the "rectification of names." (Not simply the idea that names—i.e., the terms for things—and reality must cohere, but that actuality should be made to conform to a term's innate idea, essential meaning, and behavioral manifestations.) The chapter's focus falls upon the three cords—the relationships between ruler and minister, father and son, and husband and wife—while (according to the *P'ai-hu T'ung*) the so-called six relationships exist among fathers, brothers, the clan, uncles, teachers and elders, and friends.

3
視 聽
Seeing and Hearing

Governmental measures for "seeing and hearing" refer to seeing minute forms and hearing faint sounds. Forms that are minute are not [usually] seen and faint sounds are not [usually] heard. Thus the enlightened ruler sees the minuteness of the subtle and hears the nearly inaudible beginnings of the great. He harmonizes the interior with the exterior and the exterior with the interior. Thus the Tao for governing consists of concentrating upon hearing a lot. For this reason if he listens to, investigates, and then adopts the words of the masses below him and his plans reach the ordinary officers, the myriad things will then be within the scope of his eyes and the numerous sounds will assist his ears. Thus a classic states, "The sage has no constant mind, he takes the hundred surnames as his mind."[226]

The eyes see for the mind, the mouth speaks for the mind, the ears listen for the mind, and the body provides rest for the mind. Thus a body having a mind is like a state having a ruler. When you harmonize the interior with the exterior, the myriad things will be illuminated. Observing the shape of the sun and moon is insufficient to be considered clarity, hearing the sound of thunder insufficient to be considered hearing. Thus the enlightened rulers take extensive seeing to be knowledge and extensive hearing to be spiritual. When the five notes have not been heard one has no means to discriminate *kung* and *shang*; when the five colors have not been seen one has no means to discriminate dank black and yellow.

Thus the enlightened ruler is normally like day and night. In the daytime he implements public affairs, at night private affairs arise. Perhaps he does not hear the groans of the aggrieved or deem loyal attempts to advance the good credible. When the sound of rancor goes unheard then grievances are aired; when those who advance the good are not accepted the loyal will not gain credibility and the perverse will conceal their villainy. Thus the *Book of Documents* states, "Heaven sees what my people see, Heaven hears what my people hear." This is what is meant.

---

[226] Although this statement seems like something out of the *Tao Te Ching*, it is actually from the *Shu Ching*'s (*Book of Documents*) "Kao Yao Mo."

Comment: Often dwelling in splendid isolation, the ruler could be completely ignorant of even the most monumental events and inimical developments unless he made a determined effort to keep abreast of the state's affairs. However, he was completely dependent upon an army of officials and attendants for information about the "outside" world, and thus at their mercy should they wish to conceal or distort incoming reports for their own purposes, as frequently happened over the course of Chinese history. All the military writings emphasized the need to have accurate intelligence about the enemy, but far fewer warned of the pernicious developments that could obscure his understanding.[227] Thus this chapter exhorts rulers to maximize their efforts to know the world about them, such knowledge being the requisite basis of enlightened policies and decision making.

---

227 However, in "The Great Forms of Etiquette," the *Six Secret Teachings* states: "The eye values clarity, the ear values sharpness, the mind values wisdom. If you look with the eyes of all under Heaven there is nothing that you will not see. If you listen with the ears of all under Heaven there is nothing you will not hear. If you think with the minds of all under Heaven, there is nothing you will not know. When [you receive information from all directions] just like the spokes converging in the hub of a wheel, your clarity will not be obfuscated."

4
納 言
Adopting Words

Governmental measures for "adopting words" refer to [facilitating] remonstrance and disputation in order to select from the plans of the masses below. Thus rulers have argumentative ministers and fathers have argumentative sons who, when they regard something as unrighteous, criticize it and thereby approve of their superlative aspects while correcting their deficiencies. Perversity cannot be sanctioned, goodness cannot be contravened. When perversity is sanctioned and goodness contravened the state will certainly be endangered.

When the ruler of men rejects their remonstrance, loyal ministers will not dare introduce plans and pernicious ministers will succeed in monopolizing the government. This harms the state. Thus in a state that accords with the Tao, words are bold and actions upright, but in a state bereft of the Tao there is bold action but syncophantic words. When superiors do not hear, those below do not speak. Thus Confucius did not find it embarrassing to question those below, the Duke of Chou was not embarrassed to humble himself before others. Thus their actions were complete, their names are illustrious, and later ages take them to be Sages. For this reason, when a house suffers leaks below they are plugged up above. If the leakage is not stopped above, those below cannot dwell there.

5
察 疑
Investigating the Doubtful

Governmental measures for "investigating the doubtful" are similar to investigating the colors vermillion and purple and distinguishing the notes *kung* and *shang*. Reddish purple disorders vermillion, licentious sounds can cause doubt in orthodox music. Chaos is given birth in distance, doubt is given birth in delusion. Even though things belong to different categories their appearance may have the same color. White stones look like jade so the stupid treasure them, fish eyes look like pearls so the stupid grab them. Foxes look like dogs so the stupid raise them, withered skeins look like melons so the stupid eat them. Thus when Chao Kao identified a deer as a horse the king of Ch'in did not have any doubt. When Fan Li presented beautiful women from Yüeh, the king of Wu did not find it befuddling.

When plans are doubtful there will not be any way to decide affairs; when affairs are doubtful achievement will not be realized. Thus sagacious men never take being pleased with their thoughts as enlightenment but instead trust in prognostication to determine their auspiciousness and balefulness. The *Book of Documents* states, "When three men divine, you must follow the words of two" and notes that in cases of great doubt "strategic plans should reach down to ordinary men." Thus Confucius said that "in his administration the enlightened ruler is not troubled that people do not know him but that he does not know men." Therefore, do not be troubled that the exterior does not know the interior but only that the interior does not know the exterior. Do not be troubled that inferiors do not know their superiors but only that superiors do not know their inferiors. Do not be worried that the menial do not know the noble, only be worried that the noble do not know the menial.

Thus officers will die for those who know them and women will [adorn] their appearance for those who are pleased with them. Horses race for those who whip them and the spirits prove enlightening to those who understand them. Thus when the ruler of men decides criminal affairs and imposes punishment he should be worried that he will not be enlightened, that the innocent will be judged guilty, offenders will be pardoned, the strong will monopolize discussions, the weak will be encroached upon and insulted, the upright will be unjustly defamed, the crooked will not be straightened, the trustworthy will be doubted, and the loyal will be harmed. These will all summon Heaven's contrary *ch'i*, the troubles of disaster and brutality, and the changes of misfortune and chaos.

In judging criminal cases entailing punishment enlightened rulers should question the defendant about the facts. If his speech does not appear vacuous or seem to be concealing anything, neither prevaricating nor distressed, then observe his coming and going, investigate the way he advances and withdraws. Listen to the sound of his voice and observe how he looks about. If he appears fearful and sounds grief-stricken, comes in quickly but departs slowly, looks back and sighs, these are the substance of rancor that has not been able to gain expression. If he looks down and steals glances around, shows fear when he leaves, breathes rapidly, shrinks back when listening and speaks as if expressing some deep plan from within, his words lack coherence, he comes in slowly and departs rapidly, not daring to turn about or look back, this is the behavior of a guilty person who wants to extricate himself. Confucius said, "If you look at what he does, observe his basis, and investigate what he rests in, how can a man conceal himself, how can a man conceal himself?"[228]

> Comment: The problem of similitude in evaluating both people and events was recognized early on. Especially troubling in the area of military intelligence, it also confounded attempts to fathom character and choose men for employment, as Confucius himself discovered when he misperceived the nature of a disciple. However, quite unusually, the chapter proceeds to unfold some methods for interpreting behavior within a judicial context, well justified because doubt was known to undermine faith in the equitableness of punishments as well as to paralyze decision making in general.

---

228 *Analects*, "Wei Cheng."

Pien Yi

6
治 人
Governing Men

Governmental measures for "governing men" refer to the transforming influence of the Tao, the very means to order and display [what they should do]. Thus a classic states, "Order them with Virtue and righteousness and the people will join in implementing them, show them goodness and evil and the people will know the prohibitions."[229] The masses below look up to the brilliance of the sun and moon, the myriad things accord with encompassing *Kan* and *K'un* (Heaven and Earth). For this reason the far-off Yi (people) presented offerings to Yao and Shun but the various Hsia rebelled against Kings Chieh (of the Hsia) and Chou (of the Shang). It was not Heaven that had motivated them but the transformative influence [of virtuous rulers] above that made them so.

Governing men is like raising sprouts, first eliminate the weeds. Thus, a state about to arise attacks [perversity] within the state, one about to decline imposes harsh strictures in the mountains. The governance of an enlightened ruler concentrates upon knowing what troubles people.

The lictors in black garb are minor ministers within the state. Thus it is said that there is nothing that the lictors do not grasp, no one knows the extremes to which they go. When they confiscate the people's food, hunger and deprivation arise and give birth to chaos and disobedience. Encourage [the people] in agricultural pursuits, do not snatch away the seasons. Keep the taxes and impositions light, do not exhaust the people's wealth. In this way you will enrich the state and give security to families, so aren't they appropriate measures?

Those who have states and families do not worry about being poor but about lacking security. Thus in their measures T'ang (Yao) and Yü (Shun) made it profitable for people to meet. They employed the seasons of Heaven and divided the profits of Earth in order to prepare for baleful years. In autumn there was a surplus of foodstuffs that was supplied to those who lacked. Wealth circulated throughout the realm, people did not pick up anything left on the roads, and none of the populace departed.

---

229 *Hsiao Ching.*

However, under the government of the five hegemons the impoverished were compelled to contribute to the rich and the feudal lords came to love profit. When profit flourishes people contend for it. Disaster and harm arise together and the strong and weak encroach upon each other. Those who personally farm are few, those engaged in secondary activities many. The people are then like floating clouds, their hands and feet are never at rest. A classic states, "Do not esteem goods that are hard to obtain in order to keep the people from becoming thieves. Do not esteem useless items in order to keep the people's minds from becoming disordered."[230]

Sagely government is attained when everyone manages their own official responsibilities. In antiquity, in the time of Duke Ching of Ch'i, they were concerned that the people indulged in extravagance and excess and did not follow the *li* and regulations.[231] Ch'in took what they thought appropriate from the Chou but excised the cultural and stressed substance, encouraging the people to acquire profits. Now, producing useless vessels, accumulating goods of no advantage, gold and silver, jade discs and pearls, green jade curios and unusual treasures, items produced by distant lands, these are not what the common people use. Thin brocades and embroidered clothes, fine silk clothes and imperial-looking materials, these are not what the common people wear. Engraving and inlaying, the skill of marvelous work and other achievements difficult to realize, these harm agricultural activities. Traveling about in curtained and jewel-bedecked carriages, fur robes and thonged leather coats, these are not the adornments of ordinary people. Double doors with painted animals, interior screens many feet in length, tombs and graves that exceed customary measure, all the enhancements that wealth allows, these are not the dwellings of ordinary people.

A classic states, "What the common people want is simply to plow themselves and exert their strength in bitterness, constraining themselves and their expenses

---

[230] Essentially a quotation from chapter 3 of the *Tao Te Ching*, "Do Not Esteem Worthies," a title totally contradictory to the emphasis placed upon seeking out and employing worthies found throughout the military writings. (The first two lines read: "Do not esteem worthies to keep the people from being contentious.")

[231] This is how the sentence reads, but the implications refer to the perverse and licentious behavior of the ruler, understanding it as he made a misery of the people below with his extravagance, by ignoring the rites, and other untoward actions.

in order to nourish their fathers and mothers."[232] Regulating them with wealth, employing them according to the *li*, neither being extravagant in fruitful years nor frugal in baleful ones, while collecting any surplus from ordinary years in order to prepare for later times, is the Tao for governing men. Does it not accord with the *ch'i* [vapors] of the four seasons?

> Comment: Despite the references to Heaven and the *ch'i* of the four seasons, the core of this chapter is a subject little raised by Chu-ko Liang in his purported writings but apparently the focus of their administrative efforts: promoting the people's welfare and thus the state's essential prosperity. The reference to official perniciousness merits note, but more important is the appropriation of the fundamental idea of devolution from an ideal age to one of materialism and harshness, with its attendant abuses. Protestations against extravagance are sometimes seen in the classic military writings,[233] but the impulse to simplicity is more correctly associated with the spirit and orientation of Taoism as originally espoused in the *Tao Te Ching*.[234]

---

232 *Hsiao Ching*.
233 For example, see "Fullness and Emptiness" in the *Six Secret Teachings*.
234 As also encompassed in "Superior Strategy" in the *Three Strategies*.

7
舉 措
Raising and Repressing

Governmental measures for "raising and repressing" refer to raising [introducing] the upright and repressing [removing] the corrupt. Now, governing a state is like governing one's body. The Tao for governing the body emphasizes nourishing the spirit, the Tao for governing a state emphasizes raising [appointing] Worthies. One nourishes the spirit to seek life and raises the Worthy to seek security. Thus a state having assistants is like a house having posts. The posts cannot be thin, the assistants cannot be weak. When the posts are thin harm results, when the assistants are weak [the state] is overturned. Thus, in the Tao for governing the state, when the upright are raised and the corrupt dismissed the state will be secure.

Posts are sturdy when the wood is straight, assistants are worthy when they are upright officials. Straight wood comes from dark forests, upright officers come from the masses below. Thus when the ruler of men selects [officials] he must seek them in hidden places. Perhaps they will be found among those who "preserve their treasure and leave the states to confusion,"[235] dwelling among the ranks of the ordinary officials. Perhaps despite surpassing talent they have not been sought out and invited to participate in the government. Perhaps despite being loyal, worthy, filial, and fraternal their villages have not nominated their names [in these categories of recommendation]. Perhaps they are dwelling in seclusion in order to achieve their intentions and are practicing righteousness in order to realize the Tao. Or perhaps, despite being loyal and dedicated to the ruler, they have been slandered by various cliques or parties.

Yao appointed recluses, T'ang summoned the Yu Shen [and gained Yi Yin], and the Duke of Chou selected from among the menial. In every case they gained the people they needed to attain great tranquility. These rulers dangled rewards for achievement and established positions for officers. They did not neglect ordinary officials, opened the four gates in order to make the government flourish, and offered the dark black and red silks [of office] to attract those hidden in the

---

235 *Analects*, "Yang Huo."

darkness. Thus all under Heaven gave their allegiance and the inhumane were kept distant.

Now, when those that are employed are not those they nurture and those they nurture are not those whom they employ, the poor and lowly will remain below while the wealthy and beautiful will be placed above. Slanderers and the perverse then realize their intentions, the loyal and upright are kept distant or cast away, and the practice of offering black and red silks no longer implemented. How are the worthy then acquired as assistants?

Now, the state's being endangered and ungoverned and the people being unable to be secure in their dwellings results from the mistake of losing the Worthy. It has never happened that when the Worthy have been lost the state was not endangered or when the Worthy were acquired the state was not secure. One who selects offices for people is disordered, who selects people for offices is well governed. For this reason inviting the Worthy and seeking officers is like the Tao of marriage. It has never been the case that a woman being married puts out money to become a wife. Therefore, women who desire wealth and marriage gifts cultivate their purity, officers who desire the black and red silks [that lead to office] strive to establish their names. By inviting officers [to serve] according to ritual the state will be at peace.

> Comment: Although a strong recommendation for employing the worthy and talented, this chapter is unusual in widening the scope of the quest for appropriate candidates to the realm at large, including dark and obscure places.

8
考 黜
Investigating and Dismissing

Governmental measures for "investigating and dismissing" refer to shifting the good and dismissing the evil. When an enlightened ruler is at the top, his mind shines to Heaven and he investigates and knows the good and evil throughout the four seas. He does not dare leave out the ministers of minor states and reaches down to the common people below. He advances the good and employs the worthy, forces out the rapacious and retires the incompetent. He makes clear the good above and below, his plans extend to the state's management, and hosts of worthies assemble like rain. This is what is meant by encouraging the good and dismissing the evil, arraying the successful and deficient.

Governmental measures for "investigating and dismissing" should focus on learning what the people find bitter. They find five things bitter. Minor officials pervert public interest for private gain and exploit their authority to commit villainy. In their left hands they wield a dagger-axe, with their right they govern the living. Internally they encroach upon other officials, externally they pluck [things] from the people. This is the first bitterness.

Major offenses are treated too lightly, laws and orders are not equitable, and those who have not committed offenses are judged guilty and even exterminated. Or those with serious offenses are treated generously, they support the strong and repress the weak, even imposing severe corporal punishment, contorting the situation. This is the second bitterness.

They allow free rein to criminals and evil officials but harm people who initiate lawsuits and make reports to the government. They sever discussion, conceal the true nature of events, and plunder and destroy the living. Their crookedness is exceptional. This is the third bitterness.

Sometimes the senior officials arbitrarily change the responsibilities of their subordinates in the [name of] governing. They favor those close to them and wantonly treat those that they hate harshly. They act oppressively and drastically, are prejudicial, and do not uphold the laws. They alter the taxes and impositions, take advantage of imposts to pluck profits, exploit all opportunities to cheat and deceive such as when sending off officials and welcoming new ones, and augment their wealth with the state's resources and people's labor. This is the fourth bitterness.

Some district officials desire to be known for their achievements. They exploit the rewards and punishments and otherwise profit from other people's affairs, as well as gain from the normal process of buying and selling goods and by monopolizing the prices. The people then lose their occupations. This is the fifth bitterness.

Now, these five affairs represent five points of suffering for the people. Anyone who acts in this fashion must be dismissed. Anyone who is free from these five must be shifted [to an appropriate office]. Thus the *Book of Documents* states, "From their achievements over three years [it will be apparent] who should be dismissed or advanced, who obtuse and who enlightened."[236]

---

236 *Shang Shu* (*Documents of Shang*, generally known as the *Book of Documents*), "Shun Tien."

9
治軍
Administering the Army

Governmental measures for "administering the army" refer to governing border affairs. The Tao for correcting chaos and preserving the state is to adopt awesome martial measures. Executing the brutal and conducting punitive expeditions against the contrary is the way to preserve the state and bring security to the altars of soil. For this reason, even when civil affairs prevail you must make military preparations.

All living beings with blood, even insects, invariably have claws and fangs that they can employ. When happy they play together, when angry they harm each other. People lack claws and fangs so they created weapons and armor in order to aid their defense. Thus the army assists the state and ministers assist the ruler. When their support is strong the state will be secure but when weak the state will be endangered. It all lies in who is entrusted with responsibility for command. If they are not generals for the people and assistants for the state, they will not master the army. Therefore, in governing, the state is administered with the civil, but in controlling the army the plans must be martial. Governing the state must react to the exterior, controlling the army must accord with the interior. "Interior" means the various Hsia groups, "exterior" refers to the Jung and Ti.

It is difficult to transform the members of the Jung and Ti with reason but easy to subjugate them with awesomeness. Rites and ritual [the *li*] have their employment, awesomeness its imposition. For this reason the Yellow Emperor engaged in battle at Chuo-li, and T'ang and Yao both fought [the San Miao] at Tan-p'u River. Shun attacked the Yu Miao, and Yü conducted a punitive expedition against the Yu Hu. Despite the transformative influence of their Virtue, the Five [legendary] Emperors, three kings, and subsequent sagacious rulers still had to apply awesomeness and martial power. Thus, even though weapons are inauspicious implements, when they had no alternative they still employed them.[237]

Now, the Tao for employing the army is to formulate your strategy before undertaking military affairs. Carefully scrutinize the Tao of Heaven and Earth, investigate the minds of the masses, practice with weapons and armor, make the principles for rewards and punishments clear, ferret out the enemy's plans, reconnoiter the points of constriction along the roads, determine the location of places of security and danger, fathom the relative nature of guest and host, learn where it will be appropriate to advance and retreat, accord with opportune moments, make preparations for defense, strengthen the power for aggressive punitive action, and raise the capability of your officers and troops. Only after making plans for victory and defeat and contemplating life and death can you send the army forth, entrust the general with responsibility, and unfold the power necessary to capture the enemy. These are the great essentials of employing the army.

The general is the master of the men's fate and the state's sharp implement. Only after determining his plans should he implement his orders. The army should be like billowing water explosively flowing, it should capture the enemy just like an eagle suddenly striking an animal. Their tranquility should be like stretched bows and crossbows, their action like the release of a [crossbow] trigger.[238] Wherever they are aimed is violently destroyed, the enemy exterminated by itself.

If the general does not ponder deeply, the officers will lack vigorous power. If he does not unify their minds and take sole control of their plans, even though he has a mass of a million the enemy will not be afraid. Apart from true enmity he is without rancor, apart from enemies he mounts no attacks. As for his achievements, without Lu Pan's [keen] eyes there is no way to perceive his skill; with

---

237 Concept from the *Tao Te Ching*, chapter 31, whose verses include the following lines:
    Superlative weapons being inauspicious implements,
    There are things that detest them.
    Weapons are inauspicious implements,
    Not the instruments of the perfected man.
    But when he has no alternative but to employ them,
    He esteems calmness and equanimity.
(For a complete martial translation of the *Tao Te Ching*, see Sawyer, *The Tao of War*.)

238 An analogy employed by both Sun-tzu and Sun Pin in "Strategic Military Power" and "Preparation of Strategic Power."

regard to warfare, without Sun Wu's strategies no way to put forth the turnings of his plans.

For plans and strategy you want secrecy, for attacking the enemy urgency, so that you capture them like an eagle attacking. When combat is like a river's onrush [after a dam] is broken, the enemy will scatter of their own accord without your troops being labored.[239] This is the power of employing the military. Thus those who excel at warfare do not get angry, those who excel at wresting victory are not fearful. For this reason the wise are victorious before they seek victory in battle, the benighted engage in battle and then seek victory. The victorious follow the road and improve the path [ahead of them], the defeated go off obliquely and lose their way. Such is the planning of those who accord with and go contrary to [the nature of warfare].

When the general shoulders his awesomeness and the officers unify their strength, their strategic power will not be vacuous and their movement will be like a round boulder tumbling down from the heights. Wherever it goes things are destroyed, they cannot be rescued nor the boulder halted. For this reason there are no enemies [capable of withstanding them] to the fore and no enemies to the rear. This is the result of employing the army's strategic power.

The army utilizes the unorthodox in formulating strategy and regards surpassing wisdom as foremost. The [army] can be flexible or firm, weak or strong, be preserved or perish. Its fervor is like the wind and rain, its expansiveness like the rivers and seas. When stationary it is like Mount T'ai, as difficult to fathom as *yin* and *yang*. It is unlimited as Earth, as replete as Heaven. It is as inexhaustible as the rivers and lakes, its end and beginning are like the three shinings [of the sun, moon, and stars]. Its life and death are like the four seasons, decline and flourishing like the five elements, while the unorthodox and orthodox mutually produce each other and cannot be impoverished.[240]

The army takes provisions as its foundation and the unorthodox and orthodox as its initiation. Its implements and weapons are intended for use, its

---

239 A particularly famous image from the *Art of War*, found in "Military Disposition." (Almost all of the sentences in this passage are taken from various chapters in the *Art of War*, especially the concept of achieving victory before fighting.)

240 The crucial concept of the unorthodox, already mentioned in the analytic section, is expounded in the *Art of War*'s "Strategic Military Power."

grainstores as preparation. Therefore the state is distressed when it buys expensively and impoverished by transporting provisions great distances.[241] Attacks cannot be repeated, battles cannot be engaged in thrice. Determine the strength [required] and employ it because excessive amounts are wasted. By eliminating what is not advantageous the state will be at peace; by eliminating the incapable the state will be profited.

When someone excels in attacking the enemy does not know where to mount their defense; when someone excels at defense the enemy does not know where to attack.[242] Thus those who excel in attacking do not rely on weapons and armor, those who excel at defense do not rely on fortifications and moats. For this reason high walls and deep lakes are inadequate to provide solidity, solid armor and sharp weapons inadequate to provide strength. If the enemy wants to maintain a solid defensive posture, attack where they are not prepared.

If the enemy wants to deploy their formations, go forth when they will not expect it. If you go forth and the enemy comes up, be careful about the positions you occupy. If you mobilize but the enemy halts, attack their left and right flanks. Assess how the enemy is combining their forces and begin by mounting a sudden strike where they are substantial. If they do not know where to mount their defense nor know the day for battle, the places they will need to defend will be numerous and the forces concentrated at any point therefore few.[243]

You must think about mutual preparation, about the strong and weak attacking each other, your courageous and fearful assisting each other, front and rear mutually advancing, and left and right [flanks] mutually racing forward, just like the head and tail of a snake from Mount Ch'ang simultaneously striking.[244] This is the Tao for rescuing the army.

The victorious maintain their awesomeness and complete their strategic plans by themselves. Although they know the terrain's strategic configurations, they cannot be discussed in advance. Hold discussions with the enemy to figure out their gains and losses; deceive them to learn their secure and vulnerable

---

241 From "Waging War," *Art of War*.
242 *Art of War*, "Vacuity and Substance."
243 From "Vacuity and Substance," *Art of War*.
244 An analogy found in the *Art of War*'s "Nine Terrains."

points.²⁴⁵ Analyze them to know their numerousness and fewness, display a form to determine their commitment to life and death.²⁴⁶ Ponder well to know their bitterness and pleasure and develop strategies to discover where they excel at preparations. Thus, from out of life, the army will strike the [already] dead, avoiding the substantial and suddenly assaulting the vacuous.

In mountain warfare do not approach the heights, in riverine warfare do not go contrary to the current's flow.²⁴⁷ When fighting in grassy areas do not try to transit the depths, when engaged in combat on level terrain do not go contrary to vacuities [gaps]. When fighting on the road do not go contrary to isolated forces. These five are advantageous to the army and are sustained by the terrain.

Armies are successful through employing strategic power and defeated when their plans leak out. They are hungry when provisions have to be transported far and thirsty when they have to dig wells themselves. They are labored by annoyances and disorder but lax in security and tranquility. They become doubtful when not engaged in battle and misled when they perceive profit. They retreat [at the risk of] punishments and fines but advance for rewards and gifts. They become weak when pressed but strong when strategic power is employed. They are distressed when surrounded and fearful when first to arrive. They are frightened by shouts at night, become disordered in darkness, mystified when they lose the road, [spiritually] impoverished on severed terrain, lost when [attacked by] explosive troops, but gained if they know plans beforehand.²⁴⁸

Therefore flags and pennants are set out to attract their eyes, gongs and drums struck in order to resound in their ears. The great axes [of punishment] are displayed in order to unify their minds, instructions and orders issued in order to unify them in the Tao. Offer rewards in order to encourage achievement and impose capital punishment in order to prevent artifice. Battle flags and pennants are raised in the daytime because the troops cannot hear each other; fires and drums are brought out at night because they cannot see each other. If they fail

---

245 One of the few mentions of deception in any of Chu-ko Liang's writings.
246 This sentence reflects the *Wu-tzu*'s thoughts on probing the enemy found in "The Tao of the General."
247 See "Maneuvering the Army," the *Art of War*.
248 A concept that directly contradicts the idea expressed in the *Art of War* (and embraced by most of the military writers) that the commanding general should keep everyone ignorant of his plans until the last moment in order to mystify the troops and preserve secrecy.

Pien Yi

to follow instructions or orders employ the great axes of punishment to compel them.

Anyone who does not know the facilitations offered by the nine configurations of terrain will not know the Tao of the nine changes.[249] Those who know Heaven's *yin* and *yang*, the names for the various configurations of Earth, and close associates found among Men, these three, will gain and maintain their achievement. Those who know their officers will know the enemy; those who do not know their officers will not know the enemy. Those who do not know the enemy will be decimated in every encounter. Thus for armies you are about to attack you must first know the minds of the attendants, officers, and troops. The five types of clandestine agents must be closely associated with the army and generously [rewarded] by the commander. Without sagacious wisdom they cannot be employed, without benevolence and moral worth they cannot be used. When the five agents succeed in their tasks the people can be used and the state long preserved.[250]

Thus armies that seek to survive make preparations and when they have no alternative they fight. In tranquility principles are employed to regulate security, in movement they are employed to regulate awesomeness. Do not rely on the enemy not coming but instead rely upon not being vulnerable.[251] With the nearby await the distant, with the rested await the fatigued, with the sated await the hungry, with the substantial await the vacuous, with the living await the dead, with many await a few, with the flourishing await the declining, and with ambushes await those coming forward. [When encountering] well-ordered flags and drums beaten in unison you should withstand them to the fore but overturn their rear, solidify the ravines and passes, and conspicuously set out fixed deployments. Subvert them with [prospects for] profit, soften them with harm. In this way the Tao of the army will be complete.

> Comment: "Administering (or Controlling) the Army," the lengthiest chapter in the *Pien Yi*, begins by justifying the

---

249 A concept first articulated in the *Art of War*, "Nine Changes," which includes these words.
250 In recognizing the need for intelligence, this paragraph essentially summarizes the contents and thrust of the *Art of War*'s infamous chapter on clandestine agents, "Employing Spies."
251 See "Military Disposition" in the *Art of War*.

need for military power and martial measures with the traditional argument, found in the *Huai-nan Tzu* and other early writings such as Sun Pin's *Military Methods*, that conflict is inherent to mankind. Thereafter it embarks on a sort of sweeping integration of fundamental practices and concerns, including the difficulty of suppressing external peoples and a rather unusual citation of the importance of unorthodox measures. Most of the topics and much of the language appear in the *Chiang Yüan,* suggesting the chapter may have been deliberately constructed from selected materials embedded within it. However, unlike most *Pien Yi* sections, "Administering the Army" contains numerous concepts and extensive passages derived directly from the *Art of War*. Despite being unattributed, they show a thorough familiarity with the founding text of traditional Chinese military science, as would be expected of Chu-ko Liang.

Pien Yi

10
賞 罰
Rewards and Punishments

Governmental measures for "rewards and punishments" refer to rewarding the good and punishing the evil. Rewards are the means to flourish achievement, punishments the means to prevent villainy. Rewards must be just, punishments must be equitable. When rewards are granted on a known basis, then courageous officers will know what they are dying for; when corporal punishment and fines are imposed on a known basis, the perverse and evil will know what to fear.

Thus rewards cannot be bestowed without any basis, punishments cannot be wantonly applied. When rewards are baselessly bestowed, dedicated ministers will be annoyed; when punishments are wantonly applied, upright officers will hate [the government]. For this reason, there was the incident in which harm resulted from Yang K'u not being equitably awarded a portion of the lamb roast at the King of Ch'u's defeat because he believed slander.[252] Now, the general alone controls the awesomeness of [deciding] life and death. If he spares the lives of those who should be slain and slays those who should live; his indignation and anger are not appropriate; his rewards and punishments not clear; his instructions and orders not consistent; and he takes the personal as the public, these five will endanger the state.

When rewards and punishments are not clear, orders and instructions will not be obeyed. When those who must be executed are spared, the myriad villainies will not be prevented. When those who must live are slain, the officers and troops will scatter and be lost. When indignation and anger are inappropriate, awesome martial [power] will not be prevail. When rewards and punishments are not clear, the lower ranks will not be stimulated to achievement. When the government's instructions are not appropriate, the laws and orders not followed, and the personal is made the public, people will have divided loyalties.

When the myriad villainies cannot be prevented the [state] will not long endure. When the officers and troops scatter and are lost the troops will certainly

---

[252] Yang K'u, the ruler's chariot driver, was so annoyed at being slighted that during the battle he drove straight into the enemy.

be few. When awesome martial [power] is not practiced, when they see the enemy they will not arise.[253] When the lower ranks are not stimulated to achievement, the ruler will lack strong assistants. When laws and orders are not followed, turbulent affairs will go unrectified. When people have divided loyalties, the state will be endangered.

Therefore prevent villainy with government, rectify extravagance with frugality. The loyal and upright can be employed to manage criminal cases, the scrupulous and equanimous can be employed to control rewards and punishments. When rewards and punishments are not corrupted men will die submissively. When famished people are departing by the roads while the stables contain fat horses, it can be termed losing the people while preserving yourself, being harsh to the people but generous to yourself.

Therefore the ruler first summons [and employs] someone and later grants rewards. If he issues orders first and executes afterward the people will give their allegiance, fearing yet loving him, and act without orders. If rewards and punishments are unjustly implemented without orders having been issued, loyal ministers will perish without having committed offenses and pernicious ministers will advance without achievement. If in bestowing rewards [the ruler] does not omit those with whom he is annoyed or regards as enemies he will have the strength of Duke Huan of Ch'i when he gained Kuan Chung. If in executing and punishing he does not spare his intimates and relatives he will have the fame of the Duke of Chou who killed his younger brother [for rebelling]. The *Book of Documents* states, "Without favoritism or partisanship the Tao of kingship is regular and prominent, without partisanship or favoritism the Tao of kingship is equitable and tranquil." This is what was meant.

---

253 Note that in "Tactical Balance of Power in Attacks" the *Wei Liao-tzu* states: "Now the people do not have two things that they fear equally. If they fear us they will despise the enemy; if they fear the enemy they will despise us. The one who is despised will be defeated, the one who establishes his awesomeness will be victorious."

11
喜 怒
Happiness and Anger

Governmental measures for "happiness and anger" refer to not responding with happiness to affairs that are not happy nor reacting with anger to situations in which one should not get angry. It is necessary to be clear about the categories of happiness and anger. Anger [punishment] should not be perversely imposed upon men who have not committed offenses, happiness should not follow for officers who should be exterminated. The boundary between happiness and anger must be carefully examined. When happy you cannot release the guilty, when angry you cannot execute the innocent.

The affairs of happiness and anger cannot be wantonly administered nor can preferences be practiced and achievements neglected. Generals cannot express their personal anger by mobilizing for warfare, they must employ [have] the minds of the masses. If they engage in combat merely because of personal annoyance their employment of the troops will certainly result in defeat. Anger cannot revert to joy, happiness cannot return to anger. Therefore, the civil should have priority and the martial should be subsequent. Those who seek victory first will certainly be defeated later, those who get angry first will invariably suffer regret. A morning's irritation can result in losing one's life. Therefore, the *chün-tzu* [perfected man] is awesome but not ferocious, irritated but not enraged, worried but not fearful, joyful but not happy.

Only when there is some affair that one can be irritated about should awesome martial [power] be applied. When awesome martial [power] is applied then punishments and fines are imposed, when corporal punishments and fines are imposed then the myriad villainies will be blocked. If awesome martial [power] is not applied corporal punishments and fines will not be accurate, and when corporal punishments and fines are not accurate the myriad evils will not be rectified and the state will perish.

> Comment: From the *Art of War* onward the early military thinkers cautioned against the danger of strong but

momentary emotions, especially anger and happiness, affecting judgment and prompting action, whether punitive or military. Therefore, assessment and planning must always precede martial action, and both conducted on a rational, objective basis.

Pien Yi

12
治 亂
Governing Chaos

Governmental measures for "governing chaos" refer to scrutinizing the officials and their responsibilities, eliminating the superficial (*wen*), and looking for the substantial. Silk threads that are too long will certainly have disordered knots, fine threads that are not drawn out will certainly become tangled.[254] When the three cords (*kang*) are not upright and the six relationships (*chi*) not managed chaos is given birth. When a state is well governed the round accord with the compass, the square accord with the T-square, and the foundation accords with the ends. When government accords with the Tao the myriad things can be brought to completion and the achievements can be preserved.

Now, chaos in the Three Armies, their turbulence and disorder, [are brought about] by each [commander] following his own principles. Enlightened rulers govern [with] the cords and relationships. Governmental affairs should be prioritized. First regulate the cords, later manage the relationships.[255] First regulate the orders, later the punishments. First order the nearby, later the distant. First regulate the interior, later the exterior. First regulate the foundation, later the results. First bring the strong under control, later the weak. First manage the large, later the small. First regulate yourself, afterward other men.

Accordingly, when the cords are regulated the relationships will be stretched out, when orders are managed punishments can be implemented. When you regulate the nearby the distant will be secure, when you regulate the interior the exterior will be correct. When the foundation is managed the results will be penetrating, when you regulate the strong the weak will arise. When you manage the large the small will act. If you regulate the upper [ranks] the lower ones will be upright. If you regulate yourself men will respect you. This then is the Tao for governing the state.

---

254 The idea seems to be that great disaster can evolve from the fine and minute.
255 The cords and relationships previously appeared in "Rulers and Ministers."

13
教 令
Teaching Orders

Governmental measures for "teaching orders" refer to superiors instructing those below. Unless something accords with the laws it is not spoken of, unless it coheres with the Tao it is not implemented.

What superiors do is observed by the lower ranks. Now, being lax with yourself while teaching others is termed contrary to [proper methods of] government. Rectifying yourself to teach others is termed conducive government. Therefore, only after the ruler of men rectifies himself does he put his orders into effect. When he is not personally upright his orders will not be followed. Not following orders spawns changes and chaos.

Thus the Tao for those who act as rulers is to make teaching orders primary, executions and punishments subsequent. Not teaching people but engaging in warfare with them is termed "abandoning them." The Tao for first training the officers and troops in employing their weapons consists of five measures. First, have their eyes become practiced in the changes indicated by the pennants and the techniques of [maneuvering] horizontally and vertically. Second, have their ears become practiced in listening to the sound of the gongs and drums and then acting and being inactive, advancing and halting. Third, have their minds become familiar with the severity of corporal punishments and fines and the profits of rank and rewards. Fourth, have their hands become practiced in the facility of the five weapons and in the preparations required for combat and warfare. Fifth, have their feet become practiced in turning about in formation, moving forward, running, and advancing and retreating when appropriate. These are termed the five instructions.

Teaching orders and military formations each have their own Tao [method]. In teaching the left is called green dragon, the right is called white tiger, the fore called vermillion sparrow, the rear dank martial, and the center *hsüan-yüan* [Yellow Emperor].[256] The commanding general occupies a position with spears

---

[256] Although the employment of flags to direct action and facilitate training is extensively discussed in the early military writings, names such as these rarely appear. (For one of the few instances, see "Controlling the Army" in the *Wu-tzu*.)

on the left and *chi* (spear-tipped dagger-axes) on the right, shields to the front and crossbows to the rear, with the flags and drums in the center. When the flags signal everyone arises, when they hear the sound of the drums they advance, and when they hear the sound of the gongs they halt. When they follow what is indicated the five formations will be ordered.

For rectifying the formations the flags and drums are masters. At a single drum beat a green flag is raised and they assume the straight formation. At a double beat a red flag is raised and they assume a sharp formation. At a triple beat a yellow flag is raised and they assume a square formation. At a quadruple beat a white flag is raised and they assume a circular formation. At a beat of five a black flag is raised and they assume a curved formation.

The straight formation is that of wood, the sharp that of fire, the square that of earth, the round that of metal, and the curved that of water. These five phase[257] formations revolve in a mutual production sequence and collide with each other in a mutual conquest sequence. The production sequence is employed to rescue, the conquest sequence for warfare. Production sequences can provide support, conquest relationships can empower victory over enemies.

Now, the method for unifying the five formations together is the mutual guarantee system based upon five. Five men compose a *chang*, five *chang* a *shih*, five *shih* a *chih*, five branches a *huo*, five *huo* a *chuang*, and five *chuang* an army (*chün*), completing the army's troops.[258]

Now, in order to exploit the facility appropriate to each weapon focus on knowing the constraints that should be imposed. The short [in stature] should carry spears and spear-tipped dagger-axes; the tall should carry bows and

---

257 The use of the relationships among the five phases—sometimes termed "elements"—merits note. (The five phases—wood, fire, water, earth, and metal—were correlated with all sorts of observable, especially repetitive, phenomena and considered to be inherently related through several production and conquest relationships, including wood giving birth to [or sustaining] fire and water conquering [extinguishing] it. The more esoteric military thinkers [such as Li Ch'üan and Chu-ko Liang] employed the five phases in a variety of ways, including to organize their thoughts on formations, characterize conquest dynamics, and even to deliberately obscure reality, as discussed in the T'ang dynasty's *Questions and Replies*.)

258 Although there were variations, the so-called mutual guarantee system and their structuring into hierarchical units based on five were generally considered the foundation of military organization in antiquity. However, the numbers found here are somewhat different from those normally seen in such Warring States writings as the *Ssu-ma Fa* and *Chou Li*: 5, 25, 125, 625, 3125, and 15,625 rather than 5, 25, 100, 500, 2,500, and 12,500.

crossbows; the sturdy should carry flags and pennants; the courageous should carry gongs and drums; the weak should work in provisions and animal management; and the wise should be masters of planning.[259] Village members should be gathered and bonded together by the mutual guarantee system of fives. At the first drumming they should assume proper order, at the second practice the formations, at the third arise and eat, at the fourth strictly order the camp, and at the fifth march out. After they hear the drums and gongs the pennants should be raised and the ranks sent forth in sequence. Once they have heard the drum sounded three times and the flags have been raised, those who raise their weapons and attack the enemy first should be rewarded, those who retreat should be beheaded. This is what is meant by "teaching orders."

> Comment: This selection preserves some interesting, rarely seen material on the issues and intricacies of training men for organized warfare rather than combat as individual warriors. (The need for training is clearly articulated in the *Chiang Yüan*, especially "Practice and Training.") As usual, it is through the gongs and drums that men will receive their basic orders, but "Teaching Orders" also briefly indicates how the flags are to be employed in directing changes in the formations. The use of the five phase relationships in this regard particularly merits note. (The five phases—wood, fire, water, earth, and metal—were correlated with all sorts of observable, especially repetitive, phenomena and considered to be inherently related through several production and conquest relationships such as wood giving birth to [or sustaining] fire and water conquering [extinguishing] it. The more esoteric military thinkers employed the five phases in a variety of ways, including to organize their thoughts on formations, characterize conquest dynamics, and even deliberately obscure reality.)

---

259 Essentially a quotation from *Wu-tzu*, "Controlling the Army."

Pien Yi

14
斬 斷
Beheading and Severing

Governmental measures for "beheading and severing" refer to the laws [that are applied to those] who do not follow instructions and commands. There are seven categories of law: the first is slighting [the army], the second being dilatory, the third thievery, the fourth deceit, the fifth disobedience, the sixth being chaotic, and the seventh being misleading. They should be prohibited by those governing the army. If those who should be severed are not severed you will certainly suffer disorder. Thus the awesomeness of the great axes of punishment was established in order to manage this. Execute those who do not follow orders.

Martial regulations differ [from civil ones]. If light offenses are heavily punished orders will not be disobeyed. Those who disobey orders should be beheaded. Those who fail to assemble at the proper time, who do not advance when they hear the drums, who take advantage of open spaces to hang about, who dither and halt, who are at first nearby then later far-off, who do not respond when their names are called, whose vehicles and armor are not in good repair, and whose weapons are not prepared can be said to slight the army. Behead those who slight the army.

Those who fail to pass on orders after they receive them or when they pass them on are not careful; who mislead and befuddle the lictors and officers; and who do not listen to the gongs and drums nor look at the flags and pennants are said to treat the army in dilatory fashion. Behead those who do this.

They fail to warehouse provisions and are not careful with the army's weapons. Their impositions and bestowals are not equitable, they favor those close to them, seize things that are not theirs, borrow material goods but do not return them, and snatch [severed enemy] heads from others in order to garner their merit. They can be said to steal from the army. Those who steal from the army should be beheaded.

Those who change their surnames or alter their names, whose uniforms are not fresh, whose flags and pennants are ripped or ruined, whose gongs and drums are not ready, whose edged weapons are not ground [sharp], whose implements and staffs are not sturdy, whose arrows are unfletched, whose bows and crossbows are unstrung, and who do not implement the regulations and orders can be said to be deceiving the army. Those who deceive the army should be beheaded.

Those who hear the drums but do not advance; who hear the gongs but do not halt; who do not put their flags down when ordered or raise them when instructed; who do not follow the indications of the flags; who avoid the front and move toward the rear; who induce disorder in the ranks when the army sets out; who break their bows or crossbows to the detriment of the army's strategic power; who retreat without fighting; who go right when expected to go left; or who, supporting the wounded and carrying the dead, abandon the fight of their own accord and go back, can be said to have turned their backs on the army. Those who turn their backs on the army should be beheaded.

When the army is sent forth and the general assumes command, if the officers and troops chaotically contend with each other to be first; the vehicles and cavalry follow close upon each other, choking the roads so that the rear cannot move forward; they clamor and shout so that nothing can be heard, causing the army's order and structure to be lost; they wound each other with their weapons; the long and short are not managed properly; and upper and lower splay out in all directions, this can be said to be disordering the army. Behead those who disorder the army.

Wherever they stop to encamp they ask about their fellow villagers, gather together to eat with them, and act to mutually protect each other. If they are unable to transgress the normal order they forcefully enter other squads of five. They contravene and scramble the proper order, they cannot be commanded to stop. They cross through the camp and go in and out but not through the gates. If they do not reform by themselves villainy and perversity will arise. Those who know about it and do not report it commit an offense of the same degree. Moreover, they gather with others to drink wine, boast about what they have seized and received, speak loudly and utter startling words, and mislead the lictors and officers. This can be said to be misleading the army. Those who mislead the army are beheaded.

After these [offenders] are beheaded and severed, the myriad affairs will be well governed.

Pien Yi

Comment: The *Wei Liao-tzu* includes several chapters detailing punishments for particular offenses, but mostly battlefield cowardice and similar offenses. The contents of this selection are unusual and presumably reflect actual problems that had been encountered in contemporary campaign armies.

15
思 慮
Thinking and Contemplating

Governmental measures for "thinking and contemplating" refer to thinking about the imminent and contemplating the far-off. Men who do not contemplate distant [events] will certainly experience imminent worries. Thus the perfected man's thoughts do not exceed [the responsibilities] of his position.

Thought rectifies plans, contemplation is thinking about measures to be taken for affairs. Apart from [the responsibilities of] his position the perfected man does not plan for governmental activities, apart from his own affairs he does not contemplate the measures to be taken. Great affairs arise in difficulty, minor affairs in the easy. Therefore, if you want to think about profit you must contemplate the [potential] harm; if you want to think about success you must contemplate failure. This is why a nine story tower, despite its height, invariably falls into ruin.

Thus, when looking up, you cannot ignore what is below, when observing the front cannot ignore the rear. For this reason, when Duke Mu of Ch'in attacked Cheng his two sons could foresee the harm. When the king of Wu accepted the women from Yüeh, Wu-tzu Hsü knew that defeat would result.[260] When the state of Yü received a jade disk and horses from Chin,[261] Kung Chih Ch'i knew the harm that would follow. When Duke Hsiang of Sung trained his soldiers with chariots, Mu Yi knew they would disobey. This sort of wisdom, attained through thought and contemplation, can be said to be enlightened.

Now, how can following in the tracks of defeated formations and becoming enmired in the mud be beneficial? Thus even though Ch'in achieved hegemony over the realm, they did not realize the Tao of Yao and Shun [and thus perished]. Danger is given birth in security, perishing in existence, and chaos in good or-

---

260 At the end of the Spring and Autumn period Wu had defeated Yüeh, but Yüeh's ruler, the famous King Kou-chien, embarked on a program of systematic subversion that included sending beautiful women to befuddle the king of Wu. (For a complete retelling, see Sawyer, *Tao of Spycraft*, 232–242.)

261 Ostensibly to receive the right for his armies to pass through en route to attacking another state, but of course they subjugated Yü en route back from their victory. (This later became the basis of a well-known aphorism. For further discussion, see Sawyer, *Tao of Deception*, 31–32.)

der.[262] When the perfected man sees the minute he knows the evident, when he sees the beginning he knows the end. Thus disaster has no way to begin, this is [the result] of governmental measures of thought and contemplation.

---

262 As the *Six Secret Teachings* states in "The Tao of the Military": "Existence does not lie in existence but in thinking about perishing. Pleasure does not lie in pleasure but in contemplating disaster." An ancient aphorism similarly speaks about thinking of danger while dwelling in security.

16
陰 察
Clandestine Investigation

Governmental measures for "clandestine investigation" refer to making comparisons among categories of things in order to realize their meaning. When the exterior is harmed the interior is isolated, when those above are deluded, those below will be doubtful. When they are doubtful those close to them will not be employed, when deluded those who look [at things] will lose their measure. When measure is lost plans become disordered, when plans become disordered states perish. When states perish [the people] will not be secure. For this reason thinkers contemplate the far-off. Those who contemplate the far-off will be secure while those who do not will be endangered.

The wealthy realize their ambitions, the poor lose the seasons. When excessive expense is indulged in, much of what has been stored away will be lost. If you exhaust your wealth to buy things, those without achievement will gain sole control. Those with numerous worrisome affairs become irritated; irritation is given birth by dilatoriness.

When a boat leaks water enters, when a sack has a hole the interior empties out. Small mountains are bereft of wildlife, shallow waters lack fish. When trees are weak no nests are found there, when walls are ruined houses tumble down, and when embankments break the water surges forth. Those who run fervently fall prostrate, those who walk securely are slow. Those who court danger lack wisdom, who walk on ice are fearful. Those who attempt to cross [mountain] springs drown, who encounter streams cross over. Those who lack oars do not get across, those who have lost a companion look back into the distance.

In making rewards and punishments scrutinize accomplishment. Those who lack sincerity lose credibility. When the lips are lost the teeth will be cold. When the hair is lost the skin will be exposed. Partiality perverts speech, prejudicial listening gives rise to worry. Those who are good at planning are victorious, those who are bad at planning end up being shattered. The good exhorting the evil is like spring rain moistening [the land]. Unicorns are easily mounted, worn-out horses are hard to train. Those who do not look are blind, who do not listen are deaf.

When the roots are damaged the leaves wither; when the leaves wither the flowers drop; when the flowers drop the fruit is lost. When the pillars are thin the house collapses, when the foundation is thin then the ends are unstable. When the lower [part] is small the upper collapses.

Those who do not discriminate between black and white cast aside the dirt and keep the stones and they group tigers and sheep together. Those whose clothes are ripped mend them, whose belts are too short extend them. Those who play with knives will wound their hands, who jump about will hurt their feet. Washing does not require rivers and lakes, what is essential is getting rid of the dirt. Among horses one does not need [the famous one-thousand-*li* horse] Ch'i Chi, what is important is fleetness of foot. Worthies do not have to be sages, what is essential is that they have penetrating wisdom.

In sum, there are five "virtues": the first is called preventing brutality and halting [the use of] armies; the second is rewarding the worthy and punishing offenders; the third is resting in benevolence and harmonizing the masses; the fourth is preserving the great and determining achievement; the fifth is sustaining the vexed and rejecting slander. They are termed the five virtues.

> Comment: This chapter purports to be about "clandestine investigation," but actually is nothing more than a pastiche of common sayings and observations only vaguely related to the subject. While many of them were originally insightful, by the Three Kingdoms period most had become trivialized.

III
Collateral Matter

Critical Sources

Chang Ch'i-yün 張其昀。中國歷史地圖。臺北, 中國文化學院, 2 vol., 1980.
Chang Shu 張澍. 諸葛忠武候文集, various woodblock editions.
Ch'en Shou 陳壽。三國志 (三國志集解 in 二十五史。臺北, 藝文印書館, (nd).
Chung-kuo Chün-shih-shih Pien-hsieh-tsu 中國軍事史編寫組。中國軍事史：兵略。 北京, 解放軍出版社, 1986.
Chung-kuo Li-tai Chan-cheng-shih Pien-ts'uan Wei-yüan-hui. 中國歷代戰爭史編纂委員會。 中國歷代戰爭史：Vol. 4. 臺北, 黎明文化, 1980 (rev. ed.).
Ho Chao-chi and Jen Chen 何兆吉 任真。諸葛亮兵法。 南昌, 江西人民出版社, 1996.
Hsü P'an-ch'ing 許盤清 and Chou Wen-yeh 周文業。"三國演義," "三國志" 對照本。南景, 江蘇古藉出版社, 2 vol., 2002.

Li Hu 黎虎。魏晉南北朝世論。北景, 學苑出版社, 1999.
Liu Han-hua 劉漢華。諸葛孔明的兵法。臺北, 耀文文化, 1993.
Luo Chih-lin 羅志霖。諸葛亮文集譯注。成都, 巴屬書社, 2011.
Ssu-ma Kuang 司馬光。新交資治通鑒注。臺北, 世界書局, 16 vol.,1972.
Su Pao-hsiang 索寶祥。心書。北景, 民族出版社, 2000.
T'an Ch'i-hsiang 譚其驤。中國歷史地圖集：三國, 西晉時期。 香港, 三聯書局, 1991.
T'an Liang-hsiao 譚良嘯。八陣圖與木牛流馬。成都, 成都武侯祠博物館, 1996.
Tuan Hsi-chung and Wen Hsü-ch'u 段熙仲 聞旭初。諸葛亮集。北景, 中華書局, 1960.
Wang Jui-kung 王瑞功。諸葛亮研究集成。 山東, 齊魯書社, 2 vol., 1997.
Wang Chung-hun 王仲葷。 魏晉南北朝史。上海, 上海人民出版社, 2003.
Watnabe Seichi 渡辺精一。反三國志。東景, 講談社, 1991 (Japanese redaction and translation of Chou Ta-huang 周大荒, 反三國志).
Yü Ta-chi 余大吉。中國軍事通史：三國軍事史。北京, 軍事科學出版社, 1998.

Suggested Martial and Contextual Reading

Dennis Twitchett and Michael Loewe, *The Ch'in and Han Empires, 221 B.C. – A.D. 220* (*The Cambridge History of China*)

Moss Roberts, translator, *Three Kingdoms* (translation of 三國演義, *The Romance of the Three Kingdoms*)

Ralph D. Sawyer:
  The Art of War
  The Seven Military Classics of Ancient China
  Sun Pin Military Methods
  Fire and Water: The Art of Incendiary and Aquatic Warfare in China
  One Hundred Unorthodox Strategies: Battle and Tactics of Chinese Warfare
  Tao of War: The Martial Tao Te Ching
  Tao of Deception: Unorthodox Warfare in Historic and Modern China
  Tao of Spycraft: Intelligence Theory and Practice in Traditional China
  Conquest and Domination in Early China: Rise and Demise of the Western Chou
  Ancient Chinese Warfare

Made in the USA
Middletown, DE
16 April 2020